Smiling Through the Cultural Catastrophe

Smiling Through the Cultural Catastrophe

Toward the Revival of Higher Education

JEFFREY HART

Yale University Press   *New Haven and London*

Designed by James J. Johnson and set in Monotype Baskerville and Bulmer types by Keystone Typesetting, Inc.

Printed in the United States of America by

Library of Congress Cataloging-in-Publication Data

Hart, Jeffrey Peter, 1930–

    Smiling through the cultural catastrophe : toward the revival of higher education / Jeffrey Hart.

        p. cm.

    Includes bibliographical references and index.

    ISBN 0-300-08704-7 (alk. paper)

    1. Education, Humanistic.   2. Civilization—Study and teaching.   I. Title.

LC1011 .H365 2001

370.11′2—dc21   2001022241

A catalogue record for this book is available from the British Library.

The paper in this book meets the guidelines for permanence and durability of the Committee on Production Guidelines for Book Longevity of the Council on Library Resources.

10 9 8 7 6 5 4 3 2 1

Dedicated to
Baker-Berry Library and its staff,
the library being
the most important building
on any campus

A people that no longer remembers has lost
its history and its soul.
—ALEKSANDR SOLZHENITSYN

The temples of the gods are the most enduring works of man.
—CHRISTOPHER DAWSON

To lose what is not a waste land is the very condition of being in a
waste land.
—LYNDALL GORDON (on T. S. Eliot)

Contents

Preface

In 1947 and 1948, when an undergraduate at Dartmouth, I studied with a professor of philosophy named Eugen Rosenstock-Huessy, a refugee from the Nazis. During World War I, as a soldier in the German army, he had fought at Verdun. On one occasion, during a lull in the bombardment, he wandered out into the pitted and scarred no-man's-land. Suddenly the artillery on both sides began firing again and he took refuge in a crater. He experienced extreme disconnectedness and negation. "I was a naked worm," he told the students in his classroom. In 1933, he experienced another extreme negation in the form of the Nazi revolution. Like Edmund Burke at the time of the French Revolution, he had been startled into reflection by these traumatic negations. He had felt thrust outside history, a "naked worm," as he put it, meaningless, wandering on the moon. In consequence, he had thought long and deeply about education, his masters becoming Friedrich Nietzsche and William James, both of whom he saw as attempting to bring meaning out of despair. He had two phrases he repeated so often they remained in a student's mind.

He would say, "History must be told." He explained in various ways that history is to a civilization what personal memory is to an individual: an essential part of identity and a source of meaning.

He also said that the goal of education is the citizen. He defined the citizen in a radical and original way arising out of his own twentieth-century experience. He said that a citizen is a person who, if need be, can re-create his civilization.

Goethe is often said to have been the last man to have known his civilization in its totality, that after Goethe things became too complex for anyone to achieve such grasp. Rosenstock-Huessy had a different sort of knowledge and mastery in mind. He meant that the citizen, the product of a genuine liberal arts education, should understand his civilization in the large, its shape and texture, its narrative and its major themes, its important areas of thought, its philosophical and religious controversies, its scientific development, its major works of the imagination. The citizen in this sense need not know quantum mechanics, neutron theory, non-Euclidean geometry, or the details of the twelve-tone scale, but he should know that they are there and what they mean.

That kind of knowledge is the goal of liberal education, the knowledge of the great narrative and other possible narratives, and the ability to locate new things in relation to the overall design, and the ability to locate other civilizations and other cultures in relation to it.

In a democracy such as ours the goal must be to have as many people as possible grasp their civilization this way, because they participate in the governing function either directly or indirectly and because they help to create the moral and cultural tone of the social environment we all share.

During the nineteenth century, Matthew Arnold, reflecting upon these matters in his essay "Numbers; or, The Majority and the Remnant," hoped for a "saving remnant," those who would be the educated bearers of the central ideas of their civilization. Some thoughtful educators today have felt obliged to settle for a minimum goal of that sort because of the pervasive and deadening power of mass culture. Nevertheless, it would be wise not to underestimate the general human intelligence but rather try to extend genuine education as widely as possible.

If history must be told, various narratives about Western civilization can attempt to "cover the facts." The most central, the one that goes furthest, I think, in covering the facts, has been called "Athens and Jerusalem." As used in this way those two nouns refer simultaneously to two cities and to two goals of the human mind. Athens and Jerusalem are at once actual and symbolic. In their symbolic meaning, "Athens" represents a philosophic-scientific approach to actuality, with the goal being cognition, while "Jerusalem" represents a scriptural tradition of disciplined insight and the aspiration to holiness. Together they propose the question: Is all of actuality more like a mathematical equation or is it more like a complicated and surprising poem, reflecting, as Robert Penn Warren once put it, the world's tangled and hieroglyphic beauty. Over many centuries Western civilization has answered this question not either-or but both-and, both Athens and Jerusalem. The interaction between Athens and Jerusalem has been a dynamic one, characterized by tension, attempted synthesis, and outright conflict. It has been this dynamic relation that is distinctive in Western civilization, and has created its restlessness as well as energized its greatest achievements, both material and spiritual, both Athens and Jerusalem. In such things as the Empire State Building, the Golden Gate Bridge, the hydrogen fusion reaction and the microchip, the cognitive science of Athens predominates, but spiritual aspiration is also present. In Chartres Cathedral, the music of Bach, Stanford White's triple porch of St. Bartholemew's Church, the poetry of Gerard Manley Hopkins and T. S. Eliot, the spirituality of Jerusalem is a potent force but the mind of Athens remains a presence, too. As the achievements just mentioned indicate, the great narrative could be told in terms of art and architecture, and certainly music, perhaps even science and mathematics. But here it will be told in terms of literature, which does not need to be translated from nonverbal to verbal expression.

The most important books and other works of high intellect represent a continuing revelation of Western thought and feeling. Such revelation is endless, almost by definition. Attention to it is the work of a lifetime. For the practical purposes of college education, a good introduction can consist of a single one-year course, that is, one course among many at the freshman or sophomore level. One model for such a course is the freshman Humanities I–II course at Columbia College, the seminar ancestor of which was introduced in 1919 by John Erskine, a professor of English. It begins in the fall with Homer and ends in the spring with a great novel chosen from many possibilities.

The title of this book speaks of a "cultural catastrophe," and, more cheerfully, of "smiling through it." The catastrophe is evident to anyone with eyes to see and ears to hear, but as regards higher education, one aspect of the catastrophe is the fact that of the books discussed in the pages that follow, all of them bearers of essential civilizational knowledge, few are part of the intellectual equipment even of professors in the liberal arts today, much less their students. This occlusion has been accompanied by, indeed is part of, an epistemological egalitarianism that assumes one opinion is as good as another, one book or proffered work of "art" as good as another, one idea as good as another, one "lifestyle" as good as another. Not surprisingly we have seen growing incoherence in the university curriculum, a loss of point and a loss of seriousness, and as would naturally follow, a proliferation of whimsical and shallowly ideological courses: the triumph of nescience.

But I sense that out across our nation, the dark fields of the republic as Nick Carraway called it, a growing number of students and professors long for something more serious and more lasting. Therefore my title is *Smiling Through the Cultural Catastrophe* because of the intellectual force and civilizing energy of the indispensable works to be considered. "To lose what is not a waste land," writes Lyndall Gordon in *T. S. Eliot: An Imperfect Life*, "is the very condition of being in a waste land." To claim this, and also to claim distinctive excellences for Western civilization, will doubtless seem to many culturally unforgivable. But that is part of the catastrophe.

Acknowledgments

I wish to express my gratitude to Jacques Barzun, Lionel Trilling, and Mark Van Doren. They introduced me as an undergraduate to many of the books I discuss here, and these books remained with us when we were colleagues. I am also grateful to the generations of students both at Columbia and at Dartmouth who entered the conversation to my great benefit. I must mention as representative of these, and one of the most brilliant, a young man of great promise, Kellner Schwartz, who completed his undergraduate work at Columbia in three years and then died kayaking somewhere in the direction of the Arctic Circle. RIP. Wise and learned advice during the writing of this book came from Joseph Epstein, Robert Hollander of Princeton, and Jonathan Brent of Yale University Press. I am grateful to Bill Buckley for his decades of friendship, belief in this book, and his encouragement. The staff of Baker-Berry Library at Dartmouth has been gracious and untiring. And finally, thanks to Eliza Childs, the most meticulous of editors.

PART 1

The Great Narrative

CHAPTER ONE

Athens and Jerusalem

Plato and the Prophets are the most important sources of
modern culture.

— HERMAN COHEN (1924)

In this chapter we will be considering the creative tension that arises
between Athens and Jerusalem and the fundamental importance of that
tension for Western civilization. Yet the idea of creative tension may also
be applied to individual psychology. It may well be that thought itself,
considered in its very nature, arises out of the experience of contradiction, that thought is the response of the mind to the experience of
contradiction. Thus Emile Durkheim was struck by the apparent para-
dox of the fact that the suicide rate rose not during periods of economic
depression but during periods of rising prosperity. This contradiction
provoked thought leading to theories of relative deprivation and reference groups. Perhaps thought requires contradiction. As Lionel Trilling
once observed, "whenever we put two emotions into juxtaposition we
have what we can properly call an idea. When Keats brings together, as
he so often does, his emotions about love and his emotions about death,
we have a very powerful idea and the source of consequent ideas."[1] Thus
John Keats's lyrical expression, the nightingale's song, the unheard music of the Urn, and the thin but welcome music of autumn, arose out of
contradiction.

I make no claim to originality in positing "Athens" and "Jerusalem"
as fundamental to the structure of the Western mind and the civilization

it produced. Thomas Jefferson and Friedrich Nietzsche do not appear often in the same sentence, but they agreed at least upon this. The Athens-Jerusalem paradigm is not exactly a commonplace, and certainly not one in the discussion of literature, but enough philosophers have argued for its centrality to have made this a kind of consensus. Whatever their differences in detail, such philosophers recognize that Athens and Jerusalem amount to a dialectic, and that the consequences of their interaction have been decisive for the character of Western civilization, setting it off from other cultures and civilizations both past and present. Yet, as I have said, this is not part of the intellectual equipment of the educated reader, and neither professors nor their students appear to be aware of its dynamic significance or its presence in the important books we will be discussing here, beginning with the *Iliad* and Exodus, fundamental works for Athens and Jerusalem. Indeed, with very few exceptions, these and many other works to be discussed here are but residually present today, if at all, even to professors of the liberal arts. In our present circumstances, I believe, most educated readers will experience these classics with, paradoxically, the sense of discovery felt by Keats upon first reading Chapman's Homer.

As I have said, the terms *Athens* and *Jerusalem* in this dialectic refer to the two famous cities and to the distinctive ways of looking at the world that developed in each. More broadly, they are metaphors referring to philosophy/science and to the disciplined insights of Scripture. The philosopher begins like Socrates by saying "I know nothing" and pursues knowledge through an investigation of the world. The scriptural tradition bases its view of the world on a series of received insights into the constitution of actuality. The insights are not true because they are recorded in scripture, but they are recorded there because, finally, they are true. As Paul Cantor says in his excellent recent book on *Hamlet*, "The conflict between the classical and the Christian has been central to Western civilization, and has produced the basis for both its proudest and its most deeply problematical moments."[2] As we will see later on, the strong and competing claims of Athens and Jerusalem may be central to the conflicts within the mind of the troubled prince.

Let us begin by reflecting for a moment on the "Athens" part of the dialectic. It can hardly be a matter of dispute that both science and philosophy have developed in the West with a continuity and practical authority not seen in any other civilization. Edward Grant, for example, a distinguished historian of science, has provided a persuasive demonstration of why this disciplined investigation of the world developed in the West and nowhere else.[3] Grant argues that Islam, which very early exhibited great skills in science and philosophy, distinctively maintained these activities in an intellectual compartment separate from Islamic religion. It thus failed to institutionalize the investigation of the world in its great religiously controlled universities. Within Islam, as in China, early scientific achievements remained separate from the central institutional life of the civilization. In neither was there a dialectic, an inter-action—troubling but creative—analogous to Athens and Jerusalem.

In the West such a dialectic, with its creative tension, was established as early as the first century A.D. That, according to Grant, made the historic difference. His account of this development is important and should be quoted here rather than summarized:

Although science has a long history with roots in ancient Egypt and Mesopotamia, it is indisputable that modern science emerged in Western Europe and nowhere else. The reason for this momentous occurrence must therefore be sought in some unique set of circumstances that differentiate Western society from other contemporary and earlier civilizations. The establishment of science as a basic enterprise within a society depends upon more than expertise in technical scientific subjects, experiments, and disciplined observations. After all, science can be found in many early societies. In Islam, until approximately 1500, mathematics, astronomy, geometric optics, and medicine were more highly developed than in the West. But science was not institutionalized in Islamic society. Nor was it institutionalized in ancient medieval China, despite significant achievements. Similar arguments apply to all other societies and civilizations. Science can be found in many of them but was institutionalized and perpetuated in none.[4]

This is an important piece of analysis. Its arguments apply to "all other societies and civilizations." Science was "institutionalized and perpetuated in none." Grant locates this uniqueness explicitly in a theological development, the incorporation by early Christianity of Greek philosophy, an incorporation that involved intense struggle. He writes from the perspective of the history of science, but clearly he engages much more here—that is, a uniquely Western way of looking at the world, with consequences for its culture generally. He puts his stress on Clement of Alexandria and Origen in their arguments with Tertullian, but the dialectic between Athens and Jerusalem can be traced back more than a century earlier, to the first century, to Paul and to Philo of Alexandria, a Platonizing Jewish philosopher, both of whom were contemporaries of Jesus. Grant, however, concludes that it was Clement and Origen who institutionalized the dialectic between Athens and Jerusalem and established the terms with which their successors worked: "In the second half of the Third Century, Christian apologists concluded that Christianity could profitably utilize pagan Greek philosophy and learning. In a momentous move, Clement of Alexandria (ca. 215–150) laid down the basic approach that others would follow. Greek philosophy, they argued, was not inherently good or bad, but one or the other depending on how it was used by Christians. Although the Greek poets and philosophers had not received direct revelation from God, they did receive natural reason and were therefore pointed toward truth."[5] Though Clement and Origen won this important argument, they did not do so without fierce opposition. Tertullian (ca. 225–150) sternly asked, "What, indeed, has Athens to do with Jerusalem? What concord is there between the Academy and the Church?"[6]

It is striking here that Tertullian, thus very early, uses as paradigmatic the terms *Athens* and *Jerusalem*, indicating as he does so that they were thus understood then as we understand them here, and no doubt were so understood even earlier. Tertullian tried to pry Athens and Jerusalem apart. Clement and Origen tried to pull them closer together. In its formative early centuries, Christianity, like Islam later on, might have ignored or tried to suppress Greek philosophy. As Grant says, however, the victory of Clement and Origen was momentous. The Athens-Jerusalem dialectic prevailed in the West. Neither was compartmentalized against the other.

Beginning with Homer and with Exodus, that is, here, Achilles and Moses, roughly contemporary Bronze Age figures (very approximately around 1200 B.C.), both of whom were fundamental to their civilizations, both flawed, both heroic and exemplary, we will go on to see the tensions shift within the dialectic as represented by a succession of indispensable works reflecting to a considerable degree phases of Western civilization. The heroic virtue of Achilles will be internalized by Socrates as heroic philosophy. The Commandments of Moses will be internalized by Jesus in his famous Sermon on the Mount as heroic holiness. Neither man wrote anything, and both teachers were martyrs to their truth. Exterior heroism becomes interior aspiration, in Socrates to cognition, in Jesus to perfection of the soul. Paul of Tarsus, a contemporary of Jesus, Roman citizen, Jew, rabbi, Christian, and a Greek speaker, embodies in his person the polarities of the dialectic. When he travels to Athens to make his case at the Areopagus, the scene in Acts is intended to remind us of Socrates before the Athenian jury. Augustine begins as a Roman and a neoplatonist but chooses Paul and holiness, and Dante holds the polarities together in a grand synthesis, Aristotle-Cicero-Virgil-Science, but also Paul-Augustine-Scripture-Aquinas. Hamlet contains multiple contradictions, saliently the command by the Ghost to exact revenge (heroic) but not to "taint" his mind (Christian). The Enlightenment shifts the balance toward Athens—science and cognition—but evokes in response a profound critique in literature and philosophy.

Leo Strauss, a formidable twentieth-century philosopher, was far from alone in insisting on the centrality of this dialectic. He maintained that the core of Western civilization consists of an irresolvable tension between Athens and Jerusalem. He began a famous and densely argued essay ("Jerusalem and Athens," 1968) this way: "All the hopes that we entertain in the midst of the confusions and dangers of the present are founded positively or negatively, directly or indirectly, on the experience of the past. Of these experiences the broadest and deepest, as far as

Western men are concerned, are indicated by the names of the two cities Jerusalem and Athens. Western man became what he is through the coming together of biblical faith and Greek thought. In order to understand ourselves and to illuminate our trackless way into the future, we must understand Jerusalem and Athens."[7]

Strauss insisted repeatedly that though individuals in regard to ultimate decisions might choose either Jerusalem or Athens, they at the same time must remain open to the other possibility because each pole represents a profound interpretation of actuality. Off at the edge, do we place our bets on rational analysis or on the insights of acknowledged masters? If the individual chooses one or the other, for Strauss the West must not. He went so far as to claim that Western liberal democracy uniquely inhabits the both-and tension between Jerusalem and Athens. It is the special insistence of Strauss's thought that the tension not be resolved, that civilizationally the dialectic remain open. I understand him to mean that a society based entirely on cognition (Athens) would have a pull toward totalitarianism, as in Plato's *Republic;* and that a society based wholly on the pursuit of holiness (Jerusalem) would be a theocracy and resemble a monastery. For Strauss, these two tendencies correct each other and freedom flourishes within the tension, the democratic norm being the man who knows too much to be a skeptic or a relativist but too little to be an absolutist. Strauss's reverence for the great works of Western literature has to do with the fact that, characteristically, they do not resolve the tension, though they may pull one way or the other. They refuse to simplify the experience of either Athens or Jerusalem. When that experience is lost, I understand Strauss to be saying, the West ceases to take itself seriously. There occurs, to use the language of Martin Heidegger, a "withdrawal of being."

Strauss certainly understood that in his both-and civilizational position he was quarreling with, or correcting, Nietzsche, who internalized the tension and sought to resolve it. Nietzsche experienced the tension with pain and could write about it lyrically: " 'You shall always be the first and excel all others; your jealous souls shall love no one, unless it be the friend'—that made the soul of the Greek quiver; thus he walked the path of his greatness. 'You honor thy father and mother and follow their will to the roots of one's soul'—that was the tablet of overcoming that another people hung over themselves and became powerful and eternal thereby."[8] This was one way to express the polarities and their tension: the Greek striving for excellence, the Hebrew commitment to a moral and spiritual tradition handed down by father and mother. Unlike Strauss, however, Nietzsche wanted to resolve the tension rather than maintain it, the tension perhaps being too much for his nerves. He proposed to do so through a new kind of man who would contain the opposites. "The Roman Caesar," he called it, "with Christ's soul." This new man, the Übermensch, was, as Strauss put it, "meant to unite Jerusalem and Athens at the highest level."

Of course the Superior Man "at the highest level" remains a myth. We can see distant attempts to embody a resolution in, perhaps, Charlemagne, Chaucer's Knight, Shakespeare's Henry V, soldiers with aspects of saintliness, but not at the level or intensity that Nietzsche had in mind. His Superior Man contains the contradiction without diminishing the attracting force of either pole. Not surprisingly, such a figure remains mythical, though perhaps finding expression in the lyricism of Nietzsche's prose.

Descending a bit, one sometimes encounters these polarities in unexpected places. The great historian Thomas Babington Macaulay, celebrant of material progress, sensed the polarities, however flickeringly, when he visited the Crystal Palace exposition in London in 1851. At this temple of science and progress, he records, "I made my way into the building; a most gorgeous sight; vast, graceful . . . I was quite dazzled, and I felt as I did on entering St. Peter's."[9] Macaulay admired nothing that St. Peter's represented religiously, but he had sensed for a moment the power of its spiritual aspiration.

Lest I be misunderstood here, I repeat that there have been and are great civilizations besides the Western form. Indeed, Western civilization has flourished to a considerable degree because of its eclecticism, its ability to absorb and make use of what it has found to be valuable outside itself. The alphabet that permitted the transcription of the epics

10 THE GREAT NARRATIVE

of Homer was a Semitic import by an illiterate Aegean civilization. The
numerals that now are universally used came from Islam. The arts have
been importantly influenced by the works of peoples both ancient and
modern.

Islamic scholars made important contributions to the development of
Western science, though, as has been pointed out here, Islam did not
succeed as the West did in institutionalizing science. During the general
disorganization of Europe that followed upon the collapse of the Western Roman Empire late in the fifth century, the preservation of learning
depended indispensably upon Islamic scholars and scientists who provided a "bridge" over the chaos in Europe. In addition to this, the
monastic communities that arose in Europe, islands of civilization amid
roving bands of brigands and seaborne invaders, preserved vital connections with ancient learning. Both the monastic and Islamic "bridges"
were vital to the preservation of this material and in making it available
when a degree of feudal order was established during the twelfth century.

The Greeks, the cognitive tradition of Athens, and preeminently
Aristotle, had created the foundations for a variety of disciplines—
physics, zoology, medicine, meteorology, ethics, metaphysics, logic. Islamic scholars living in and around Alexandria, for centuries a crossroads of philosophy and science, translated, commented extensively
upon, and modified the works of the Greeks. For example, the translator
Hunyuan ibn Ishaq (died ca. A.D. 873) translated three dialogues of
Plato, four works of Aristotle, fifteen Hippocratic medical texts, and
ninety works of the Greek physician Galen. Living as he did in the ninth
century A.D., this Islamic translator and his colleagues had no counter-
parts in a disintegrating Europe that was unable to establish a minimum
of civilized order, though the embattled monastic communities aided the
effort at preservation. It is no denigration of the Islamic scholars to say
that when order began to be restored Europe was able to make use of the
vast material handed down in ways that Islamic society was not prepared to do. The Islamic inhibition had to do with its belief system, the
basic presuppositions of its culture, and this was certainly a tragedy
for Islam.

I will risk a bit of repetition here because of the importance of the following point. Beginning in the first century A.D., and importantly articulated by Clement and Origen in the second and third centuries, the main Western tradition has held that Athens and Jerusalem, though in tension, are compatible. There would be shifts of emphasis, yes; but there would be no divorce. This amounted to the assumption that very ultimately there is a single truth available to both Athens and Jerusalem, toward which they converge, even if the two paths may not finally meet within human understanding. The dominant Islamic tradition, in contrast, evolved a tradition of compartmentalized truths. For Islamic thought during its decisive phase, a proposition might be true in science and philosophy but false in religion. The central Western tradition, with its roots in the first century, held with Greek logic that a proposition cannot be both true and false at the same time. Western truth, both scientific and religious, had to be unitary. There could be no contradiction. If a miracle is alleged to have occurred in time and space, it must be validated like any other event.

The Great Wall and the Forbidden City are strikingly different symbols from those we take for granted as Western, which certainly include Odysseus and Columbus, Oxbridge, Harvard, CalTech, and the Sorbonne, Chartres Cathedral, the Empire State Building, and the Golden Gate Bridge, philosophy pressing to the edges of the time-space continuum and maybe beyond, space exploration, and Dante's unifying symbol, the "Love that moves the stars." When students encounter the material we will be dealing with in this book, that is, major works of intellect and art in the Western tradition, they always sense that they are dealing with matters of the first importance. They are retracing one of the greatest adventures in the history of mankind, and they are on their way to becoming citizens.

Of the works we will be considering in the chapters that follow, beginning with the *Iliad* and Exodus, a strong and lasting consensus judges all to be absolutely fundamental. Many have enjoyed such classic status for centuries. Some of the earliest reach tantalizingly back into prehistory. Of course books discussed or even mentioned here do not exhaust any list of major works, and new books, written today or tomorrow, will gather a consensus and be added to the lists. Works forgotten for one reason or another are rediscovered, and any list is subject to re-evaluation and revision. But when all is said and done, the works dealt with here have endured, and for good reason. Tradition is both cognitive and democratic; it extends the vote beyond the minority living at any given moment.

Each work to be examined here challenges the reader, including this writer, sometimes with its difficulty, sometimes with strangeness, which is an attribute of originality. Often within the work itself there are reservations and contradictions that are part of the total world of that work of art. Such internal contradictions exist because the author's mind was aware of just such complications in actuality and necessarily included them within the whole he was fashioning.

To each of these works countless scholars have devoted their lives. Needless to say, I can claim a degree of expert knowledge in only a few of them and probably will commit errors even about those. A reader reads a strong book, but such books as these also silently read the reader, demanding effort and aspiration, and always issue a silent judgment on the quality of the reading and the reader. A brilliant young professor with whom I once shared an office at Columbia became so challenged and tested by what he found in Shakespeare that he almost became unhinged, and though he was an astonishingly effective lecturer found himself unable to organize a doctoral thesis about so powerful a writer.

But it is by no means a bad thing, short of such self-immolation, for a student lulled by our egalitarian culture to be obliged to deal with authors who dramatically surpass him in intellect and imagination. We are not the peers of these great writers. But they have the power to make us more intelligent for a while, and perhaps better, than we ordinarily would be. In a formulation worth pondering, Robert Frost once remarked that strong writing made us consider life "with greater regard."[10]

On the frieze above Butler Library at Columbia are engraved such names as Homer, Virgil, Augustine, Dante, Montaigne, Cervantes, Voltaire, Plato, Aristotle, Milton, Shakespeare, Goethe. Such names are there, and permanently, because they deserve to be. And I suppose they are out of chronological order because the architect meant to say that greatness is a more important thing than time. I once overheard a Columbia student, who looked to be a freshman, rather charmingly observe that the writers listed there are "the first team."

"Humanity," wrote C. S. Lewis, "does not pass through phases as a train through stations: being alive, it has the privilege of always moving yet never leaving anything behind. Whatever we have been, in some sense we still are."[11] I take this to mean that we can participate imaginatively, both as individuals and as a culture, in past modes of being and adapt them to our present consciousness. Achilles, Odysseus, Moses— these and the other great figures never died. The modes of being and insight represented by these works are absolutely permanent things, and the great conversation that goes on among them and between us and them is immensely important.

CHAPTER TWO

Athens: The Heroic Phase

Plato, four centuries after Homer's epics were written down, tells us that Homer was the educator of Greece. It was this authoritative standing that moved Plato to try to displace Homer and project a new ideal of nobility for Greece and, beyond Greece, for mankind. Plato fully absorbed Homer and was inspired by him but tried to go beyond him, knowing that his contest with Homer was epic in character. As against the older nobility of the battlefield, Plato proposed the superior heroism of the mind.

The name Plato was a friendly nickname for a youth who must have been one of the most astonishing schoolboys who has ever lived. His given name was Aristocles, the son of Ariston, and he was born in 428 or 427 B.C. His family were upper-class Athenians. Tradition has it that the name Plato was given him by his young friends because of his exceptionally wide forehead.

In the Athenian schools, he, like the other students, read the *Iliad* and the *Odyssey*, committed passages to memory, and commented on the poems extensively. He no doubt was acquainted with the developing tradition of Greek philosophy, which included such figures as Heraclitus, Democritus, Thales, and Pythagoras. What he accomplished was to combine the epic stories of Homer with philosophy in a new synthesis. He tried to replace Homer's noble chieftains with Socrates, who would be not a prince of Greece alone but of philosophy itself, an explorer of the human essence and of the cosmos. Plato thought he saw beyond

Homer to universal truths that remained only implicit in the great poet. He meant to dislodge Homer as the educator of Greece and establish himself as the better teacher.

The Homeric epics thus had enormous civilizational consequences, both in themselves and as refracted through the mind of Plato. They belong to a much wider epic tradition and have features and themes in common with such other ancient epics as *Beowulf, Roland, Niebelungenleid,* and *Gilgamesh.* As we will see, the Homeric epic material has roots in common with the other major epic emerging in the Middle East, the epic of the patriarchs and Moses in the Hebrew Bible.

The Homeric epics became fundamental for two large reasons. The great poet we call Homer possessed enormous talent. *Beowulf, Gilgamesh,* and the others cannot compete. In addition, Greek culture did something unique with his epics. As the *Iliad* and the *Odyssey* moved through Aegean culture they engaged a developing Greek philosophical tradition that existed long before Plato and which, with hindsight, we call the "pre-Socratics." This ancient philosophical tradition, of which we have little more than fragments, sought universal truths, often conceiving of them in ways that now may seem bizarre. As its greatest exemplar and refiner, Plato sought to complete their thought and, as against such Homeric heroes as Achilles and Odysseus, put forward his universal hero of the intellect, Socrates.

It is important here to stress that in Plato, Homer is always there, a named and unnamed presence, antagonist and inspirer. His dialogues are combats of the mind, comparable to the mortal combats on the field before Troy. These dialogues describe a long mental journey, comparable to the long journey of Odysseus from Troy to his home in Ithaca. Yet if Plato came forward as the heroic philosopher challenging the heroic poet, he himself was also challenged. He surely knew that in order to prevail he would have to match or beat Homer in literary and intellectual power. He accepted that challenge, and we have his extraordinary dialogues.

Nonetheless, Homer is always there. When Socrates, who could have saved himself from execution, instead chooses death and immortal glory, he makes the choice Achilles made. Death is as nothing compared with honor. Plato's own style is as distinctive as Homer's. Readers often speak of the special "music" of Plato's dialogues; and music itself was of great importance to him, both for its own sake and as a mode of knowledge. As a mode of knowledge, music was comparable to, for example, geometry— an expression of the underlying order of the cosmos. Eric Voegelin's brief sentences on the death of Plato amount almost to a philosophical poem: "Plato died at the age of eighty-one. On the evening of his death he had a Thracian girl play the flute to him. The girl could not find the beat of the *Nomos*. With a movement of his finger, Plato indicated the measure."[1]

The accounts we have in epic literature are stories with roots deep in the prehistoric past. We naturally regard this material with some skepticism about its worth as history; yet it would not be wise to dismiss the legends as purely fictitious. They are memories of memories, no doubt embellished, but perhaps preserving a core of historical truth. Those archaic preliterate peoples cared deeply about their legends, a precious mode of self-understanding, and the bards told the old stories again and again. Originally they were transmitted orally, by wandering performers, and were written down only with the discovery of writing, that is, rather recently in the West. The Greeks acquired a written alphabet around 800 B.C., about five hundred years after the events described by Homer are supposed to have happened.

The narratives coming to us from what I have been calling Jerusalem's heroic phase have similarly ancient roots. In what follows, this heroic phase will be represented by the epic of Moses, by the *Mosead* as it might be called, consisting of the first five books of the Hebrew Bible. The chronologies here, as in all ancient works, are complicated and subject to dispute, but, strikingly, Genesis seems to have been written down at about the same time as the *Iliad* and the *Odyssey*, around 800 B.C. The epic of Moses moves from the creation of the universe in Genesis through the escape from Egypt, the reception of the Law on Sinai, various wanderings and military campaigns, and ends with the epic death of Moses as he views the Promised Land across the Jordan River.

The stories that come down to us in Homer and in the Pentateuch passed through many narrators before they were written down and are not strictly speaking history as we use the term. Yet this does not mean that they are fiction. The Athenians of the fifth century, contemporaries of Thucydides, were highly literate and knew what history is; yet they believed that "something like" the Homeric stories had actually happened in what we would call the thirteenth century B.C., long before the Greeks had a written language. Such people as Achilles, Odysseus, Hector, Helen, Paris, Priam, Agamemnon, and all the others had existed, they thought, their stories handed down by bardic storytellers and finally by the greatest of these, Homer.

Whether Homer himself could write remains a matter of scholarly dispute, but he lived on a hinge of history that led to a leap in consciousness. With a Semitic script new to Aegean culture, he or someone else wrote down his bardic stories and allowed the legendary figures to live upon the written surface and thus the Athenian stage, and also helped shape Greek philosophy.

It would certainly be exciting for us to push back in time with the archaeologists to the forever silent, preliterate peoples. Homer's Troy is still there today, at least its traces. In the ancient world a city destroyed often provided the foundation for another city, and it now seems established that the Troy described by Homer met this fate. Archaeologists, beginning with the inspired and eccentric Heinrich Schliemann and continuing through many others, have found in the sixth layer of material there a Bronze Age city whose remains appear to be those of the city Homer describes. Homer's description of the area corresponds to much that can be seen today. His topography, including the famous adjacent islands, is accurate. Sediment has changed the old beach where the Greeks landed, but insofar as we can check Homer's account, the poem is startlingly accurate.

Again, I would issue a warning, memory among these preliterate peoples must have been different from modern memory. We have archives, they had stories handed down, but they seem to have clung to accuracy. Much of their view of the world depended upon it. I find it dangerous to doubt serious and central oral tradition in any comprehensive way.

I suppose it likely that most of us do feel some attraction to and curiosity about those ancient silent peoples who lived not only before writing but before now-remembered oral narrative. We no longer hear their voices. All we have of some of them are a few artifacts, including such silent wonders as the cave murals at Altamira, Lascaux, and Avignon.

The deeds of Achilles had been sung, but he did not have a transcribed voice until more than five hundred years after his supposed death. With Homer these archaic Bronze Age figures come to us out of prehistoric time, all of a sudden visible, speaking, acting, knowable. Imagining ourselves back in time, when the sixth level of our archaeological dig was Troy of the many high towers, we can see through the eyes of old King Priam the approach of Achilles, who Priam knows is death to Troy: "And old Priam was the first to see him coming, surging over the plain, blazing/like the star that rears at harvest, flaming up in brilliance . . . So the bronze flared on his chest as on he raced."[2]

Homer suspects that the worried king might well have been the first to see the approach of this most dangerous of warriors. Homer's Achilles blazes and flames, as indeed Priam's city would burn. The word *harvest* suggests the coming autumn of Troy. And this is the Bronze Age, so Achilles' bronze armor flares in the distance.

If Homer's Achilles is a memory of memories of a great Bronze Age warrior, so Moses comes to the written narrative through centuries of recollection. He is much more solidly placeable in history than Achilles, yet there is no important evidence that Moses ever lived. There is no independent evidence that the Hebrew tribes in fact were slaves in Egypt, or that Moses led them out and through the desert to Canaan. There are confirmatory scraps and inferences, as we will see, but that is about all we have in the way of history. Experts on the issue of the historical existence of Moses seem to have reached a rough consensus that "someone like" Moses had to have existed unless subsequent events in history are not to be left floating in air. There must have been such a powerful personality to rally the disparate tribes, form them into a people on their march through the desert, deliver the Law, and through endurance and successful warfare lead them to the bank of the Jordan across from Jericho. The passage about his death at the end of Deuteronomy is one of the great things in literature, fully equal in epic literature to the death of Achilles, for which we have to wait until book 24 of the *Odyssey*. No one knows where the grave of Moses is, on the wrong side of the Jordan River, as he was forbidden by God to cross into the Promised Land. In this epic narrative, Moses, like Achilles, is flawed in many ways; yet he remains the colossal figure of Michelangelo's famous statue, the great epic hero of Jerusalem in its heroic phase.

So far as chronology is concerned, we could start the narrative of Western civilization either with Homer's epics or with the Hebrew Bible. They are the primary documents. For the heroic phase of Greek culture, either the *Iliad* or the *Odyssey* would serve; or, better still, both of them together. Many of the same characters appear in both poems, and both raise the same important questions in different ways. The *Iliad* is intense, high pressured, tightening the knot of tragedy to the point of madness. The *Odyssey* is spacious, like the seas sailed by Odysseus, full of blue water and sunlight, sensuous, often amusing, often polite, and fortunate at the end. Dante knew the two stories only in summary and distorted form, but he must have had both poems in mind when he makes Virgil call Homer the "sovereign poet." Virgil combined elements of both in his *Aeneid*. Achilles and Odysseus figure in Dante's *Divine Comedy*, Odysseus brilliantly. As we see here, the greatest books tend to talk with one another in continuous dialogue.

The *Iliad* and the *Odyssey* were brought to Athens in their present form by Pisistratus, who ruled, with interruptions, from 560 to 527 B.C. As has already been mentioned, Homer himself may not have been able to write, since Homeric culture was illiterate. But at about the time of Homer, during the ninth century B.C., the peoples of both the Greek islands and the mainland borrowed from the Phoenicians, their trading partners, a Semitic alphabet that they began to use in limited ways, as in brief inscriptions. It is not known whether Homer ever saw this notation used for wider purposes. What we have as the texts for the *Iliad* and *Odyssey* may have been taken down by a scribe or team of scribes as a bardic performer sang or recited the hexameter verses, perhaps to the accompaniment of a stringed instrument. We can imagine such celebratory entertainments taking place at the small courts of local rulers and nobility, as the chieftains listened to the narrative depictions of their heroic ideals. By the time these narratives were written down they probably were too well known to have admitted of much variation. For the civilization of Greece, these poems became more than magnificent narratives. They had much of the character of scripture. Schoolboys read them with care, memorized passages, and commented on them from an ethical perspective. The *Iliad* and the *Odyssey*, along with much else, were part of the Greek *paideia*, or character-shaping curriculum. The goal of the curriculum was *areté*, a special kind of excellence. If one combined all the excellences of the various heroes and heroines of the Homeric poems, and for a moment forgot their flaws, one could construct a model of *areté*. One could discuss the various excellences and rank them according to degree of excellence—the courage and grandeur of Achilles; the cleverness and eloquence of Odysseus; the sheer strength of Ajax; the urbanity and courage of Hector; the filial nobility of Telemachus; the moral strength, cunning, and politeness of Penelope; the courtliness of Nausicaa; the experienced wisdom of Nestor and Mentor. Of course there were the defects to be considered: the rage of Achilles, the catastrophic misjudgment of Agamemnon, the narcissistic erotic carelessness of great and beautiful Helen. All of these would have been the subject of discussion and analysis.

In Homer's two epics, the heroes strive toward the comprehensive excellence of *areté* in every aspect of their being.[3] The ideal of *areté* combines battlefield prowess with courtly manners, constant awareness of ancestors and other noble examples, eloquence, and musical ability. Such a hero is both eloquent in speech and heroic in action. All the great figures in Homer strive for *areté*, even in the athletic games, which are more than games in the Homeric epic. Human nature is assumed to be uniform, and *areté* is its highest achievement. Thus Ajax embodies strength, Odysseus eloquence, but Achilles combines the two, in addition to all the others. The degree of *areté* a hero has achieved cannot be known until his death. Surely great Hector lost in this competition when he fled from Achilles in that terrible scene, running terrified around the walls of Troy; yet, all in all, he deserved his enormous funeral pyre at the end of the *Iliad*. In the pursuit of *areté*, every heroic action deserves eternal glory through recollection and celebration in art. The characters in Homer know their stories will be sung by the poets. Aristotle drew the elements of *areté* together in a pedagogical synthesis in his portrait of the magnanimous man in the *Ethics*. He also composed a hymn to his friend Hermias, prince of Atarneus, who had died for his moral and philosophical ideals. The hymn explicitly connects Aristotle's own conception of permanent pattern with Homer. The gods and goddesses already have their perfection, as Homer conceived it, because they are immortal.[4]

The remarkable thing about Homer's epics is that, magnificent narratives as they are, they were also implicitly philosophical. They had enough latent intellectual content to provide a basis for the reflections of high Athenian philosophy. The bond among Homer and Socrates, Plato and Aristotle is the striving toward an abstract idea of pattern or form, as in *areté*. But, and this is an enormously important point, Homer's *areté* is not only the human goal of heroes but is striven for by animals and inanimate objects. It is latent in the speed and spirit of noble horses, in the perfection of physical objects, such as swords, shields, goblets, musical instruments. Such things have their goals of excellence, often genealogies, and they strive for their ideal forms with the rest of Homer's universe. This is not as mysterious as it might sound. We can imagine that every "thing" is trying to be the best "thing" of its kind—whether that "thing" is a cat, a tree, or a wave of the sea. Of course, some "things," like many humans, fall far short. In comparison with the Form, they are misshapen, while others in varying degree approach ideal Form. Homeric actuality is a vast Olympic games, striving toward the permanence of perfection. There can be no doubt that Socrates, Plato, and Aristotle were enormously aware of this dominant quality in Homer and in the civilization that took Homer for its text. Plato, who said that

Homer was the teacher of Greece, envisioned reality as an unchanging pattern of Forms or Ideas finally subsumed in the One, the Good, the ultimate Form of the cosmos. The perception of Forms leading to the Form was to be the goal of an arduous intellectual or spiritual quest. If you desired to undertake it, you might enroll at Plato's Academy in Athens. Plato understood this intellectual and spiritual ambition as derivative from the striving of the Homeric hero for the perfect Form of *areté*. Aristotle also studied *areté* in Homer, and it underlay his concept of "pattern," which, like Plato's Forms, transcends the particulars. It is here, in the high philosophy of Athens, and in the schools of thought derivative from it, that a connection occurs with the biblical monotheism of Jerusalem, there "from the beginning." The philosophers were moving toward a philosophically derived monotheism, a logically derived language of talking about ultimate things that was not derived from myth or scripture. "Plato's whole philosophy," writes Werner Jaeger, "is built on the creation of 'patterns.' . . . And he describes the ideas as 'patterns' established in the realm of 'Being.' The Idea of the Good, that universally applicable pattern, is directly descended from the models of heroic *areté*, which were part of the old aristocratic code."[5]

The Olympic gods and goddesses in Homer are related to these developments. They are an immortal aristocracy, immune to any serious consequences of their rivalries and foibles, jealousies, angers, and vices. They provide an immortal background against which human action strives for an immortality of honor, memory, and artistic celebration. But in Homer, and as later developed by Socrates, Plato, and Aristotle, there is an aspiration in Homer's divinities to move beyond the many toward one divine power that would be beyond squabbling, specialized, local divinities. In Homer, final power resides with a sometimes negligent Zeus. From another perspective, the Olympic gods and goddesses in Homer represent a sort of halfway house in religious development, lodged somewhere between the rich substratum of popular cults, many of them of dark and barbaric character, and the final perceptions of Greek philosophy as represented by Socrates and developed by Plato and Aristotle.

These Olympian gods and goddesses represent a religious reform, a cleaning up of dark material reaching far back into archaic time. They seem to have been brought to the Aegean area around 1500 B.C. by nomadic Greek-speaking warriors, who encountered a richly developed matriarchal culture, notably on the island of Crete, where they conquered the inhabitants. The matriarchal mythology was not entirely obliterated. Zeus married Hera, female divinities are prominent in the Olympian pantheon, and the Homeric epics are full of impressive women. Despite the reformist victory of the aristocratic Olympian pantheon, it continued to have competitors in the form of popular cults, mystery, fertility, animal worship, and so on, including the observances of which were often chthonic.

In the Olympian gods and goddesses, as much later in Socrates, Plato, and Aristotle, we see a movement in the direction of monotheism, and a potential opening to concourse with Jerusalem. It was a "gradual unfolding," writes Werner Jaeger, "of the essential elements in the earliest forms of the Greek spirit, which throughout all the variations of its history remains fundamentally one and the same."[6] Thus, as I have said, ultimately the Homeric striving for *areté* became a cognitive pursuit in Socrates, Plato, and Aristotle, an internalization of epic heroism in the form of heroic philosophy, Socrates dying for cognition as Achilles died for *areté*.

In the Homeric epics, at the dawn of the Western literary and religious tradition, the gods and goddesses function as an immortal background against which mortal human beings work out their fates, yet the immortality of these Olympian divinities gives rise to extensive philosophical development. Homer and his contemporaries did not work out an exact sense of the timeless or immortal, which would go beyond memory and celebration. By the time we reach Socrates, the subject of immortality is up philosophically, as in the *Phaedo*. We have noticed that characters in these poems are well aware that their stories will be sung "forever" by the poets, nor were they wrong. Probably every educated person, even today, knows at least something, however sketchy, about Achilles, Odysseus, and Helen of Troy. Writing millennia after Homer, Milton refers to this view of immortality as "the last infirmity of noble mind." His word *noble* there is complicated. The idea that fame constitutes immortality is a noble idea in the sense that it is characteristic of Homer's aristocratic culture. It is also noble in the sense of "admirable." Yet it is a "last infirmity," since Milton thinks the Christian sense of immortality a vast improvement upon it. Yet Homer meant a great deal to him. His own great character Satan, the fallen archangel, is a descendant of Achilles. Satan is a defiant hero of the old kind, unfortunately caught in a Christian universe. Milton even gives him a great shield, like that of Achilles. It also seems likely that Milton's Adam had red ("hyacinthine") hair because Achilles also did.

Although Homer's gods and goddesses are immortals, they often intervene in human affairs, favoring one hero or another, siding with Greeks or Trojans. Homer is not saying, however, that they determine the results of the action. His characters are not puppets. The interventions of the gods reflect a universal human experience, of being affected by larger "forces," of falling in love or experiencing sudden anger or, as the Chinese have it, possessing, or losing, "the mandate of Heaven."

"Rage—Goddess, sing the rage of Peleus' son Achilles,/Murderous, doomed." This is the opening line in Robert Fagels's fine translation of the *Iliad*. On the evidence of that line the poem might have come down to us as *The Achilead,* or "poem about Achilles." During the fifth century, however, the historian Herodotus referred to it as the *Iliad,* or poem about Ilium (Troy), and the name stuck. These competing possibilities tell us something important about the poem. It is the tragedy of Achilles, his overpowering rage and its consequences, of the greatest of warriors dying young for immortal fame. But it is also the universal tragedy of civilization, as Homer's world saw it, the ever-recurring defeat of the city as part of the endless cycle of destruction and creation. It is thus the tragedy of the civilized city, the highest known form of human association. In Homer's world, there is no relief from this cycle. Troy will be sacked and burned, its women become booty and its men slaughtered; but such as Troy was will all cities be, including Athens. As Kipling warned the British Empire in "Recessional," it too one day could crumble into dust with Nineveh and Tyre.

Within this cycle of destruction and creation, there are only a few palliatives, for the Homeric world is icy cold. The brevity of life is resisted by heroic action, which gains for the hero immortal fame. Achilles is the exemplar of this ethos, the noblest, bravest, and most eloquent of them all, who has chosen brief life and immortal glory over long life and mediocre obscurity. Even as he slaughters the Trojan prince Hector in book 22, Hector prophesies, correctly, that Achilles himself will be killed by Paris before the walls of Troy. The vast funeral pyres of such heroes as Achilles, Hector, and Patroclus celebrate their greatness and blaze out as affirming flames against the darkness of the Homeric world. Resistance to the darkness also comes from creation, the rebuilding of the civilized city—while knowing that it too will fall—and in the perfection of all areas of life through art, whether shown in a goblet or a palace. The Homeric world and the Bronze Age Homeric heroes in this poem are colder than anything we are likely to know. In another realm are the gods, that immortal aristocracy, who temporarily involve themselves with human affairs but, secure in their deathlessness, are essentially indifferent to transitory humans.

In this poem, very importantly, Troy, the Civilized City, is the highest form of civilization known to Homer's world. Situated on the coast of today's Turkey, at the southern end of the Hellespont (Dardanelles), the city is far more attractive than the ferocious Greek military encampment on its beach. Troy, with its local allies, is large enough to field a formidable army (about 10,000 men), yet small enough to form a community in which the leading members at least know one another. Homer very finely evokes the beauty and civility of Troy, the work of its architects and artisans and its high civilization. Its goddess Athena, powerful and vengeful when crossed, also embodies intelligence. It has its temples, palaces, festivals, monuments, and tombs. King Priam's palace is a splendid structure:

> And soon
> He came to Priam's palace, that magnificent structure
> built wide with porches and colonnades of polished stone,

> and deep within its walls were fifty sleeping chambers
> masoned in smooth, lustrous ashlar, linked in a line
> where the sons of Priam slept beside their wedded wives,
> and facing these, opening out across the inner courtyard,
> lay the twelve sleeping chambers of Priam's daughters,
> masoned and roofed in lustrous ashlar, linked in a line,
> where the sons-in-law of Priam slept beside their wives.[7]

The Trojans are courteous and accustomed to restraint. They are not even vindictive toward Helen, who now understands, too late, that her adulterous and solipsistic affair with Prince Paris has brought war and danger to the city and was itself a form of self-destruction. Prince Paris, indeed handsome and luxurious, suggests the wealth and also the vulnerabilities of this high civilization. The Trojan hero Hector, for example, is more civilized than Achilles and, unlike Achilles, is divided in his will. A formidable warrior, he is also drawn strongly to his wife Andromache and their infant son Astyanax. In the scene where Hector, leaving for battle, frightens Astyanax with his Bronze Age armor and his plumed helmet, Homer sums up a great deal about the actuality of war:

> In the same breath, shining Hector reached down
> for his son—but the boy recoiled,
> crying against his nurse's full breast,
> screaming out at the sight of his own father
> terrified by the flashing bronze, the horsehair crest
> the great ridge of the helmet nodding, bristling terror—
> so it struck his eyes. And his loving father laughed,
> his mother laughed as well, and glorious Hector,
> quickly lifting the helmet from his head,
> set it down on the ground, fiery in the sunlight,
> and raising his son he kissed him, tossed him in his arms,
> lifting a prayer to Zeus and the other deathless gods.[8]

Andromache will disappear from history as a slave in Greece, and Astyanax will be hurled from the battlements in the final destruction of the city.

Within this poem about Troy there is also an *Achillead* about a warrior very different from Hector and capable of being both much more and much less than the human norm. Although not a god, he is godlike, the son of Thetis, a sea goddess, and King Peleus of the Greek Myrmidons. He will die young, but immortal fame will be his approach to divinity. The more civilized Hector could not have reached the depths of fury felt by Achilles after the insults from King Agamemnon and would not have become the killing machine that was Achilles after the death of his friend Patroclus. For most of the poem, Achilles is absent from the battlefield, but when he returns he makes all the previous fighting seem tame. When he wades through the slaughtered Trojans and finally has Lycaon at his mercy, his words are subzero cold:

> Come, friend, you too must die. Why moan about it so? Even
>   Patroclus died,
> a far, far better man than you. And look, you see how handsome and
>   powerful I
> am? The son of a great man, the mother who gave me life a deathless
>   goddess.
> But even for me, I tell you, death and strong force of fate are waiting.[9]

There is no pity at all here, no admiration for a fallen but worthy foe. This archaic hero out of the Bronze Age is both icy and remorseless, at once great and barbaric. He kills Hector and desecrates his corpse by dragging it in the dust behind his chariot.

Yet Achilles is also a prince, and we do glimpse other qualities when he is not consumed by rage at Agamemnon's insults. His manners, when he is calm, are regal. He is well versed in the traditions and rituals of his civilization. If there are furies within him and a barbarism that seems to go beyond the warrior qualities of those around him, it is also possible to think that these aspects of him are inseparable from his greatness. His red hair distinguishes him from most of the Greeks around him. His passion for life often reaches heights of lyrical expression intensified by the carnage and death that fill the poem. His love for Patroclus (and there is no indication that they are sexual lovers) is as intense as his contempt for Agamemnon or his savage determination to destroy Hector. Toward the end, he goes to battle with a great shield made for him by Hephaestus, armorer to the gods, on which is epitomized all of human existence that was known to Achilles or to Homer, war and peace in the form of two cities, the city of calamitous war and the city of fruitful peace. Achilles is formidable, more than a great warrior: he is the epitome of the heroic as imagined by his archaic society. He dominates every scene in the poem, even those from which he is absent.

The leader of the Greek armies, who have been fighting unsuccessfully for nine years on the plain before Troy, is called in most translations King Agamemnon, but he is not an absolute monarch in the Renaissance sense. He is a prince among lesser but also powerful princes. Whether Achilles, a much younger man and commanding the largest personal army in the alliance, is really lesser in standing than Agamemnon remains ambiguous. Agamemnon, unsuccessful here for nine years, may well be anxious about his position and also worried about the prestige of Achilles when he decides to humiliate him at the beginning of the poem. In its large sweep, the narrative moves from that disastrous quarrel at the outset to the great funeral pyre of Hector at the end. By this time, Achilles has achieved his revenge for the killing of Patroclus, and his normal courtesy, however shakily, has returned. The funeral rituals for Hector are thus also a celebration of the heroic ideal itself, to which Achilles has returned. For the death of Achilles we must wait, as I have said, for Homer's account in the last book of the *Odyssey*.

Achilles' enraged quarrel at the beginning may seem to a modern reader to spring from trivialities, at least in comparison with the disasters that result from it. The quarrel ostensibly concerns booty seized by the Greeks in a local raid. This includes the young woman Chryses, who is assigned to Agamemnon, and Briseis, who goes to Achilles. But because Chryses is the daughter of Calchas, a priest of Apollo, a plague descends upon the Greeks and Chryses must be returned. Agamemnon demands compensation from Achilles for this loss, they quarrel, and his heralds seize Briseis from Achilles' lavish headquarters stockade. During the quarrel Achilles, hand upon his sword, is ready to kill Agamemnon but is restrained by Athena, who here embodies something like good sense, or perhaps doubt or prudence, on the part of Achilles, given his situation.

Yet Achilles, Agamemnon, and everyone else know that Agamemnon has deliberately insulted Achilles, negated the roots of his being. The meaning of Achilles' existence is that he is a prince and a great warrior, destined to a short life but immortal "honor." The female person of the young woman Briseis is beside the point here, which is the total meaning of Achilles' short life. These ancient Greek nobles are the equivalent of medieval knights, though without the chivalry, and demand that their honor be respected. It is an objective fact, validated by their deeds and testified to by their reputations and by future poets.

Very incautiously, Agamemnon declares: "You are nothing to me." This is an astonishing statement, a hole in the cosmos, nihilistic. Yet in the entire course of the poem Agamemnon never apologizes for this violation. It remains nonnegotiable, though he tries to bribe Achilles back into the Greek alliance with gifts and flattery. "Rage—Goddess, sing the rage of Peleus' son Achilles, murderous, doomed" is Robert Fagels's fine translation of the opening lines, yet no English translation can capture the clangorous sound of Homer's bardic hexameter verse, in which the opening of the poem sounds like an overture to universal doom.

Achilles' rage at Agamemnon is fully justified. Agamemnon has insulted him and in so doing denied the meaning of his existence. Yet Achilles' rage goes far beyond righteous wrath, is condemned by his friends and peers, and becomes destructive madness. Perhaps it would have been better to have killed Agamemnon right there in the heat of justified anger, during the quarrel, and despite Athena. That might have been better than to have precipitated the sequence of events that now unfolds. The passionate Achilles plunges into a downward moral spiral and spreads destruction around him. He withdraws his army from the Greek alliance and does so in a militarily vulnerable moment. He prays on the shore to his mother Thetis and implores her to petition Zeus to turn the fortunes of war against his own side (he commits treason). Driven by rage over the death of Patroclus, who is wearing Achilles' own bronze armor when he is killed by Hector (Achilles betrays friendship), he emerges to destroy Hector. But when he slaughters Hector, he desecrates the body (sacrilege) by dragging it behind his chariot and denying it suitable funeral rites. The godlike Achilles, son of a goddess, a Greek warrior prince, plunges to the bottom of his own moral universe. Almost certainly, Hector, with his civilized restraints, would have been incapable of reaching this nadir. Hector is not "godlike."

The recovery of Achilles is not altogether complete, though to a considerable extent he is redeemed within his Greek moral universe. With Hector's desecrated body lying unwashed, the aged King Priam of Troy makes his way alone to Achilles' headquarters to plead for his son's body. The still-enraged and steely heart of Achilles is moved, not by pity but by a perception of the old man's courage. After all, Achilles could have killed him in an instant. Priam, here, is affirming Achilles' own code. It is possible to think that, here, Priam, a king, redeems the insult to Achilles by Agamemnon, reasserts the code through his own courage. Achilles thinks of his own father, Peleus. Yet he grows impatient when Priam asks for the return of Hector's body: the very sight of Hector's corpse might rekindle his fury. He might flare up into rage again, cut the old king down, and break the laws of Zeus.

Achilles is no penitent. His heart is not broken with pity or guilt. Yet when the corpse of Hector is bathed and wrapped in a braided battle-shirt, Achilles lifts it in his own arms, places it on a wagon, groans, and begs for forgiveness—very importantly, not forgiveness from Priam or Zeus but from the dead Patroclus. His cold, savage heart is not tamed.

What he accedes to here is a reaffirmation of the code violated at the start by Agamemnon. He submits to his religious duties, and the atmosphere of madness brought on by Agamemnon's insult dissipates with the great funeral of Hector.

There is of course a great deal to be said about all this, and much of it has been said for tens of centuries. Homer described here a universal pattern by no means limited to archaic Greece. Great poets have told stories like that of Achilles again and again. We cannot but feel that the rage of Achilles went beyond humanity, into godlike rage. He had battered against the boundaries of the human in other respects—his eloquence, his passion for life, his prowess in battle. He had battered against the boundary between the human and the gods. He was "godlike" but therefore plunged further down than other humans would. The higher the form of being, the lower it can plunge. That is the chilling and prophetic demonstration of the *Achillead* within the *Iliad*.

Montaigne commented memorably on the impulse in mankind to rise above its own humanity. "They want to be beside themselves, want to escape from humanity. That is madness: Instead of changing into angels, they change into beasts: instead of winding high, they crash down."[10] Pascal later made the same observation in his *Pensées*, perhaps paraphrasing Montaigne: "Man is neither angel nor brute, and the unfortunate thing is that he who would act the angel acts the brute."[11]

In the *Iliad*, Achilles' female counterpart is Helen. She has betrayed her husband, King Menelaus, and willfully run off to Troy with the handsome Prince Paris, who also acts without consideration for the fate of his city. But Paris is trivial compared with both Achilles and Helen. Achilles is godlike, Helen is goddesslike. Her beauty is so extraordinary that it is almost irresistible. In this, she resembles Achilles on the battlefield. The classical scholar Bernard Knox well says that Helen is a sort of human Aphrodite, goddess of sexual passion.[12] Within the *Iliad*, however, she is in the process of coming to her senses, returning to civilization. Her passion for Paris is gone and she realizes regretfully what she has wrought. Homer and his audiences, and his later interpreters, including Plato, did not consider this depiction mere moralism but rather something like scientific fact about human nature. An extreme form of behavior, often connected with greatness, leads almost inevitably to moral blindness and destruction. Neither Homer's audiences nor we have tired of this awe-inspiring story, which is always being brought up-to-date.

Homer sets up another parallel between Achilles and Helen: both have asserted individual will against community, Achilles the fury over honor outraged, Helen her imperial erotic will. Both share responsibility for the deaths of thousands. Yet Achilles returns to fight and is reintegrated into the Greek forces. In the *Odyssey* (book 4) we learn Achilles' fate from King Menelaus, now at home in Sparta and reconciled with his wife, Helen.

Her fate is surprisingly fortunate. After the destruction of Troy she has returned to Sparta and Menelaus and now is a great lady. She has re-entered that world and her manners are queenly. Whenever she appears before men in the great hall of Menelaus's palace, her maids place before her the symbols of womanhood—the distaff, an instrument for winding cotton or wool, and her work box, both of which are golden. When she leads a conversation with Odysseus's son Telemachus, she ceremoniously but perhaps truthfully compliments him on resembling his father. Having destroyed the Civilized City through her erotic profligacy, Helen has returned home as a civilizing presence. Homer's lines about her entrance to the great hall are virtually a hymn to high civilization and its order:

> Helen emerged from her scented lofty chamber—
> Striking as Artemis with her golden shaft—
> And a train of women followed . . .
> Adraste drew up her carved reclining chair,
> Alcippe brought a carpet of soft-piled fleece.
> Philo carried her silver basket given by Alcandre,
> King Polybus's wife, who made his home in Egyptian Thebes . . .
> His wife presented Helen her own precious gifts,
> a golden spindle, a basket that ran on casters,
> solid silver polished off with rims of gold.
> Now Phylo her servant rolled it in beside her,
> heaped to the brim with yarn prepared for weaving;
> the spindle swathed in violet wool lay tipped across it.[13]

Helen thus becomes, remarkably, a perfect fit for her queenly role. She has learned tragically the destructive power of the erotic (the goddess Aphrodite). But Achilles remains the greater figure. There remains something deeper and more disturbing about him.

Homer presents him as fulfilling his choice of dying young, killed by an arrow shot by Paris, of all people, who at that moment has heavenly favor. The Olympic gods may not be entirely reconcilable to Achilles, nor he to them. Unlike Helen, Achilles can step into an abyss outside the very possibility of civilization. The death of Patroclus can for him lead to nihilism, total negation, profoundly felt mortality annihilating all known criteria for behavior. Whatever he does, heroic or not, he tells his mother Thetis, the sea goddess, is useless to the dead Patroclus, who died as a result of Achilles' rage over Agamemnon's insult to his honor. Thus there is that extraordinary moment in book 9 when Achilles actually calls into question the role sacred honor has played in his behavior, contemplates a black hole in the code that informs his life with meaning.

> The same honor waits
> for the coward and the brave. They both go down to Death,
> the fighter who shirks, the one who works to exhaustion,
> and what's laid up for me, what pittance? Nothing—
> and after suffering hardship year in and year out,
> staking my life on the mortal risks of war.[14]

Achilles is the only one in the poem who can thus step outside the code of *areté* and question it, testing it against the mortality of his young friend Patroclus. Let them warm their hands at the great funeral pyres! All is darkness anyway. Achilles fights and has his own pyre. No doubt in the *Iliad* this moment is pedagogical. If you waver, experience despair, abyss, remember great Achilles, who also did so.

But there is something else to say here. If Achilles glimpses that honor may not reside in his heroic code, then where does honor really lie? Here Homer, no doubt with Plato listening, swings wide the door to Greek philosophy.

The idea prevailed for a long time that Homer was a "bard," perhaps illiterate, no doubt primitive, and therefore "authentic" in comparison with later and more polished writers. Yet Homer is anything but primitive and unpolished. Close attention to the *Iliad* and the *Odyssey* shows that he was astonishingly intelligent and subtle, a profound explorer of the human mind. Even if, perhaps, he could not write his poetry down, he certainly could think, and there is no reason to consider him less intelligent or sophisticated as an artist than Dante or Shakespeare.

Before leaving the Homeric epic I would like to notice just one among the many episodes that make these narratives so powerful. This is that strange scene by the sea in which the insulted and devastated Achilles pleads with his mother Thetis to turn the war against the Greeks. Never was treason committed with such lyric sweetness, even as Achilles initiates the sequence of events that will take him to the bottom of his moral world and result in the death of Patroclus. I quote here a few lines from the rendition by the modern poet Christopher Logue.

> Sometimes
> Before the gods appear
> Something is marked.
> A noise. A note, perhaps. Perhaps
> A change of temperature. Or else, as now.
> The scent of oceanic lavender.
> That even as it drew his mind
> Drew from the sealcolored sea onto the beach
> A mist that moved like weed, then stood, then turned
> Into his mother. Thetis, mother lovelost face.
> Her fingers, next that lift his chin, that push
> His long, red currant-colored hair
> Back from his face, her voice, her words:
> "Why tears, Achilles?
> Rest in my arms and answer from your heart."
> And the sea so still
> It looks like a metal plate.[15]

In narrative writing, a "theophany," a showing forth of the god, is not easy to manage. Homer and Logue manage it beautifully here, a Botticelli in verse, a sea goddess coming in a sea mist. And here the great Achilles, the prince and battlefield terror, the godlike Achilles, becomes a boy weeping to his mother. One cannot imagine Hector doing that. He was too civilized. Here, again, we touch the emotional range and greatness of Achilles and the subtlety of his creator.

CHAPTER THREE

Moses as Epic Hero

Like Achilles, Moses is a great epic hero, indeed a Bronze Age hero roughly contemporary with Achilles, but his story cannot begin in the middle of things as does the story of Achilles. Monotheism is at the center of Moses' life, and challenged at every side, monotheism cannot be assumed in the narrative but must be established at the beginning. This was the first task of the narrators who shaped this epic material, and they undertook it in Genesis.

In the *Mosead,* as I have suggested it might be called, the great epic hero does not appear until the second of the five books of the Pentateuch, Exodus. He is climactic as the heir of the patriarchs. Like a Homeric hero he dies immortal in fame at the end of the fifth book, Deuteronomy, in a scene as moving as those recounting the deaths of Achilles and Hector. Like Achilles, Moses is an archaic figure of enormous stature, flawed and astonishing.

Indeed, two eminent scholars, Cyrus H. Gordon and Gary Rendsburg, have argued persuasively that the biblical and Homeric epics have common roots in the ancient Near East, writing recently: "the Bible must be understood in its ancient Near East context more fully than is generally recognized. But the origins of Greek culture also lie to an appreciable extent in the ancient Near East. At no time during the broad sweep of ancient Near Eastern history were Greece and the Near East not in contact. . . . Out of this interaction in the East Mediterranean

came the heroic ages that inspired the early literature of both the Hebrews and the Greeks."¹ Gordon and Rendsburg describe a vast process
in which early civilizations arose in the Fertile Crescent, the valley of
the Tigris and Euphrates Rivers, spread energetically westward to the
shores of the Mediterranean Sea and thence to Cyprus, Crete, and the
mainland of archaic Greece, and even into the Balkans. Then, in a
countermovement, Aegean culture spread eastward with trade, population movement, and warfare. The Trojan War in the *Iliad* reflects one
aspect of this. "The early histories of the Hebrews and Greeks," write
Gordon and Rendsburg, "were intricately interrelated, and neither can
be understood in isolation from the other."² They demonstrate this
through a detailed examination of the ancient epic tradition in that area
and through strong archaeological evidence of Aegean and Semitic cultural interaction. The foundations of the European mind, that is, the
Western mind, were laid down originally not in what came to be known
as Europe but in the archaic cultures of the eastern Mediterranean and
Near East.³

Yet there is one decisive way in which the epic, by the time of Homer,
breaks with the Hebrew epic of Moses. Homer could begin "in the
middle of things" with the "rage of Achilles" at Agamemnon. The
Mosead cannot begin with Moses because the Israelites forced the question back far beyond the birth of Moses. The originality of the *Mosead*
epic lies in the fact that it is also an epic of monotheism, and that before
it can begin his story it has to go back to its major premise, the beginning
of everything. Until much later, Greek poetry and philosophy left the
question of the "beginning" shrouded in mystery. The Hebrew epic, in
contrast, forced the question back and back, asking, "Why is there something rather than nothing?" and "Why is there motion rather than
stasis?" and "Why is there sound rather than eternal silence?"

If they had not thus forced the question back in time, the *Mosead*
could easily have started with the remarkable story of Moses himself in
Exodus; but there had to be a first book, about the beginning of the
beginning, entitled Genesis, which is about Creation—about the original

creation of the universe and, derivatively throughout, about human creation in terms of sexuality, families, and dynasties.

The ancient Hebrew theological poets were not astronomers, but their primal insight has now been validated by modern astrophysics. There is now no doubt that the universe had a beginning. Until quite recently, such a beginning was a controversial question. Albert Einstein, for example, very reluctantly gave up the hypothesis of the eternity of matter, also a conviction of the ancient Greeks. But in 1965 Arno Penzias and Robert Wilson of the Bell Laboratories detected and measured diffuse radiation from the explosion that began the universe, thus confirming earlier mathematical calculations. The universe is approximately twenty billion years old.[4] What was "there" before the universe is a question that cannot be addressed by science. It was addressed by the ancient Hebrew theologians and theological poets. Their revolutionary deduction was monotheism.

Hebrew monotheism came as a profound and wholly unwelcome shock to the settled cultures of the Near East, and even to the nomadic and less settled Israelites. It entered history like a tornado, tearing away at established polytheisms, and made its way amid bitterness and cruelty as well as joy. Today the monotheistic premise is taken for granted, even among atheists, because of the completeness of its triumph. That is, atheists today do not bother to disbelieve in Thetis, Pan, Hera, Zeus, Moloch, or Baal. Atheists disbelieve in the God of monotheism.

This God entered history through a unique intuition among the ancient Israelites about what makes a god God. Probably this intuition arose as a negative reaction on the part of a nomadic desert tribe against the established polytheisms of Egypt, Mesopotamia, and Canaan (roughly, modern Israel). But it was also a positive—indeed, quasi-philosophical—intuition that there must have been something "there" before the beginning.

A sense of the radical strangeness of monotheism is difficult to recover today, when everyone assumes monotheism when the term *God* is used; but it struck the ancient world as a radical deviation. The great and strange first book, Genesis, is littered with traces of polytheism, dead and wounded polytheism on an archaic battlefield, even among the Israelites themselves.

The original patriarchs, Abraham, Isaac, and Jacob, were certainly not comfortable with this monotheistic God. Joseph, an Egyptian viceroy though a Hebrew, a monotheist at ease in Egypt, is a singular case. If we pay careful attention to the highly concentrated Genesis narrative we can recover some sense of the surprise, the radicalism, and the torment of this permanent leap in human consciousness.

We hear the voice of this God again and again in the Hebrew Bible. In contrast to the gods and goddesses in Homer, this Hebrew God speaks but is not seen directly. He is outside time and space. When he manifests himself it is through such "theophanies" as a burning bush, a mist, a pillar of fire, or mysterious visitors. All of this must represent very early religious experience. This Hebrew God has absolutely no aesthetic appeal because he is entirely other. He really did not have to forbid the making of images of him because there can be no images. The Greek gods and goddesses have charm, but the last quality we would ascribe to this God is charm. Here, to look upon God's face is to die. We hear his voice, to be sure, in the opening of Genesis: "Let there be light." We hear about his six days of creative activity. Throughout the Pentateuch he speaks powerfully to individuals and even argues with them, submits to their scornful laughter. Often he can be powerfully angry. Later, when Job challenges him from the standpoint of the human idea of justice, God—I should think quite inevitably—appeals from such "justice" to the original Creation, which he evokes in language that has reverberated through the ages: "Do you give the horse his strength or clothe his neck with a flowing mane? . . . [Leviathan] makes the deep churn like a boiling cauldron and stirs up the sea like a pot of ointment. Behind him he leaves a glistening wake; one would think the deep had white hair. Nothing on earth is his equal, a creature without fear."[5] This voice is shocking. At first it seems unfair, yet its appeal is not entirely to power but also to wonder. It appeals unconditionally to the original Creation, to all that we can see, and reminds Job that he is not his own creator. It contains a kind of logic and demands recognition of God's complete primacy. In his first encounter with God on Mount Horeb, Moses asks God his name, and God replies, momentously, "I AM THAT I AM." The compact Hebrew terms are variously translated, but they boil down to a statement pointing, as in the passage from Job just cited, to the original Creation. This God is Being itself, there before time and prior to all existing beings within time. He does not "exist" in the ordinary sense but is the condition of all existence. Syntactically, he is the subject, while everything else is a long predicate. In the phrase of the modern theologian Paul Tillich, God is the "ground of being."[6] Job pleads eloquently for justice; God reminds him to whom he is speaking. The book of Job is not about justice, but about the ultimate basis of everything.

Not surprisingly, throughout the Hebrew Bible there is recurrent tension, indeed often agony, in the relationship of the Israelites to this God. His demands are stern and total, and he can produce destruction—though it is always followed by renewed creativity at a higher level. One is not surprised that in their relationship to him, the Israelites are often recalcitrant, "stiff-necked." That expression is a metaphor arising out of the experience of this rural people. Before the yoke can be placed on an ox, the animal must relax its neck muscles and bow its head. The stiff-necked Israelites repeatedly resist, pulling away from the yoke of the monotheistic God.

And no wonder. Unlike all other gods, this God is related to nature in an uncomfortable and ambiguous way. He manifests himself variously as a burning bush, whirlwind, cloud, or human-seeming messengers, but he is not identical with any part of nature. Thus he is different from all the polytheisms and pantheisms, ancient as well as recent. Because there is an unbridgeable gap between this God and the nature we know, he is ultimately unknowable. As I recalled earlier, no image is to be—indeed can be—made of him. He can be experienced but not seen. Mostly, he speaks. I suppose it follows that the ancient Israelites are not known for their visual arts, for painting, sculpture, or architecture—unlike the Babylonians, Egyptians, Greeks, or Romans. They are however known

for their words; they are the people of the book (or scroll). The monotheistic God speaks, and his people answer him with words, which include great poetry, as in the Psalms.

The historical victory of monotheism in the West is not without
elements of pathos, even tragedy. Defeated at last, at least in high culture, were the old familiar and sometimes friendly gods and goddesses of
wood and stream, hearth and crop, cloud and ocean. The familiar gods
depart, and also the frightening ones, the gods of fire and flood, war,
human sacrifice, holy prostitution, infanticide. The triumph of monotheism involved a theodicide. Millennia later the young John Milton,
holding in tension his classicism and his Christianity, both celebrated
and mourned this theodicide in his great poem "On the Morning of
Christ's Nativity":

> In consecrated Earth
> And on the holy Hearth
>   The *Lars* and *Lemures* moan with midnight plaint,
> In Urns, and Altars round,
> A drear, and dying sound
> Affrights the *Flamins* at their service quaint.[7]

Throughout the Hebrew Bible itself we find traces of the residual
polytheism. Many biblical scholars think the destructive serpent in the
Garden of Eden derives distantly from the Mesopotamian river dragon
who rises at flood time on the winding, serpentlike Tigris-Euphrates.
The representation of God appearing as on Sinai amid thunder and
lightning, clouds and fire, seems an adaptation of imagery previously
associated with Baal, the Canaanite god of war.[8] Similarly, the tent
Moses orders erected as a tabernacle for God is fiery by night, covered in
mist by day, like the volcano imagery associated with Baal. It is as if the
composers of these narratives drew on polytheistic imagery familiar to
them in order to represent the theophanies of the monotheistic God for
whom they had no cultural precedent. The birth of this God in human
consciousness is like a painful parturition. The Israelites are repeatedly
tempted back toward polytheism, as in the episode of the Golden Calf,

which scholars think was a young bull, to whose worship Israelites flocked even at the base of Sinai. What the *Mosead* epic recounts is the drama of a revolutionary monotheism being carried into history by the turbulent and often rebellious tribes of Israelites. But before that narrative can unfold, and before we get to the hero of the *Mosead*, the premise of monotheism must be established.

Because of its high degree of concentration and organization, the brief account of the Creation that opens Genesis can be regarded as a magnificent theological poem, a grand overture to an astonishing story. It comes at the beginning and is about the original beginning—some twenty billion years ago, to use another vocabulary—and is fundamental to the entire Hebrew epic of monotheism. Apparently written down in the eighth century B.C., it undoubtedly draws upon a long oral tradition and offers a summarizing answer to the perennial question: "Why is there something, rather than nothing?" Centuries later, Thomas Aquinas would observe that if there ever were absolutely nothing for a split second, there never could be anything at all.[9] What the Genesis poem does is offer an account of what happened just before, and then at, the "beginning." Its account is highly organized, its verbal form as well as its content reflecting the view that there exists an underlying form and purpose to the universe.

The Book of Genesis begins: "In the beginning God created the heavens and the earth" (Genesis 1:1). Just whose is the voice that announces this? We can never know. A long tradition exists that this is the voice of Moses himself; this, historically, is very doubtful. But why this tradition exists is quite understandable. That opening sentence announces the theme of Moses' life.

The mysterious narrator of Genesis continues: "And God said, 'Let there be light.'" To whom does God address this command? Surely there is no one else there for him to talk to before the beginning. Is God talking to himself? Linguistic scholarship comes to our rescue. The biblical scholar Jack Miles tells us this: "The sentence 'Let there be light,' so stately in English, translates just two quick words in Hebrew: *yi 'or*.

The one-word sentence 'Light' would be a defensible English translation; for if the sentence is a command, it is not spoken commandingly. One does not speak commandingly to oneself. It is rather as if a carpenter reaching for a hammer were to speak the word 'hammer' aloud. Compliance with a command is not even remotely at issue."[10] The poet of Genesis thus tries to epitomize in language the first moment of the Creation, advancing to the frontiers of the knowable.

The Creation poem that follows is organized in beautifully symmetrical patterns, its language reflecting a sense of cosmic design. The poet speaks of the six "days" of Creation. These, of course, are not six twenty-four-hour sun days, but units of unspecified time, and as we now know, very long units. That they are not our sun days is indicated in that the sun does not even exist until the fourth day. The poet/poets are metaphorically representing God's creative activity in terms of a human work week.

The catalogue of representative created things, moreover, exhibits pattern and suggests an overall designing intention. The first four days move from the initial "light" to the sun, moon, and stars. The following two days introduce "swarms of living creatures," birds, whales, cattle, and creeping things and culminate in mankind, created "in our image," God using the royal plural. On the seventh day, God "rests," completing the metaphor of the human work week and giving divine sanction to the Sabbath.

What I have tried to do here is indicate the rich suggestiveness of the Creation poem and its essential and logical priority in the epic of monotheism. In the unfolding of this narrative, the commandment "be fruitful and multiply" turns out to issue in horror as well as joy and triumph as it works its way out in history. Some of the episodes are as dark or darker than anything in Aeschylus.

Our principal focus in this chapter will be on Exodus and on Moses, a Bronze Age hero in many ways comparable to his very approximate contemporary Achilles, not least in his capacity for rage and violence. Yet it is impossible not to pause here with an example of the narrative depth achieved by Genesis, devoting a few words to Abraham, with whom the narrative comes forward with a huge figure recognizable as a particular human being in history. Before Abraham, all the characters— Adam and Eve, Abel and Cain, Noah and his daughters—are simplified figures of a folklorish quality. Abraham is something entirely different. There is also the great interest of that dark episode of the sacrifice of Isaac. In view of Abraham's character as developed in the compact narrative, the usual interpretation may be wrong. Abraham's apparent willingness to sacrifice his only son may not be an example, as Søren Kierkegaard thought, of total obedience and heroic faith.[11]

From first to last, Abraham is anything but docile. At the beginning of chapter 12, we have that concentrated moment when God first speaks to Abraham, pulling him out of his customary life and into epic history: "And the Lord God said to Abraham: 'Go forth from your land and your birthplace and your father's house to the land I will show you. And I will make you a great nation and I will bless you and make your name great, and you shall be a blessing. And I will bless you. And I will bless those who bless you, and those who damn you I will curse, and all the clans of the earth through you shall be blessed.' And Abraham went forth as the Lord had spoken to him" (Genesis 12:1–4). From Abraham here we hear nothing. He obeys, but silently. There is even something rude about this encounter, no customary salutation as "Abraham!"—and no acknowledgment such as "Here I am." Abraham certainly does not give thanks for the great mission assigned him by the highest authority. We might well think that Abraham does not quite like the sound of this offer. He, now the first Jew, has been chosen. But there may be resistance in his silence, and the absence of ceremonial courtesy suggests God's awareness of his tough and skeptical character.

We soon find out a great deal to support this. Abraham is a successful merchant on the caravan routes extending from the fertile crescent of the Tigris-Euphrates down through Canaan. He has a wife, a harem, slaves, camels, tents. What goods he deals in is not clear, but throughout he is a tough bargainer and a successful man. He can easily afford the precious gifts needed to arrange a marriage for his son Isaac to Rebekah. When his aged wife Sarah dies at Hebron, he refuses the gift of a burial ground and insists on paying the Canaanites four hundred silver shekels and receiving a deed at the gates of the town, before Hittite witnesses, to make it official. Before Sodom and Gomorrah he rashly bargains with God, asking him first whether he will destroy the cities if there are fifty just men there and, receiving the answer no, proceeds to bargain him down to ten. The tough caravan bargainer probably does not dare push God further. No doubt he has enjoyed using justice as a lever against God.

When Abraham and Sarah grow old without a male heir, Abraham complains to God, who lyrically renews the promise first made in chapter 12: "I will bless her so that she will be the mother of nations; kings of peoples will come from her" (Genesis 17:16).

Abraham's response is vivid. He laughs out loud at God. The original deal is looking worse all the time. He is "ninety-nine" years old (that is, "very old"). In the next chapter, when God again promises offspring, it is old Sarah who laughs from within her tent, her shriek having a cosmic quality as it rings out over the desert. The laughter of Abraham and Sarah is bitter and skeptical.

When Abraham in chapter 22 appears willing to obey God by killing his sacred heir Isaac, is God testing Abraham's obedience, or is it the other way around, as Jack Miles suggests, Abraham holding God to his bargain?[12] The scene slows down in narrative pace and is agonizingly detailed: the wood, the donkey, the binding of Isaac, the altar, the butcher's knife. But Abraham must be well aware that if Isaac dies, God will have gone back on his original and reiterated covenant. The tough and stiff-necked bargainer of the caravan routes may figure that he has God on the hip here. And God gives in, intervening with a messenger at the last moment. If this interpretation is correct, it is consistent with Abraham's character. He, like the Israelites later on, has never been easy for God to deal with.

Moses develops the understanding of monotheism evolved in Genesis. Obeying a new definition of the divine mission, that of the law and nation-building, he becomes a powerful rebel against the Egyptian polytheistic system, along with its derivative monarchy and bureaucracy, hands down a Law rooted in the nature of Being, unifies the tribes under the Law, leads them in years of warfare against the surrounding polytheistic tribes, and dies within sight of the territory of his new nation across the Jordan River in Canaan.

The hero of this stage of monotheism, Moses, is well represented by Michelangelo's famous statue, which expresses his power as prophet, commander, and founder. Michelangelo, with justice, transforms the Bronze Age Moses into a European Renaissance figure and ratifies his place in the European pantheon. One of the vital projects of the Renaissance was the attempt to consolidate the modern nation-states. Michelangelo could see Moses as a Renaissance man because in the four books that tell his story, he is susceptible to that interpretation.

In general, it is not very useful to try to get "behind" a narrative such as this about prehistoric events and search for historical fact; but Moses is much more locatable in history than Achilles or Odysseus. Gordon and Rendsburg, for example, have made plausible deductions about the likely date and circumstances of the Israelites' exodus from Egypt and, derivatively, about the likely dates of Moses' life.[13] The Pharaoh Ramses I ruled very briefly from about 1309 to 1308 B.C. and commenced a vast building project that included temples, palaces, and colossal statues. Upon his death, his vice-regent, named Seti I, became Pharaoh (1308– 1291 B.C.) and continued the imperial projects. He was succeeded by Ramses II (1291–1224 B.C.), whose long reign was of great importance. Two texts from this reign allude to the use of slave labor, presumably for the ambitious construction projects.

According to Gordon and Rendsburg, the exodus of the Israelite slaves probably occurred during the reign of the next Pharaoh, Ramses III (1182–1151 B.C.). They base this upon an enigmatic passage in Exodus 13:17, which states that the Israelites fled from Egypt at a time when there was warfare in the north and therefore took a longer alternate route through the Sinai desert in order to reach Canaan: "God did not lead them by way of the land of the Philistines, though it was near, for God said: 'Lest the people change their minds when they see the fighting and return to Egypt' " (Exodus 13:17). It is a fact that during the reign of Ramses III, the north of Egypt was under assault from the sea, probably from the direction of Philistia, near Gaza. The Hebrews were aware of these people (see Genesis 10:5), and it looks as if the Egyptians faced a landing by a ferocious expedition of warriors. Gordon and Rendsburg surmise that the exodus led by Moses coincided with this warfare in the north, around 1175 B.C. They further observe that archaeological evidence indicates that Hebrew settlements began to be established in Canaan around 1150, or about twenty-five years after the assault of the Sea People upon northern Egypt.[14] Of course these surmises are fascinating in themselves, attempts to discern events however dimly in the remote depths of time. They also indicate that the epic of Moses has a firm grip on actual history.

To sum up: Gordon and Rendsburg think that the Pharaoh named Seti I, successor to Ramses I, was the ruler who elevated Joseph to his high post in Egypt; that Ramses II, enormously powerful, was the Pharaoh who "knew not Joseph"—that is, was not friendly to the Israelites, enslaved them and then ordered the slaughter of their firstborn because of their threatening fertility; and that the great exodus of more than 600,000 Israelites led by Moses occurred during the reign of Ramses III.

In the extremely compact narrative of the first two books of Exodus every sentence is important. Here we learn a great deal about Moses. The pervasive theme is opportunity and danger, poles between which Moses lives from his birth until his death. In him we have division of mind, conflict of cultures, ferocity of temper, and heroic resolution.

Initially, it must strike the reader as odd that, after so much attention to genealogy in Genesis, the text does not mention the names of Moses' parents. They are merely "a man of the house of Levi" who "took to wife a daughter of Levi." Thus these parents are certainly Hebrews. The failure to name them here may foreshadow the complex upbringing of Moses: they both are and are not his parents. Soon Moses will be a man of two worlds, Hebrew and Egyptian. We have to wait until Exodus 6:20 to learn that their names were Amram and Jocchabed; we learn still later that Moses has a sister named Miriam and a brother named Aaron.

The narrative focuses sharply on Moses and pushes his Hebrew family into the background.

Like many epic heroes, Moses has a remarkable and dangerous infancy. Because of Pharaoh's order to kill firstborn Hebrew infant males, Moses' mother hides him for three months, then laces him in a caulked basket that she floats among the reeds near a riverbank. From this hazardous situation he is rescued by a daughter of Pharaoh, an Egyptian princess who decides to save him though she knows that he is a Hebrew. No doubt this princess is acting from humane motives; but she is also defying the orders of the god-king, a disobedience ultimately very dangerous to the empire. The violation she commits is both religious and political. In effect, she is rebelling against the Egyptian system itself, her disobedience extending to the imperial court. This may be a hint that the entire system, and the polytheism that undergirds it, is vulnerable.

After rescuing him, the Egyptian princess names him, performing as a surrogate mother. She names him "Moses" because "I drew him from the water." As Eric Voegelin points out, however, this name has an ambivalent relationship to the Egyptian and Hebrew languages.[15] On one hand, in Egyptian the relevant verb is *masheh* (mes, mseu: born) and is used in such nouns as Thutmose, Ahmose, and so on, "mose" meaning "son of." The princess very likely would have given him his name in this sense, the "son of" some favorite Egyptian god. In that case, it is possible to speculate that Moses, when he turns wholly against Egypt, shortened his name to Moses by dropping the name of the god. On the other hand, the Hebrew word *masha,* meaning "drawn out of the water," is the etymology supported by Exodus 2. It is possible that the princess, knowing the child to be Hebrew, secretly gave him a Hebrew name. In this case the child indeed had a rebellious surrogate mother.

These are not just scholarly minutiae. The alternative etymologies reinforce the sense of Moses as a man between two cultures. He is neither Egyptian nor fully Israelite, a man on the edge. Not surprisingly, he has great difficulties with "his" Hebrew people throughout his long life.

The tension continues in his treatment by the kind princess. Knowing him to be a Hebrew, she provides him with a Hebrew nurse who turns out to be his actual mother, Jochabed. At the very least, this is strange behavior on the part of the princess, though we do not know the roots of its strangeness. As we go on in this very compact narrative, we see that Moses must have been brought up as a sort of Egyptian of the upper classes, indeed close to the throne, and must have received an appropriate Egyptian education. As the surrogate son of the princess, he was almost an Egyptian prince. At the same time, he had been nursed by his real mother and felt a strong emotional tie with his Levite brethren. (Much later on, Moses will order his Levite brethren to slaughter some 3,000 Israelites for heresy in the famous episode of the Golden Calf.)

There is nothing in the narrative that tells us what the content of Moses' Egyptian education might have been, yet some speculation is almost irresistible. About seventy-five years before Moses, an unusual Pharaoh ascended the throne and tried, by force, to overthrow the Egyptian polytheistic system and the established institutions that went with it. Amenhotep IV, known as Akhenaton, sought to reform the empire by abolishing its polytheistic religious system and installing a monotheistic god in its place.[16] He was a political and religious reformer, an aristocratic reformer from the top down, and he failed. All that we have left of him is the poem "Hymn to the Sun," the sun here being a symbol of the monotheistic god, a poem he may have written himself as a celebration of monotheism and an anthem of the reformed Egyptian state. The profound scholar Eric Voegelin pronounces it to be a "new" voice in history.

> The Aton is the creator god:
> O sole god, like whom there is no other!
> Thou didst create the world according to thy desire,
> While thou wert alone

Evidently the Egyptian system proved to be too strong for the reformer's efforts, too entrenched among its priests, magicians, officials, and institutions. Yet seventy-five years later, a young and aristocratic Moses might well have been aware of Akhenaton, who would have remained at least a memory for some of his aristocratic peers. And Moses surely knew the oral tradition of Hebrew monotheism as embodied in Genesis I. Judging by his subsequent behavior, he could have concluded that monotheism had its real roots there, among the lowly tribes, slaves though they were, and not burdened by the massive weight of Egyptian tradition and institutions.[17]

Given the spare and compact narrative, all of this is speculation. Yet within that narrative it is clear that the young Moses knows the Egyptian system well. This enables him to mount a comprehensive attack upon it. When he does assault it, the challenge is political, military, and above all religious. As Jack Miles says, his challenge is not on behalf of "national liberation."[18] Still less is it based on Wilsonian "self-determination." Moses is demanding that Pharaoh honor the claims of the monotheistic God, in other words honor a God who singularly claims to be superior to the polytheism that undergirds and legitimizes the entire Egyptian structure, including the throne Pharaoh is sitting on. Not surprisingly, Pharaoh's heart is repeatedly hardened during the tense negotiations with Moses and Aaron, and this is why ultimate force must be brought to bear upon him, and why agreeing but not agreeing he sends his army after the fleeing Israelites and into the disaster of the Sea of Reeds near the Red Sea.

In those negotiations Moses and Aaron, undoubtedly dressed as magicians and speaking Egyptian, appeared at Pharaoh's court. Their contest with the magicians is at bottom religious. The power of the magicians stems from ritual and spells, that of Moses from Yaweh. After proving ritualistically that he can change his staff into a serpent (some think crocodile), Moses visits Pharaoh with ten plagues which, whatever else they may be, are symbolic attacks on Egyptian polytheism. The first three plagues are menacing nuisances rather than genuinely dangerous. They attack minor deities in the Egyptian pantheon, such as Hapi, the god of the Nile, and Hequet, the frog goddess of life. But the later attacks are upon the chief god Re, as locusts blot out the sun at noon and then the sun is darkened for three days. Moses is showing not only that he has something like a cosmic weapon up his sleeve, but that he represents something much greater than the gods of the Egyptian theology.[19]

Of course it is possible to suppose that the afflictions visited upon the Egyptians had a naturalistic explanation. If the Nile turned red with blood, this might have been algae or clay falling from the banks. Locusts and sandstorms could blot out the sun. And so forth. But under the circumstances, these things would have carried their symbolic weight at a court drenched in magic, and everyone there would have understood that Moses was not speaking like such an intellectual reformer as Akhenaton but as a radical monotheistic revolutionary attacking in a fundamental way the entire Egyptian system.

Long before Moses reaches this fateful confrontation at the court of Pharaoh his relationships with his Hebrew brethren and his aristocratic Egyptian peers have been turbulent and often sinister, as two famous and important episodes attest. They also demonstrate Moses' quick, dangerous temper, which will be characteristic of him throughout. Indeed, as a serious imperfection, this dangerous volatility may well be one reason why he is finally forbidden to cross the Jordan River into the Promised Land.

In the first of these two revealing episodes, Moses is aware of the "burdens" now being borne by his brethren, the Hebrew slaves. He "goes out" to them to see them, concerned evidently, but at first keeping a spectatorial distance. "One day, after Moses had grown up, he went out to where his own people were and watched them at their hard labor" (Exodus 2:11). No doubt his courtly status keeps him at an emotional distance from them, but they indeed are his brethren, and suddenly his ready anger erupts. He acts violently and dangerously. "He saw an Egyptian beating a Hebrew, one of his own people. Glancing this way and that and seeing no one, he killed the Egyptian and hid him in the sand" (Exodus 2:13).

When we understand that relatively harmless beating was a fairly standard Egyptian labor practice and might be an assertion of status rather than actual punishment, we may see Moses' rage as a comprehensive rebellion against Egypt itself. Still, he is careful during the murder. He tries to make sure there are no witnesses and buries the corpse. Very likely he would have been executed for murder, and perhaps rebellion, had he been caught. But for the moment he is still Egyptian.

The next incident occurs immediately after this in the text. Evidently his brethren are not grateful for his intervention against the Egyptian, and are willing to use their knowledge of it against him. "The next day he went out and saw two Hebrews fighting. He asked the one in the wrong, 'Why are you hitting your fellow Hebrew?' " The rejoinder of the offender must have been devastating to Moses: "Who made you ruler and judge over us? Are you thinking of killing me as you killed the Egyptian?" The mockery in the word *ruler* must have been wounding. Moses is acting like an Egyptian prince. In his depths, he knows he is a Hebrew. As a semi-prince, he has tried to intervene in Israelite quarrels. Where does his authority as a "judge" come from? Good questions. Worse, this Hebrew has seen Moses murder the Egyptian and has the power to blackmail him or inform on him. "Moses was afraid and thought, 'What I did must have become known.' " Indeed, word does reach the court of Pharaoh, and Moses must flee Egypt.

It is not easy at this juncture to fathom Moses' state of mind. In his depths, he knows that he is a Hebrew, yet he has been Egyptianized. As a semi-prince, he has tried to intervene in Israelite quarrels and been rejected. He seems to wish that his brethren were better than they seem to be. Yet they see through his Egyptian persona and threaten his life. When Pharaoh hears about the murder committed by Moses, "he tried to kill Moses. But Moses fled from Pharaoh and went to live in Midian, where he sat down by a well" (Exodus 2:15).

In the exile, or exile on top of exile, it is clear that Moses has time for prolonged reflection. He is a divided man, a prince alone and in exile. What roots he had have been severed. He will be a supreme Israelite hero and a world-historical figure, but he has been rejected by the Egyptians and also by his own people. The phrase "he sat down by a well" is poignant because at this low point in his history he commences a new life.

As he sits by that well in Midian—such a well being a local meeting place, and make of the symbolism what you wish—a group of local sheep herders try to drive off the daughters of a local priest who seek to water their flock. Moses, typically, intervenes. He is successful, as the daughters report back to their father: "An Egyptian rescued us from the shepherds. He even drew water for us and watered the flock" (Exodus 2:19). We notice that the Midianite daughters see Moses as an Egyptian. Also that he must have been formidable enough to prevail with the hostile shepherds. Indeed, we have seen that he has a history of physical violence.

The local priest, Jethro, impressed by the report he receives from his daughters, invites Moses to join his household, where Moses seems temporarily content. He marries one of the daughters, Zipporah. Of course the priest Jethro is a polytheist, about which Moses must be entertaining some major doubts. Moses' situation remains strange. He is not an Egyptian, he is not a Midianite, and he has been rejected by the Hebrews. He is a "prince" living among shepherds. He is some sort of monotheist living among polytheists in a provincial backwater. Years pass in this exile. Zipporah gives birth to a son. The following verse in the narrative has great poignancy: "Zipporah gave birth to a son, and Moses named him Gershom, saying, 'I have become an alien in a foreign land'" (Exodus 2:22). The Hebrew *ger* means "stranger." In the narrative the birth of Gershom seems to precipitate a crisis for Moses. However content he may or may not have been in Midian, I think we understand that he cannot be content to have Gershom also live there. Whatever interpretation we want to make of this, extraordinary events follow, as the narrative leaps ahead to the experience that transforms Moses from isolation in exile to the Moses of his great mission, the decisive experience of God that Moses has on Mount Horeb ("Holy Mountain"). The final verses of Exodus 2 mark the transition. The Pharaoh dies after years have gone by, perhaps indicating that Moses' crime has been forgotten by the authorities, thus allowing him to return, and there, "The Israelites groaned in their slavery and cried out, and their cry for help because of their slavery went up to God. God heard their groaning and he remembered his covenant with Abraham, with Isaac and with Jacob. So God looked on the Israelites and was concerned about them" (Exodus 2:23–24).

So ends the second chapter of Exodus, with so much packed into it, an extraordinary piece of writing. In these transitional lines, which lead into the still more remarkable chapter 3, we can pause to wonder what God "heard" and what "God remembered his covenant" might mean. Perhaps God had forgotten about the Israelites until this particular moment—*this* moment, because Moses' experiences have ripened him to the exact point where he is ready for his destiny. Moses' total experience has made him a unique instrument. In any case, in chapter 3 Moses has a religious experience that changes the history of the world: "Now Moses was tending the flock of Jethro his father-in-law, the priest of Midian, and he led his flock to the far side of the desert and came to Horeb, the mountain of God" (Exodus 3:1). At this moment all of Moses' past seems to come together in a new synthesis. His disparate identities, Hebrew infant who narrowly escaped slaughter, educated Egyptian prince, exiled monotheist living among the polytheists of Midian, a man of undoubted force and ability, all of these combine into something that could not have happened earlier. Indeed, his mission is so novel that even his Hebrew brethren do not accept it easily and repeatedly rebel against it.

If we take an overall view of the Moses epic, from Exodus through Deuteronomy, we see that it contains three distinct and important "mountain" experiences. The first occurs now, at Horeb. The next takes place at Sinai when he delivers the Law that forms God's people out of refractory and rebellious Hebrews. The third occurs on Mount Nebo when, now old, he sees the Promised Land across the Jordan but is forbidden to cross over to it and dies and is buried there in an unknown grave.

On Horeb, Moses experiences a theophany that the narrative expresses in terms entirely new to the Bible. Clearly the creators of the oral and then the written narrative meant listeners and readers to understand that something happened to Moses on Horeb that was different from anything that had happened to Abraham, Isaac, or Jacob, even though we have just been told that God "remembered" them.

Specifically, on Horeb God commands Moses to challenge Pharaoh directly, and Moses understands all that this will mean. Moses' courage seems to flicker, as God has to talk him into this mission. Here we may remember Abraham's silence when challenged in this way. At one point Moses' reluctance "angers" God. God also uses a new term with regard to the Israelites, calling them collectively the "son of God" and "my firstborn." This is new and designates them collectively as the bearers of monotheism. They too, like Moses, will be reluctant. All this is completely new, nothing earlier having prepared for it. Later on, at Sinai, this seems to be modified as Moses himself becomes far more preeminent, himself becoming the God-bearer to the people.[19]

Not only is the burning bush imagery of the experience on Horeb new to scriptural narrative, but the descriptive passage is highly wrought and full of significance. The word *bush* is repeated thematically, emphasizing its importance and novelty: "The messenger of the Lord appeared to him in flames of fire from within a *bush*. Moses saw that though the *bush* was on fire it did not burn up. So Moses thought, 'I will go over and see this strange sight, why the bush does not burn up' " (Exodus 3:2, emphasis added). Eric Voegelin finds a connection between the Hebrew word for bush (*seneb*), which is repeated here, and the noun *Sinai*. This reinforces the relation between the two events that together create the conditions for the new Israel: the establishment of Moses as the leader on Horeb and the transmission of the sacred Law on Sinai.[20] This second event, to anticipate, is very far from being a matter of mere local significance. The Sinai experience links the moral Law (ethics) with the transcendent monotheistic God who is the creator of the universe in Genesis. Thus the moral Law handed down on Sinai is rooted in the order of the universe and is anything but tribal and relativistic. This, again, is something radically new and potentially universalistic.

On Horeb Moses speaks the fateful words: "God called to him from within the bush: 'Moses, Moses!' And Moses said, 'Here I am.' " Moses, estranged from Egypt and from his own people, and a stranger in the land of Midian, has reached the point where he is ready for a destiny he does not yet understand. It is possible to find such a moment in the lives of other great men in history who have become ready at a crucial moment to accept a new and at least partially mysterious mission, uncertain of its nature and outcome.

In the ensuing dialogue, a kind of agon involving Moses and God, Moses is willing to listen ("Here I am") but also doubtful and resistant. In Moses' resistance we may find reminiscences of the struggles of Abraham, Isaac, and Jacob, but the overall point is the continuing demands and stern requirements of monotheism. It is not surprising that Moses on Horeb resists the charge of taking command of the turbulent Israelites, who after all showed him little friendship and whom he may regard as a rabble, and then in their name challenging the Egyptian empire not only politically and militarily but at its religious roots: " 'So now go. I am sending you to Pharaoh to bring my people, the Israelites, out of Egypt.' But Moses said to God, 'Who am I that I should go to Pharaoh and bring the Israelites out of Egypt?' " (Exodus 3:10–11).

Much more than modesty is involved here. Moses can have no doubt as to his interlocutor, yet he resists. Even in these circumstances there is something hard and irreducible about Moses. In this dialogue, Moses' resistance goes past the point of acceptability and finally angers God. Thus despite God's promise to be "with him"—which Moses has no reason to doubt—Moses still demurs. Why? Is he still divided as to Egypt and Israel? Is he still residually an Egyptian prince? Does he condescend to the Israelite tribes and doubt their ability to challenge the Egyptian empire? After all that has so far transpired on Horeb, Moses still tries to beg off, pleading personal unfitness for the task because of a speech defect. Given the circumstances, given the power of theophany and the evident power of the staff God gives him, this is almost comic: "But Moses said to the Lord: 'O, my Lord, I have never been eloquent, neither in the past nor since you have spoken to your servant; I am slow of speech and tongue' " (Exodus 4:10).

God rebukes him, as well he might: "Who gave man his mouth?" And, "Now go, and I will help you speak and teach you what to say." "But Moses said, 'O, my Lord, please send someone else to do it.' Then the Lord's anger burned against Moses" (Exodus 4:10–13).

If Moses is stubborn, in chapter 4, appearing to doubt the commands and promises of the monotheistic Creator, some defense might be made of him. The mission he is being commanded to undertake is after all a daunting one, to challenge the Egyptian empire, the most powerful political entity he has ever known, present to him from birth in its grandeur. Yet in these exchanges we also notice that God appears to be constrained, or is at least willing to seem constrained. He is angered by Moses' stubbornness but does not use preemptory force. There is no flood this time, no rainbow of restored concord, no destruction of Sodom. God may be constrained by his irrevocable choice of Moses and the Israelites, constrained by these prior decisions. He is bound by his own covenant, yet he is dealing with Moses, who is no passive figure like Noah, but gritty and aggressive like Abraham.

In the event, Moses wins the tug of war depicted in chapters 3 and 4. God comes up with a rather pedestrian compromise. Instead of instantly curing Moses' speech defect he settles with Moses by appointing his brother Aaron as his spokesman (Exodus 4:14–17).

All of this is complicated. Moses does not quite reject his mission and may to a large degree desire it, yet he may fear its implications. Although he was a stranger in Midian, life there was not bad. Moses knows the Egyptian system, but is a monotheist. He will have to confront Pharaoh, but needs Aaron to speak for him. He knows that his intuition of monotheism is right, but hesitates to carry it forward against the visible strength of the great Egyptian empire. And, of course, his relations with the Israelites have been turbulent.

In Exodus 5, Moses and Aaron commence their mission, demanding of Pharaoh that he free the Israelites. Strikingly, Pharaoh immediately grasps the religious root of their challenge: "Who is the Lord that I should hear his voice and let Israel go? I do not know the Lord, and, moreover, I will not let Israel go" (Exodus 5:2). He responds by ordering the Israelite taskmasters to make conditions more harsh, for which they blame Moses and Aaron, not Pharaoh: "When they had left Pharaoh, they found Moses and Aaron waiting for them, and they said, 'May the Lord look upon you and judge you! You have made us a stench to

Pharaoh and his servants and have put a sword in their hands to kill us' "
(Exodus 5:20–21). Moses, not Pharaoh, is their enemy here, and their
danger. He, in turn, rebukes God: "O, Lord, why, why have you brought
evil upon this people? Is this why you sent me?" (Exodus 5:22). One
gathers from this that Moses' confidence in his mission remains shaky,
that the Israelites themselves are anything but persuaded as regards the
mission, and that at least some of them consider life in Egypt to be
tolerable. This tension between Moses and his people persists all the
way to the Red Sea and then takes different forms in the long journey
across Sinai.

Moses eventually wins in his negotiations with Pharaoh; indeed, he
certainly won in terms of the sweep of history, but the Israelites remain
refractory. They do escape from Egypt. Remarkably, they set out carrying with them the mummified corpse of Egyptianized Joseph. This detail
in the narrative picks up from the last verse in Genesis (50:26): "So
Joseph died, being a hundred and ten years old, and they embalmed
him, and he was put in a coffin in Egypt." The emigrating Israelites do
not leave the body of Joseph behind: "And Moses took the bones of
Joseph with him" (Exodus 13:19). Carrying Joseph's mummy out of
Egypt no doubt signifies continuity with the events of Genesis and with
the patriarchs. Yet Joseph got along very well with the Egyptians, rising
to a high place in the government. What changed at the beginning of
Exodus was the menacing reproduction of the Israelites, that is, their
obedience to the original command to "Be fruitful and increase in number" (Genesis 1:28). It is this that has precipitated their present situation;
and Moses possesses the insight that they cannot remain in Egypt. Ironically, no such reverent care is taken of Moses' bones at the end of
Deuteronomy.

How many Israelites undertake this trek out of Egypt behind Moses?
According to the census in Numbers, the figure is 603,350 adult males, to
which must be added women and children, perhaps a total of one mil-
lion. This will do for the purposes of the narrative, though most historians regard the claimed number as excessive. However that may be,
the Israelites are still rebellious against Moses, and he faces a possible

insurrection at the Red Sea. At this juncture, they sight the approach of Pharaoh's pursuing army. "As Pharaoh approached, the Israelites looked up, and there were the Egyptians, marching after them. They were terrified and cried out to the Lord. They said to Moses, 'Was it because there were no graves in Egypt that you brought us to the desert to die? What have you done to us by bringing us out of Egypt? Didn't we say to you in Egypt, "Leave us alone, let us serve the Egyptians?"' It would have been better for us to serve the Egyptians than to die in the desert'" (Exodus 14:10–12).

This rebuke to Moses is drenched in anger and sarcasm. So there were no graves in Egypt? That is why we have to die out here in the desert? The Israelites are far from persuaded of the wisdom of the exodus. Perhaps, they say, Egypt was all right (even though Pharaoh was killing their male children?). These views on the part of his followers confirm the necessity for Moses' leadership, and, therefore, the validity of the Horeb insight. Without the Horeb experience, an experience foreign to the ordinary life of the Israelites, there would have been no challenge to Pharaoh, no exodus, no Sinai, no Law, and no Promised Land.

The powerful and climactic Mount Sinai experience (Exodus 19:34) develops much further the Horeb or burning-bush theophany. What was implicit at Horeb becomes fully explicit at Mount Sinai. The fire of the burning bush became the much greater fire and cloud that envelop Sinai. Perhaps reminiscent of the warlike god Baal, who lives in a volcano, this fire imagery reinforces Moses' aspect, by now amply proved, as a military chieftain, even as he transmits the Commandments of the Law to his people.

Perhaps it is not surprising by this time that in the midst of these great events Moses is confronted by another rebellion, as there is an upsurge of polytheism in the episode of the Golden Calf (some biblical scholars suggest that this idol more accurately be described as a young bull). We understand that the rigors of monotheism are too exigent for the Israelite defectors. The seriousness of the rebellion is shown by the fact that Aaron actually joins it or at least does not oppose it (Exodus 32:15–35), and that Moses interprets it specifically as resistance to the forthcoming Law. Approaching the camp with the Tablets, Moses hears singing in the distance; then, when "Moses saw the calf and the dancing, his anger burned and he threw the tablets out of his hands, breaking them to pieces at the foot of the mountain. And he took the calf they had made and burned it in the fire; then he ground it to powder" (Exodus 32:19–20). Moses has returned from Sinai to find a polytheistic celebration going on, probably a ritual celebration in full swing. His familiar temper leads him to smashing the two Tablets, on which, after all, God has written, to the ground. Then he moves quickly not only to destroy the idol but to slaughter the idolaters: "So he stood at the entrance to the camp and said, 'Whoever is for the Lord, come to me.' And all the Levites rallied to him [Moses is a son of the house of Levi]. Then he said to them, 'This is what the Lord, the God of Israel, says, "Each man strap a sword to his side. Go back and forth through the camp from one end to the other, each killing his brother and friend and neighbor." ' The Levites did as Moses commanded, and that day about three thousand people died" (Exodus 32:26–28).

No human relationship can stand in the way of this slaughter, not brother, friend, or neighbor. (One thinks back to Abraham and Isaac.) The First Commandment is absolute, because it is the premise of all the rest: "You shall have no other gods before me."

Later in the journey of Moses and the Israelites toward the Promised Land a still more serious rebellion meets with even sterner rebuke from the embattled monotheistic Moses.[21] It is recounted in Numbers 25, when the Israelites and their army reach Shittim, where there occurs a large defection toward the Baal of Peor, a warrior-fertility god. Moses himself is a great warrior, and the imagery associated with him is often very much like that associated with Baal, who lives in a volcano: fire, clouds, mist. Baal is especially dangerous to Moses and his mission because he is attractive to the Israelite warriors and because his worship involves ritual sexual intercourse with the temple holy prostitutes, who are his priestesses. This episode is worth quoting at some length because of its special ferocity.

> While Israel was staying in Shittim, the men began to indulge in
> sexual immorality with the Moabite women, who invited them to the
> sacrifices to their gods. The people ate and bowed down before these
> gods. So Israel joined in worshipping the Baal of Peor. And the Lord's
> anger burned against them.
>
> The Lord said to Moses, "Take all the leaders of these people, kill
> them, and expose them in broad daylight before the Lord, so that the
> Lord's fierce anger will turn away from Israel."
>
> So Moses said to Israel's judges, "Each of you must put to death
> those of your men who have joined in worshipping the Baal of Peor."
>
> Then an Israelite man brought to his family a Midianite woman
> right before the eyes of Moses, and the whole assembly of Israel while
> they were weeping at the entrance of the Tent of Meeting. When
> Phineas son of Eleazar, the son of Aaron, the priest, saw this, he left
> the assembly, took a spear in his hand and followed the Israelite into
> the tent. He drove the spear through both of them—through the
> Israelite and into the woman's body. Then the plague against the
> Israelites was stopped, but those who died in the plague numbered
> 24,000. (Numbers 25:1–9)

The plague here was inflicted directly by God, not through the
agency of Moses, as in the heresy of the Golden Calf, where Moses
punished the malefactors. The heresy of worshipping the Baal of Peor
was much more serious, and the numbers killed commensurately larger.
The brutal action of Phineas turns God's anger away from the Israelites.

Although peace of a sort has descended, Moses now sends a military
expedition against Midian. The Israelite army is victorious and extermi-
nates all the Midianite men. But the soldiers bring the women and
plunder back to Moses, who is outraged. "Have you allowed all the
women to live?" He asked them. "They were the ones who followed
Baalam's advice and were the means of turning the Israelites away from
the Lord in what happened at Peor, so that a plague struck the Lord's
people. Now kill all the boys and kill every woman who has slept with a
man, but save for yourselves every girl who has never slept with a man"
(Numbers 31:15–18).

This savagery, chilling as it is, has its motivation in the embattled and fragile condition of the Israelites' monotheism. Jack Miles makes an important point about this, touched on before. Whatever brand of polytheism the Golden Calf represents—and biblical scholars are uncertain—Baal is a special temptation for the warrior Israelites at this phase of their history. Moses himself is associated with imagery used in connection with Baal—thunder, lightning, mists. Moses himself is a ferocious leader of warriors. The boundaries between Moses and Baal must have seemed problematic to many Israelite warriors, especially with the temple prostitutes available for active worship. But from the perspective of monotheism the boundaries between God and Baal are absolute. The Baal worshippers are dealt with so harshly because the temptation is so dangerous to monotheism.

But, right here, it is worthwhile to think of that other Bronze Age hero, Achilles, the "destroyer of cities." He and Moses were approximate contemporaries, the siege of Troy not distant from the Near East of Moses. Achilles slaughtered with merciless rage, as did his Trojan enemies. Troy itself was destroyed to its foundations, infants hurled from its battlements, and women seized as slaves. Achilles' motivation was the pursuit of *areté* and immortal fame. Moses was unyielding in his defense of pure monotheism. But when we contemplate both epic heroes a vast chill reaches us from the Bronze Age.

But to return here to the decisive Sinai experience, which unfolds between Exodus 19:1 and 34:26. From a purely narrative point of view this account is seriously flawed by long interpolations (20–23, 25–31), which interrupt the narrative by setting forth in great detail the rules and practices for implementing the fundamental Law. Much of this material has little to do with the condition of the Israelites at this juncture, a people and an army on the march. It applies rather to a later and settled community and is anachronistic here. No doubt the scribes who assembled this material wished to give it special authority by associating it with Moses. The reader of the narrative will understand this, perhaps reading the interpolations lightly while following the narrative closely. Exodus 19:3–6 commences the Sinai event with a majestic prologue: "Then

Moses went up to God, and the Lord called to him from the mountain and said, 'This is what you are to say to the house of Jacob and what you are to tell the people of Israel: "You yourselves have seen what I did to Egypt, and how I carried you on eagles' wings and brought you to myself. Now if you obey me fully and keep my covenant, then out of all nations you will be my treasured possession. Although the whole earth is mine, you will be for me a kingdom of priests and a holy nation." These are the words you will speak to the Israelites.' " God, in epic manner, declares his credentials and summarizes the content of the impending covenant, its nature, and its goal. There then follows 19:7–25. Moses returns to the elders of the people, who solemnly agree: "All that the Lord has spoken we will do." The whole people therefore is consecrated and ready to receive the Law. The rest of chapter 19 recounts the preparations for Moses' second ascent of Sinai and the delivery of the Law in chapter 20.

The consecration of the Hebrew tribes, persuaded by Moses and the elders, permanently transforms their situation, binding them together as a people new to history. They are a nascent polity under God and under a Law transmitted through Moses. The Law has cosmic backing, since the God who promulgates it is the God of Genesis 1, who created the universe. With the Law, he again brings order out of chaos, this time in the religious, moral, and political spheres, which in this Law are interrelated. The tribes become Israel, a newly constituted body. Moses adds the role of nation-builder to his list of extraordinary roles. After Sinai, the Israelites are ready for their long and testing expedition through the desert, an account given substantially in the book Numbers and concluding at the Jordan River at the end of Deuteronomy. At Mount Sinai they make the transition from Egypt (false gods, to which in various forms some of them still remain drawn) to service in a new understanding of the territory they still must win.

The commandments Moses brings down from Sinai (Exodus 20) are repeated in more concise form in Deuteronomy 5, as if by a now aged Moses summing them up from memory. Most of us are so familiar with the ten commandments that we usually do not notice their logic and compactness, the shape of the overall statement they make, and their implicit potentiality for further development. The Decalogue is a fundamental document in political philosophy, and it is of world-historical importance.

The First Commandment asserts the monotheistic premise of all that follows: "You shall have no other gods before me." Everything else follows from that. In the great Psalm about the Law, 119, the longest and most elaborately wrought of the Psalms, the psalmist describes the Law as "true" (*emeth*). That is, the Law is rooted in Being, in actuality, in the way things are. Its religious and ethical injunctions are not opinions or recommendations; there are moral and religious rules that are true just as there are observable principles operative in the world of nature.[22]

The next three commandments derive logically from the first: "Thou shalt not make thyself any graven images of anything that is in the heaven above. . . . Thou shalt not take the name of thy Lord in vain. . . . Remember the Sabbath Day by keeping it holy." Of course images of God are excluded because he is wholly Other. Nor, moving to the street level, are we to use the name of God frivolously. And, such is human nature, we require a day, the Sabbath, to remind ourselves of our place in the cosmos.

After this compact theology, the Fifth Commandment makes the link between what has gone before and the social implications that are to follow: "Honor thy father and thy mother." The family unit is the indispensable building block of society. This commandment is highly traditional in its bearing. The family does many things: it communicates the religious and ethical teaching as well as much of the rest that we call culture. The Fifth Commandment honors the importance of accumulated teaching and experience.

The remaining five commandments set forth the laws—the rules proved by experience and codified here—governing behavior in the society established by the first five commandments: Thou shalt not commit murder, commit adultery, steal, bear false witness, or covet thy neighbor's wife or property. These last five commandments deal with the human community and outline a human order within which its members can grow peacefully in relation to the divine reality of the great monotheistic premise.

Taken as a whole, the commandments outline a model, and indeed constitute a verbal model, of a society founded with its ethics rooted in the origin and structure of the cosmos.

> Thou shalt have no other gods before me.
> Thou shalt not make thyself any graven images.
> Thou shalt not take the name of thy Lord in vain.
> Remember the Sabbath Day, to keep it holy.
> Honor thy father and thy mother.
> Thou shalt not commit murder.
> Thou shalt not commit adultery.
> Thou shalt not steal.
> Thou shalt not bear false witness.
> Thou shalt not covet thy neighbor's wife or property.

God here is a rather good political philosopher; and, given the compactness and logic of the whole, he is also a literary formalist. Indeed, the formal organization here, like the formal organization of the Creation poem, reflects the order of the cosmos, of the nature of things. As indeed is appropriate. We are seeing the creation of a people and a society.

What strikes the reader afresh in contemplating this list is how relatively modest they seem, at least at first. They do not seem to require heroic behavior or extraordinary virtue. They merely set forth the basis of a community that will be monotheistic, will respect the Sabbath and family tradition, and will agree to adhere to the rules set forth in the last five commandments, which are far from requiring heroic restraint. Yet, carefully considered, the First Commandment, the basis of it all, could be seen as virtually infinitely demanding: the awareness of the fact that God comes before everything.

The Sixth Commandment, misleadingly translated as "Thou shalt not kill," might seem to enjoin a heroic pacifism, but this is not the case. The Hebrew rāṣaḥ demands "Thou shalt not murder." This is supported by the evidence that Moses himself, who is promulgating this

Law, immediately orders his Levites to kill some 3,000 Hebrews who are blasphemously worshipping the Golden Calf. He is not having them murdered but rather executed for sacrilege. They have been insulting the God of the First Commandment and seriously threatening the basis of the new community.

All ten of these commandments repay long mediation. The first is the most important by far, but the tenth is important too and helps to frame the whole. Commandment One, about the worship of other gods, is about preferring the lower over the higher good and is directed at human pride and folly. Standing first, that commandment is a theological and cosmic formulation. The Tenth Commandment, completing the list, is about the basis of social existence and the great social evil of envy. The man who covets his neighbor's wife and goods is the envious man, not a good basis for social existence and, arguably, the greatest of social evils. This Tenth Commandment, indeed, is stern about a man's property and takes care to list several examples. The principle of property here is at the basis of society, as the assertion of the First Commandment has to do with the order of the universe.

The form of the commandments does invite further development in that they are put negatively. The Israelites are not to do this and that bad thing. They thus establish a limiting basis for the community and a minimum of spiritual order. At the same time they do not exclude the development of positive virtues. Yes, do not commit adultery; but yes, too, love thy wife. These positive possibilities will appear as monotheism works its way out through history. The poets and the prophets will have their contributions as the Law makes its way through culture. The many rich books of the Hebrew Bible constitute a carefully selected compendium of various insights consistent with but also elaborating upon the founding documents of Genesis and Exodus.

After the long interpolation (Exodus 25–31) about later rules and regulations, and after the Golden Calf rebellion, in which Moses smashed the two original Tablets, Moses again ascends Sinai (Exodus 34), is instructed to cut two more stone Tablets, upon which he will write the same words that had been on the first two, presumably the Ten

Commandments. In this second experience, however, Moses is both more intimate with God and more alone with him, as it were both separated from his erring people and also more necessary to them. This is surely a result of the Golden Calf uprising but perhaps also of Moses' smashing of the two original Tablets. Both Moses and his people may be imperfect instruments of monotheism in history.

Toward the end of chapter 35, Moses comes down from Sinai with the Tablets, and: "Moses did not know that the skin of his face shone because he had been talking with God. And when Aaron and all the people of Israel saw Moses, behold the skin of his face shone, and they were afraid to come near him" (35:29–30). This detail might well be taken as a purely symbolic statement, and such physical illumination occurs from time to time in the narrative. It may, however, be taken literally in that there are verifiable accounts of something like it.[23]

The astonishing book of Exodus ends one year after the escape from Egypt. At that point God moves into the tent Tabernacle erected for him by Moses. "The Lord filled the Tabernacle" in the form of a cloud by day and fire by night. Here we seem to be in the presence of a second Creation. Genesis had begun with an enormous creative act by God. Exodus ends with the warrior God imagery suggestive of a volcano as the Israelites march forth behind Moses and his generals with years of trial, suffering, and warfare ahead of them.

The remainder of the Moses narrative occurs for the most part in the book of Numbers, which takes its title from the census of the Israelites conducted in it. In the Hebrew Bible the more appropriate title is "In the Wilderness." This narrative book is sandwiched between the books Leviticus and Deuteronomy. In the former, God speaks to his people and transmits a lengthy codification of prescribed practices. In Deuteronomy Moses (supposedly) does the same. This oration, serene and confident in tone, is presented as the last utterance of Moses before his death. On internal evidence, this cannot be an utterance by the Bronze Age figure we know as Moses. This raises no problem. The author(s) of the oration no doubt meant that they were speaking in the spirit of Moses as they extrapolated the Law for later usage. It can be taken as a "Mosaic" oration. The lengthy legal prescriptions of both Leviticus and this part of Deuteronomy, however, and even though they have great religious importance, are not part of the epic concerning the Bronze Age epic hero.

Nevertheless, it is possible to appreciate these lengthy codifications of the Law through an effort of the historical imagination. For a people struggling to actualize the implications of their monotheism in history, the strict specifications of the Law no doubt functioned as a barrier against temptation and deviation. Throughout the Pentateuch, an epic indeed, of monotheism, the narrative has made plain enough the power of polytheism to produce rebellion time and again, including among Moses' own followers. Thus in the Psalms, several of the songs express lyrical gratitude for the codification of the Law. Psalm 119 claims that studying the Law is like finding treasure, like music, like the taste of honey. To the modern reader much of Leviticus and Deuteronomy are bound to seem dry and tedious. To the ancient community, however, they must have seemed cleansing and salvific. We are not ourselves closely acquainted with pagan practices, but if we were there is no doubt that we would find many of them repulsive, abhorrent—the festive and probably orgiastic worship of the Golden Calf, the ritual prostitution of the priestesses of Baal, human and animal sacrifice, the infanticide offered to Moloch, and much else.

The book of Numbers, placed between Leviticus and Deuteronomy, picks up the story one month after God has taken up residence in Moses' Tabernacle tent. He orders that a census be taken of the encampment, and when this has been completed the Israelites set out en masse into the Sinai desert. "So they set out from the mountain of the Lord and travelled for three days. The ark of the covenant of the Lord went before them during those three days to find them a place to rest. The cloud of the Lord was over them by day when they set out from camp" (Numbers 10:33–34).

The catalogue of the tribes and their leaders as the people and its army assemble has majesty and reminds us of the catalogues of cohorts, leaders, ships, and the like in the classical epics. Rebellion, however, is never far beneath the surface, as in Numbers 11:1: "Now the people complained about their hardship in the hearing of the Lord, and when he heard them his anger was aroused. Then fire from the Lord burned among them and consumed some of the outskirts of the camp." The detail that the fire "consumed some of the outskirts of the camp" has a certain brutal resonance, reminding us of the punishment meted out to other rebellions.

The Book of Numbers is comprised of the important census of the Israelite tribes and the narrative of the long march across the Sinai desert, the first raids on Canaan from the south, the decision to invade Canaan across the Jordan River, and the victories at Heshbon and Bash, the two small Amorite kingdoms on the east side of the river. The book ends with the Israelites encamped east of the Jordan opposite Jericho and preparing to invade Canaan.

The principal theme of this book is the continuing but difficult and contentious progress of the Israelites, who are stiff-necked and complaining. This is reflected in the growing weariness and irascibility of Moses as he grows older. In Numbers 20, a curious incident occurs at a place called Meribah, where Moses himself seems impatient with God. The Israelites have run out of water for themselves and their cattle and another rebellion is at hand as they berate Moses for leading them out of Egypt. Moses and Aaron go to the Tabernacle Tent and the Lord instructs Moses that he should take his staff with him and "speak to that rock before their eyes and the rock will pour forth water." And so it does, but the episode ends with what appears to be a condemnation of Moses: "So Moses took the staff from the Lord's presence, just as he commanded him. He and Aaron gathered the assembly together in front of the rock and Moses said to them, 'Listen, you rebels, must we bring you water out of this rock?' Then Moses raised his arm and struck the rock twice with his staff. Water gushed out, and the community and their livestock drank. But the Lord said to Moses and Aaron, 'Because you did not trust in me enough to honor me as holy in the sight of the Israelites, you will not bring this community into the land I give them" (Numbers 20:9–12).

Neither Moses nor Aaron will cross the Jordan and enter the Promised Land. Throughout the narrative, both have been found wanting in various ways. Notably, Aaron was complicit in the Golden Calf worship. Moses angers easily and moves quickly to violence, and at Meribah he shows characteristic impatience in striking the rock twice. Perhaps the judgment passed by God is sweeping—"Because you did not trust in me enough"—and may go all the way back to Mount Horeb, when Moses, despite the burning bush and the voice speaking from it, argues with God about accepting his mission. Perhaps the negative judgment even goes back to Moses' childhood, divided between Hebrew mother-nurse and princess surrogate mother, and to his Egyptian upbringing and the princely airs he assumed. However we interpret the judgment at Meribah, there is a serious flaw in this great and heroic figure who in fact accomplished so much. His experience in the Sinai is painful in other ways. His sister Miriam dies and is buried in Kadesh. God repeats his condemnation of Moses and, this time, Aaron at Mount Hor, and is especially hard on Aaron: "At Mount Hor, near the border of Edom, the Lord said to Moses and Aaron, 'Aaron will be gathered to his people. He will not enter the land I give the Israelites, because both of you rebelled against my command at the water of Meribah. Get Aaron and his son Eleazar and take them up Mount Hor. Remove Aaron's garments and put them on his son Eleazar, for Aaron will be gathered to his people; he will die there'" (Numbers 20:23–25). Aaron will not enter the Promised Land, he will not gaze upon it across the Jordan, as Moses finally does. The judgment upon Aaron seems severe, and in his case as well as that of Moses it may embrace more and reach further back than the incident at Meribah.

In Deuteronomy 6, however, amid much Mosaic instruction in the Law, and after a brief exposition of the Ten Commandments, Moses, however flawed, makes an eve-of-battle speech. This is his own commandment and may amount to a recollection through oral tradition of some of his last decisive instructions to his people. It is a central text for the history of Israel:

"Hear, O Israel: The Lord our God, the Lord is one. Love the Lord your God with all your heart and with all your soul and with all your

strength. These commandments that I give you today are to be upon
your hearts. Impress them on your children. Talk about them when you
are at home and when you walk along the road, when you lie down and
when you get up. Tie them as symbols on your hands and bind them on
your foreheads. Write them on the doorframes of your houses and on
your gates" (Deuteronomy 6:4–8).

Of course, at this point, the Israelites are still in the desert and the
battle of Jericho remains in the future, and Joshua will succeed Moses as
leader. The long and stirring address attributed to Moses amounts to a
summing up and a prophetic urging to conquest, and, most important,
an anticipation of the Promised Land. Whether Moses actually uttered
these words we cannot know, but some such summing up would have
been appropriate for the great figure we have met in the narrative, and it
certainly has its architectural place in the epic sweep of the story.

Many battles and triumphant anthems later, the long journey of the
Israelites brings Moses to the eastern bank of the Jordan River, where his
life will end. Chapter 34 of Deuteronomy ends with one of the great
scenes in all of literature, in which the turbulent and now aged hero
gazes out from the highest pinnacle of Mount Nebo over the land he was
promised but now is forbidden to enter.

In Moses, as in earlier figures in the Hebrew Bible, there has existed a
strong current of resistance and impatience. This is quite different from
the relationship to the gods of the heroes of the *Iliad* and the *Odyssey*.
Achilles does not argue with Hera, let alone Zeus. The Homeric world is
much more a *given*, the world of the Hebrew Bible one of process and
new creation. We have seen that Abraham resists his world-historical
mission at the beginning and tested God outside Sodom and Gomorrah
and may have challenged God again at the commanded sacrifice of
Isaac. Moses perhaps had been negligent in the matter of the Golden
Calf. He irascibly smashed the Tablets at Sinai and was impatient with
God at Meribah concerning water from the rock. Imperfection is present from the beginning in the Hebrew Bible. In its first line, "In the
beginning God created the heaven and the earth," there is a grammati-

cal ambiguity. The Hebrew verb *B'rashit bara* literally means "in the beginning of." In the beginning of what? There is no object for the preposition. Thus you cannot get past the first line of the Hebrew Bible without sensing the presence of radical questioning, even within the symmetries of the great Creation poem that begins Genesis 1. The narrative throughout is, so to speak, stiff-necked and quarrelsome, as is the ox resisting the imposition of the yoke. We may think that the yoke of this monotheism is morally harsher than the relationship of the Greek gods to the heroes below Olympus. But perhaps it is this element of skepticism and realism in the Hebrew Bible that opens the way toward affinities between Jerusalem and Athens.

So now we have Moses, a Bronze Age hero comparable to Achilles, dying on the wrong side of the Jordan, gazing out over the Promised Land as far as the "western sea," the Mediterranean. That sea here may suggest mystery, permanence, and power. That he can see all this and not enter there below certainly represents an ambiguous success and perhaps is cruel, but it is consistent with a life marked by ambiguity from the start.

> Then Moses climbed Mount Nebo from the plain of Moab to the top of Pisgah, across from Jericho. There the Lord showed him the whole land—from Gilead to Dan, all of Naphtali, the territory of Ephraim and Manasseh, all the land of Judah as far as the western sea, the Negev, and the whole region from the valley of Jericho, the city of palms, as far as Zoar. Then the Lord said to him, "This is the land I promised on oath to Abraham, Isaac and Jacob when I said, 'I will give it to your descendents.' I have let you see it with your own eyes, but you will not cross over into it."
>
> And Moses the servant of the Lord died there in Moab, as the Lord had said. He buried him there in Moab in the valley opposite Beth Peor, but to this day no one knows where his grave is. Moses was a hundred and twenty years old when he died but his eyes were not weak nor his strength gone. The Israelites grieved for Moses in the plains of Moab thirty days, until the time of weeping and mourning was over. . . .

Since then no prophet has risen in the land like Moses, whom the Lord knew face to face, who did all those miraculous signs and wonders the Lord sent him to do in Egypt—to Pharaoh and to all his officials and to the whole land. For no one has ever shown the mighty power or performed the awesome deeds that Moses did in the sight of Israel. (Deuteronomy 34:1–12).

So ends the epic of Moses. Monotheism has burst free from polytheistic Egypt, has conquered the various tribes and come in from the desert. From the top of Mount Nebo the western sea is already in view. The Israelites will conquer the land of Canaan, establish themselves as a divinely constituted society, ground ethics in Law and Law in the structure of Being, and change the world.

CHAPTER FOUR

Socrates and Jesus: Internalizing the Heroic

Socrates and Jesus now become absolutely central figures. Socrates brings the central tendency of Athens to a sharp focus and Jesus does the same for Jerusalem. Socrates, as we see him in Plato's accounts, internalized the Greek heroic tradition that came down to him as refracted through Homer. The heroism of the battlefield and the pursuit of *areté* became heroic philosophy and the pursuit of truth, even at the cost of life itself. Socrates embodied in pure form the heroism of cognition or knowing. Jesus radically internalized the heroic tradition of the patriarchs, Moses, and the Prophets, refining it to an intense concentration on the inward condition of holiness, anchoring the older Law in the purified soul. The Homeric *paideia* was the education of Athens. Socrates internalized it as the new education of cognition. Exodus was the heroic *paideia* of the Israelites. Jesus internalized the Law as the concentration of holiness. Both drove toward universality, Socrates through reason, Jesus through the aspiration to holiness.

Socrates thus becomes in the great narrative the iconic figure of Western philosophy and science, Jesus the iconic figure of Western religion and spiritual aspiration. It is not too much to say that what is valuable in us, what is most essential, and whether we know it or not flows directly or indirectly from Socrates and Jesus. The profound tendencies of mind they epitomize came together in an uneasy but creative fusion during the first century A.D. in the Hellenized culture of Jerusalem and the Near East.

It is true that for a long period of Western history (ca. A.D. 500–1500) Socrates was little more than a name, and not much of Plato was available. The cognitive tradition we have been associating with Athens was carried forward powerfully by Plato's pupil Aristotle. Yet Socrates belongs there at the beginning as the iconic figure of cognition, made so by Plato's account of his life, death, and teaching in the *Dialogues*.

The most recent experience I have had dealing with some of this material in a classroom was as a visiting professor at a small college in Massachusetts.[1] Our seminar room was in a college building, but next to this building was a large brick church dating from about the time of the Civil War. The symbolism of our situation was striking. Socrates pursued the truth at the cost of his life. Although he wrote nothing, his disciple Plato founded an academy in Athens to carry on his work and also left us compelling narratives about his life and death. Plato's Academy was the first important Western "university," and here we were in its direct descendant in contemporary America. But we could also gaze through our large windows at that church. Jesus sought holiness, and did so at the cost of his life. And though he, like Socrates, wrote nothing, his disciples founded a church in Jerusalem to carry on his work and, like Plato in the example of Socrates, left us rich narratives about his life, death, and teaching. University and church, the embodiments of Athens and Jerusalem, were physically present there in our classroom, and in their essence did not seem distant from us.

In thinking about Socrates, a cautionary word is in order. Although we have other evidence about him, the Socrates who matters comes to us through Plato. In the *Dialogues*, a formidable theory of knowledge is proposed, yet for our purpose here it does not matter whether that theory be judged valid. What matters is that Socrates, as presented by Plato, brought to a climax the quest for "knowing" already existing in earlier Greek philosophy, a quest that indeed had been anticipated in the epics of Homer, a major theme of which is knowing what constitutes nobility of character or *areté*. The Socratic quest for truth necessarily was based upon questioning all previous assumptions. It sought to know "actuality," which ultimately had to include everything, and do so independently of religion, myth, and received tradition. In this it menaced the local particularity and tribal gods of the ancient world and laid the universal basis of science and philosophy.

Remarkably, this cognitive quest began at a specific time and place, that is Ionia, a region on the seacoast of the Near East, around 550 B.C. So far as we know, a few philosophers on the seacoasts of the Aegean and on the numerous small islands nearby began to investigate and speculate about the visible world and about the nature of the whole or cosmos. This was a startling development. No such detribalizing movement of mind had ever been known before. These pre-Socratics, as they now are known, wondered, independently of religion and myth and tradition, what the "world" really is. They proposed answers that may now seem strange, but Western science and philosophy were born because they began to ask those questions. Socrates and Plato, and then Aristotle, a pupil of Plato, stood on the shoulders of those ancient Ionian thinkers and made a leap in consciousness, and how we lead our lives is still based on their reasoning. Let us pause for just a moment here to remember and honor those distant pre-Socratics, with whom we enter a mental universe very different from the one emerging in the Hebrew Bible.

Part of their appeal is that as a group they possess intellectual charm. There is something enormously poignant about these philosophers, gazing at the sea without myth, looking at the stars, at the waves, thinking about mathematics, music, the regularities and surprises of nature. We admire these early efforts as such, but also for their very "pastness," an appeal they have that the philosopher A. O. Lovejoy called "the pastness of the past."[2] Thunder and lightning, the anger of the sea, were in the process of being understood, not in terms of the moods of Zeus or Poseidon but as natural events within the cosmos.

Here we come to a further important point. The idea that there is a whole, or cosmos, is not, after all, necessary to the practical demands of everyday living. These earliest philosophers were beginning to make a separation between the workaday world and the independent activity of observation and speculation. They thus began a sustained critical and intellectual quest for truth for its own sake, for cognition as an independent value, and this was a unique occurrence in human history.

Attempts have been made to find the beginnings of critical speculation in Egyptian mathematics and Babylonian astronomy. Some influence upon the Greeks is tenuously possible, but Egyptian mathematics was rudimentary and practical, confined to such matters as redefining fields after a flood on the Nile, and never approached the advancing knowledge of the Greeks. Babylonian astronomy was more akin to astrology and largely had to do with divination. Both societies were dominated by myth and by priestly bureaucracies and what they achieved had nothing to do with the pre-Socratics.

One might ask why this happened in Ionia and nowhere else in the then-known world. One theory holds that the Greek mainland was in a condition of relative chaos because of barbarian incursions beginning in the eleventh century B.C. Far away in Ionia there existed a continuous civilized tradition and the leisure necessary for philosophical reflection. Homer belonged to that Ionian world, though of course his material derived from much earlier events and legends.

Only fragments of the pre-Socratic philosophers survive, available in convenient modern editions. Their written works were often voluminous but have been lost, and much of what we know about them comes from Aristotle's much later comments about them. These may not be entirely fair to them since his concern was often to refute them, but they are nevertheless valuable. Let us pause a moment to witness the birth of Western philosophy and science.

A man named Thales probably deserves to be called the first philosopher-scientist. Born in the small city of Miletus, he flourished in the early sixth century B.C. He is said to have predicted an eclipse of the sun later mentioned by Herodotus, which modern astronomers date as occurring on May 28, 585 B.C. He probably had some knowledge of planetary movements. In legend he is credited with discovering some of the theorems Euclid (ca. 300 B.C.) used in his *First Book* of geometry. According to remarks made by Aristotle in his magisterial *Metaphysics*,

Thales concluded that the primary underlying substance of the cosmos is water.

Initially this sounds ludicrous. Much later Montaigne included it in a catalogue of ancient absurdities. Still, the very idea that there is a fundamental unifying factor or substance in the cosmos is momentous—central, indeed, to Socrates and Plato, not to mention modern quantum physics and the aspirations of its superconductor project, or speculations based upon the apparently limiting reality of the speed of light. Later Greek philosophy would call this underlying and unifying principle the Logos and engaged in profound debate about what it might be.

There might even be a word to say in defense of Thales' choice of water. We can see that most things around us change all the time. But the Aegean does not change. The waves that lapped the shore near Thales' Miletus lap that shore still. Plato refined out a very different conception of the underlying and unchanging order of the cosmos, but Thales may have invented philosophy by gazing at the unchanging waves of the Aegean and seeing beyond the flux of appearances to the unchanging universal of water.

Two younger philosophical associates of Thales, both of them also citizens of Miletus, posited other fundamental entities. Anaximander taught that the fundamental reality beyond all change is an indeterminate substance out of which things come and into which they disappear. His colleague Anaximines developed a theory that the fundamental substance is air, observing that "Just as our soul, being air, holds us together, so do breath and air encompass the whole world." Anaximines had to account for solids, which he did by deciding that they are concentrations of air. What we share with these ancient Miletans is the perception that there are regularities in actuality and also the impulse to search for a principle behind them. They too had the desire to see the world as intelligible rather than as mere chaos.

Pythagoras had some important contributions to make. Born on the island of Samos, not far from Miletus (ca. 532 B.C.), he exiled himself for political reasons to southern Italy, where he established a philosophical academy. It comes down to us, in part through references in Aristotle, that Pythagoras believed mathematics to be the principle underlying the order of the cosmos. As the legend goes, Pythagoras one day was playing a musical instrument and noticed that it produced its harmony in mathematical relations consisting of simple ratios, such as 1:2, 2:3, and 3:4. It seems, and this is charming, that Pythagoras was offended by the ungainly number of pi in relation to the circle. We know that pi expresses the ratio of the diameter of any circle to its circumference and that pi equals 3.1416. We do not know what value Pythagoras assigned to pi, but whatever it was he found the fraction ungainly and possibly immoral. This is amusing, but we must recall that modern physicists often speak of an "elegant" solution.

Atomic theory did not begin with Albert Einstein, Niels Bohr, and Werner Heisenberg. It seems to have begun with Democritus (b. ca. 460 B.C.), who grew up in the small town of Abdera in Thrace. His wealthy father is said to have entertained the Persian emperor Xerxes on his way to invade Greece before suffering military catastrophe at Salamis. Democritus is supposed to have written seventy books, none of which has survived. He thought that the universal building blocks of the universe are atoms, that they move in a void according to universal patterns, and that they are not reducible to smaller entities. Centuries later the Roman poet Lucretius (96?–55 B.C.) turned such atomic suppositions into a great poem of epic length, *On the Nature of Things.*

The darkly mysterious but imposing philosopher Heraclitus was born around 500 B.C. in Ephesus, north of Miletus. He taught that the fundamental reality of the cosmos is eternal flux; yet he also seems to have sought within the flux a principle of stability, a pattern or Logos. There are hints of a Logos among the fragments we have of his work: "Although universal reason is known, most people live as if they had a private reason."[3] As these brief observations suggest, Heraclitus, who in fragmentary form creates an atmosphere of profundity, was known in his own time for his obscurity. Diogenes Laertius, a third century B.C. chronicler of the ancient philosophers, hands down the following anecdote: "They say that Euripides gave [Socrates] a copy of Heraclitus's book and asked him what he thought of it. He replied, 'What I under-

stand is splendid, and I think what I don't understand is splendid too."[4]
Another picturesque anecdote has the aged Parmenides (b. ca. 500 B.C.)
meeting the young Socrates in Athens.[5] Parmenides, a leader of the
Eleatic school, wrote in verse and taught that fundamental reality simply
is, and is unchanging, and that all the phenomena we know through the
senses are therefore transitory illusions. He thus made a fundamental
break between sense experience and permanent philosophical truth.
This would be central to both Socrates and Plato. When Parmenides,
then about sixty-five, met the already famous young Socrates in Athens,
he brought with him a code of laws he had drawn up for his native Elea.
This meeting between men of different generations in Athens is a crux of
history. In Socrates and Plato the characteristic pre-Socratic issues of
permanence and flux, truth and opinion, and the nature of the cosmos
would receive a grand attempt at solution.

This brief excursion among the pre-Socratics brings us to Socrates and
to his younger disciple and commemorator Plato, and probably we
should start with what for excellent reasons has always been the most
popular of Plato's dialogues about Socrates, the *Symposium*. At the time
of the events described here, seventeen years before Socrates' execution
in 399 B.C., Socrates, forty years older than Plato, was at the height of
his fame in Athens. The account, however, is an elegiac celebration,
composed by Plato around 385 B.C., or about fourteen years after Socrates' execution.

   In the *Symposium*, the occasion is a banquet at the villa of the playwright Agathon, who has just won an important prize for his plays. The
guests are an extraordinarily appealing group, young Athenian aristocrats and future leaders of the city, drawn to Socrates because of his
intellectual power. They include Agathon, the prize-winning playwright;
also the future general Alcibiades, a Byronic figure and later the leader
of the disastrous military expedition to Syracuse; the great comic playwright Aristophanes; Phaedrus, a literary man; Pausanias, Agathon's
lover; Eryximachus, a physician; and an admirer of Socrates named
Aristodemus. They all speak marvelously in character; despite Agathon's

recent prize as a dramatist, they are all drawn here by Socrates' presence. The scene has been compared to the elegant figures in an Athenian frieze or on an ancient urn.

Here we will focus on the performance of Socrates himself in the *Symposium,* though the dialogue throughout is very rich. He appears tardily, having become abstracted through thought along the way. Looking like Silenus—bald, with protruding eyes and a snub nose—Socrates wears a clean tunic for a change, also sandals, and has even been to the public baths. Socrates' normal indifference to social appearances is the signature of his commitment to thought. C. S. Lewis has remarked that Socrates, Jesus, and Samuel Johnson are three of the most recognizable individuals in history.

One notices that throughout the *Symposium* there are references to Homer. For example, Alcibiades refers to Homer when he offers to tell the group of a remarkable incident and compares Socrates to Odysseus in the citation about "another exploit that the hero dared."[6] This is a key reference, but there are many others. Like Odysseus and Achilles, Socrates has been a warrior, but Plato has something much larger in mind, Socrates as a hero superior to anyone in Homer. In the *Symposium,* Homer appears through allusion; elsewhere, in *Ion* and the *Republic,* Plato takes him on directly and at extensive length: Homer has been the guide for the Greeks about the most important things, but his inadequacy makes necessary the philosophical quest for the truth, and Socrates must make a private study of the things in the heavens and under the earth. Socrates is indebted to Homer and to tradition, but in seeking the truth he must break with them in order to move to a higher level of theory and of consciousness. The harmony of the cosmos is to be grasped not by the practical man but by the theoretical man. Philosophy is superior to the best that poetry can offer; Socrates is superior to the Homeric heroes. Plato presents Socrates as a better teacher than Homer.

In the banquet at Agathon's villa, the subject proposed for the evening is the nature of Love. Each contributor has his characteristic thing to say, but before we come to the climactic utterance of Socrates let us consider the anecdote Alcibiades tells about him after comparing him with Odysseus. Alcibiades presents Socrates as a soldier on the battlefield at Potideia, but as much more than a soldier. This anecdote is so important that we must pay close attention to it. Alcibiades says:

> I have told you one tale and now I must tell you another, which is worth hearing, "another exploit that the hero dared," while he was on the expedition. One morning he was thinking about something which he could not resolve; he would not give it up, but continued thinking from early dawn until noon—there he stood, fixed in thought; and at noon attention was drawn to him, and the rumor ran through the wondering crowd of soldiers that Socrates had been standing and thinking about something ever since the break of day. At last, in the evening after supper, some Ionians out of curiosity (I should explain that this was not in winter but in summer) brought out their mats and slept in the open air that they might watch him and see whether he would stand all night. There he stood until the following morning; and with the return of light he offered up a prayer to the sun and went his way. I will also tell if you please—and I am bound to tell, of his courage in battle.[7]

Thus before the battle Socrates thinks, philosophizes. His very location on a "Homeric" battlefield is important, as is his prowess in battle, in which he may do Homeric deeds. But his real heroism is of another order—and neither Alcibiades nor the other soldiers who look at him with wonder can come close to participating in it.

What could be more striking as a visual representation of the teaching of Socrates and Plato than this episode before battle? No more dramatic example can be imagined of the distinction between the practical and philosophical realms. Socrates has completely internalized the best heroism of the warrior, the highest nobility imagined by Homer, and turned it into something else—philosophy, at least as Socrates and Plato understood philosophy. In the teaching of Socrates and Plato, the greatest heroism is a thing internal to the mind; and, beyond that, they believed that the cosmos, the totality of everything that we understand as real, is penetrable by the human mind, because the cosmos operates according to logical rules that are analogous to the operations of the mind itself—that is, when the mind has been trained and disciplined by philosophy.

But just what mental operations is Socrates going through when he stands there in a long philosophic trance before the battle, then awakens to pray to the sun? The *Symposium* lets us and the others into the interior of Socrates' mind in his discourse on Love, which comes after the others have spoken. Curiously, what Socrates does in his discourse about Love is "report" the teaching once given him by one Diotima, supposedly a priestess of Manitea. Very likely, Diotima is a polite fiction on Socrates' part, since what he says is so superior to the remarks of the others that he wishes to avoid embarrassing them by delivering the discourse as his own.

Socrates' speech amounts to a brilliant exposition of the Platonic ascent to true knowledge motivated by the driving force of Love, under-stood as the desire for perfect knowledge. Love, the desire for what one lacks, moves the mind from the world of the senses, which always changes, to the world of permanent Forms, which never changes. The perception of these Forms allows one to see reality as a connected whole culminating in the Form of the Whole, or Logos, the culmination here of the philosophical quest for final order, which had been articulated among the pre-Socratics and continued in other branches of Greek philosophy. The ascent demands the severe intellectual training, athletic preparation, and ascetic discipline described in the central books of the *Republic*.

The exposition of the ascent by Socrates in the *Symposium* has a seductive music, apparent logical coherence, and rise to philosophical ecstasy. The Knower and the Lover—they are the same thing—begins with the sensible world we all know and makes his way "upward by a right use of feeling." There is room here for only a brief, but representa-tive, citation from Socrates' discourse:

> This is the right way of approaching or being initiated into the mys-
> teries of love, to begin with examples of beauty in this world and using
> them as steps to ascend continually with that absolute beauty as one's

aim, from one instance of physical beauty to two and from two to all, then from physical beauty to moral beauty and from moral beauty to the beauty of knowledge, until from knowledge of various kinds one arrives at the supreme knowledge whose sole object is that absolute beauty, and knows at last what absolute beauty is. . . . What may we suppose to be the felicity of the man who sees absolute beauty in its essence, pure and unalloyed, who instead of a beauty tainted by human flesh and color, and a mass of perishable rubbish, is able to apprehend divine beauty where it exists apart and alone.[8]

Thus one could begin with several objects ordinarily considered beautiful, and by meditating on them abstract from them their principle of beauty, and by repeated such exercises arrive at the principle of beauty in general. One could do this with any sensible object, person, or quality, such as justice, ethical behavior, or the state. At the distant end of such a process, accumulating these permanent essences, one might rise to the interconnection of all essences, the permanent idea of the whole, the Logos, the principle of permanence, for which the pre-Socratics had striven.

Anyone can see that this is a severe and perhaps repellent teaching. Aristotle studied at Plato's academy in Athens for twenty years, until Plato's death, and later founded his own university, the Lyceum. The teaching in the *Symposium* is severe, and to some repellent, because few are ready to accept the proposition that the things and living beings we love are mere perishable rubbish, tainted beauty at best. There is a ferocious asceticism about this teaching. Nevertheless, there is a heroic drive in Socrates and Plato, a drive that is willing to pay any price, abandon the "color and mass" that we love here and now for a vision of the ultimate and permanent reality. In the *Symposium*, when Socrates stands all night on the battlefield at Potideia, we understand that he is at some stage of the ascent through abstraction to the vision of the whole, symbolized by his prayer to the sun. Despite his severity and asceticism, Plato is much too powerful to be dismissed.

Coming down from these heights, the *Symposium* ends in humorous— or tragic?—chaos. Alcibiades, the brilliant but unruly youth, bursts drunk into the banquet and brings the discussion of Love decidedly to an end. As Alcibiades staggers in, the banqueters hear outside in the street drunken revelry and a girl playing a flute. The contrast of this with heroic philosophy of course is comic, but the scene also suggests the human reality that such philosophy must deal with, probably failing.

Alcibiades now tells the group of an attempt he had made to seduce Socrates homosexually. Socrates, true to his philosophy, had rejected this as being merely love for his body rather than for his mind. In Alcibiades, carnal desire has not even begun the ascent to pure intellectual love. Indeed, the erratic behavior and inner disorder he exhibits here is no doubt inferentially connected with his later military disaster at Syracuse. At the end of the *Symposium*, the man of ordered soul, Socrates, is the only drinker still wide awake.

Common sense is bound to ask, however, what these permanent Forms actually "are." Are they merely mental constructs in the mind of the philosopher? Are they somehow latent in the natural world itself? Or do they exist in some realm that is real though different from ordinary experience? To this it can be replied that there is a Platonic aspect to ordinary experience. Language itself is an abstraction from things themselves. The word *dog*, for example, is an abstraction embracing the immense variety of actual dogs. Unless we had an Idea of dogness, all we could do would be number each individual animal (itself another abstraction).

If we see that cognition thus depends upon abstraction, we can imagine that the immense variety of everything (the cosmos) might also, with great and prolonged effort, be embraced by the final abstraction or Idea. For Plato, this master abstraction is the One, the Good, the Logos and contains all the other Ideas or Forms. For Plato, the cosmos is knowable by mind, because the cosmos is ultimately rational and can be apprehended by rational mind. Plato is a rationalist but not a skeptic. That is why it said over the entrance to his Academy in Athens "Let no one ignorant of geometry enter here" and why mathematics and the relations of musical notes meant so much to him. The difficulty of ascending the cognitive ladder is so great, however, that Aristotle, for example, spent eighteen years studying at the Academy. The Ideas or Forms are real, more real by far than the flux of transitory things, and they are immortal in the Logos. To repeat, the importance of Socrates and Plato does not rest on whether one accepts or rejects this theory of knowledge. Their importance rests on the fact that they acted on their belief that the cosmos was penetrable by philosophy (and, by extension, science), and that they were pioneer heroes of cognition.

What can be said with certainty is that Plato's theory of knowledge—the Forms as ultimate reality, the Logos the Form of the cosmos—has had enormous influence on Western culture. As will be seen here, Hellenistic thought pervaded the Near East during the formative early centuries and had important effects on early Christianity. After about A.D. 500, Plato's pupil Aristotle became the dominant philosophical force; he carried forward the cognitive enterprise of the Academy. Aristotle's own Dialogues are lost, but in his prose the model of Plato's dialogue method is often a presence, as in such a passage as this from the *Ethics* (book 10) on the subject of pleasure: "One school maintains that pleasure is the Good; another, on the contrary, that it is wholly bad: some of its members very likely from a conviction that it is really so, and others believing that it is better with a view to the conduct of our lives to represent pleasure as a bad thing, even if it is not; because (they say) most people are inclined toward it and are the slaves of their self-indulgence, so that they need to be urged in the opposite direction; for in this way they attain to the mean. But probably this view is not correct . . . "[9] This is the beginning of a dialogue minus the *dramatis personae*. Yet even though Aristotle was dominant after A.D. 500, Plato also came forward through various channels, and his texts, those that were recovered, commended great interest after about 1500. Plato's theory of knowledge does have problems, but so do alternatives to it. For example, it becomes difficult not to be an essentialist about some matters. Socrates can handle a skeptic with a few swift moves. Do you think that some things are essentially, or really, wrong and not just wrong according to transitory "opinion"? How about mass murder? The Holocaust? Serial murder?

Sadism? Betrayal? As your list grows longer, you too may be finding that actuality is a structure of unchanging essences. In thinking of Socrates and Plato I myself think unavoidably of St. Augustine and Dante, but also of Henry Vaughan, a seventeenth-century English-Christian platonist, who wrote the following stanza some two thousand years after Socrates:

> I saw eternity the other night
> Like a great ring of pure and endless light,
>   All calm as it was bright.
> And round beneath it, Time, in hours, days, years,
>   Driven by the spheres
> Like a vast shadow moved, in which the world
>   And her train were hurled.[10]

Although Plato famously condemned Homer and the other poets in the *Republic*, he often used poetry, or "art," himself in order to teach his philosophy. Indeed, he probably thought his dialogues as good or better than the great works of the Athenian stage. Let us conclude here with his great philosophical simile, expressive of his entire philosophical view, from book 7 of the *Republic*.

The simile consists of an underground Cave that has an opening to the outside sunlight. Inside the Cave are people chained so that they can see only the rear wall. Between these prisoners and the mouth of the Cave there is a fire, and between the fire and the prisoners there is a wall acting as a screen. Along the top of this barrier men move statues of various objects so that the fire casts their shadows on the rear wall of the Cave. The prisoners cannot see one another, only their own shadows on the rear wall, along with the shadows of the objects moved on the wall behind them.

The prisoners in the Cave represent the majority of people, who are not enlightened philosophers and see only shadows of reality, including shadows of themselves. The objects moved along the top of the wall and casting shadows too, are works of art, representations of objects. The men behind the wall moving these objects are artists. The shadows cast by the representations, what the prisoners see as art, are only shadows of representations of actual objects.

However, if one of the prisoners breaks loose and manages to approach the statues on the barrier, he sees the representations instead of the shadows of the representations. If he manages to reach the mouth of the Cave, he will see actual objects themselves, bathed in sunlight. Finally he will see the sun itself, the symbol of the Whole. The Cave represents our world of illusion. The sunlight is the light of philosophy. The objects bathed in sunlight are objects seen directly and gateways to the Forms.

It is possible that in the *Republic* itself, Plato's projected ideal polis intellectually self-destructs. Following his discussion of the Cave, Plato remarks that if someone climbing out of the Cave and into the philosophical revelation of the sunlight actually went back into the Cave of ordinary perception, he would be unable to see because of the darkness—passion, interest, folly—and would make himself ridiculous (Socrates' dishevelment and poverty). If he tried to free one of the prisoners, who are used to the darkness and consider the shadows on the wall to be real—that is, rescue ordinary people from everything they love and are accustomed to—he would certainly be killed by the prisoner.

In this tragic view of the relation of his philosophy to the actual life of a polis, Plato certainly has in mind the execution of Socrates in 399 B.C. at about age seventy-one, condemned by an Athenian jury. Indeed, in his unapologetic speech to the jury, Socrates had said exactly what Plato would say in the *Republic:* "Please do not be offended if I tell you the truth. No man on earth who conscientiously opposes either you or any organized democracy, and flatly prevents a great many wrongs and illegalities from taking place in the state to which he belongs, can possibly escape with his life. The true champion of justice, if he intends to survive for a short time, must necessarily confine himself to private life and leave politics alone."[11] The charge against Socrates in 399 B.C. was that he was devising new gods and also corrupting the youth, the latter following from the former. Of devising new gods he is certainly guilty. With a few swift moves, as in *Euthyphro,* he can demolish the traditional

Olympian gods—and he means to replace them with philosophy, the Forms, and the Logos. But the gods were social as well as religious entities, part of the existence of the city with their holidays, temples, priests, and priestesses. To discredit them with influential young men was no trivial matter. Yet, even though Socrates (in the *Apology*) mounted an unyielding defense based upon his loyalty to truth and suggested that he should be given a state pension for his work, the large jury of 501 citizens convicted him by only 60 votes. In the immensely moving *Crito* and *Phaedo,* Socrates refuses a plausible opportunity to escape into exile: he is loyal to Athens and before serenely drinking the cup of poison, he discourses very movingly on various things, including the likely, he rationally argues, immortality of the soul.

In Jesus of Nazareth we encounter a figure who in many ways stands in relation to his tradition as Socrates and Plato stood to the epic tradition of Homer. Socrates internalized Homeric heroism as heroic philosophy, the heroic dedication to cognition and truth. Jesus internalized Moses' Commandments and the teaching of the Prophets as heroic holiness. To an unprecedented degree he demanded inner purity of intention as well as obedience to the Law. Holiness was to be not a whitewashed tomb with corruption within, but pure white all the way through. Socrates and Plato understand their relationship to Achilles and Homer. In the visionary Transfiguration scene (Mark 9:2–4), Jesus appears "on a mountain" talking with Moses and the prophet Elijah.

The man we call Jesus was surely named Joshua (*Yeshua*), since there is no name Jesus in the Hebrew lexicon. Although he is an official religious figure in Western culture, we will here treat him from the perspective of the humanities rather than as the subject of devotion and prayer. That is, I will seek to find out what the narratives and other sources tell us about him. The Jesus of goodness, of gentleness, and innocent suffering will give way to a personality marked, for our sensibilities, by a special "strangeness." He will strike us as stranger than Moses, stranger than Achilles.

As we read the four gospel narratives, one literary fact surges into the foreground. There is a wide discrepancy, a chasm, between the voices of the four third-person narrators and the voice of Jesus himself. The voices of the narrators are adequate to their tasks but pedestrian, John's perhaps the least so but, after chapter 1, not especially striking. The voice of Jesus is very different: eloquent, memorable, often mysterious. Into the world of the narrative voices there comes this entirely different voice. A "red-letter" edition of the Gospels, in which Jesus' statements are printed in red, indicates this immediately. What this seems to show is that Jesus could not have been created as a fictional or semifictional character even by men who were close to him but virtually had to be part of a recollection they shared, however derived, of an extraordinary person. Those who wrote the narrative prose could not have imagined the man who spoke as their central figure.

In spite of the fact that this material has official religious standing in our culture, I need to address the question of its historical value. First, the chronology of the narratives is important. The four gospels are not the earliest evidentiary material we have about Jesus. They were written, it is generally agreed, late in the first century, all of them about thirty to sixty years after Jesus' death.

The consensus among biblical scholars is that Paul's Epistles to the various Christian congregations around the eastern Mediterranean represent our earliest documents regarding Jesus and were composed between 49 and the middle 60s B.C., when Paul was beheaded in Rome. Paul did not know Jesus. The Epistles evidently draw on oral accounts of his life and death and include quotations that derive from such oral accounts or possibly from written material that has been lost.

The best estimates for the dates of the first three gospel narratives are as follows: Mark, A.D. 65–70; Matthew, around A.D. 75; and Luke, around A.D. 85. The case of John, the fourth narrative, is more complicated. Although generally assigned a later date, it also seems to contain material from much earlier in the first century and thus may draw upon another tradition of recollection, either oral or written. Therefore John is now dated 75–120 B.C. Our third principal source, the Book of Acts, a narrative about Peter, Paul, and the early church, is a continuation of the narrative of Luke and on internal evidence was composed about A.D. 75–80.

These issues of dating have considerable importance. Clearly the evidence available to us about Jesus is not as good as the evidence we have, say, about the assassination of John F. Kennedy. A gap exists of some thirty years between the death of Jesus and the earliest written evidence we have about him. The bridge between the events and the written narratives is that "oral tradition." However, as we have seen in the case of Homer's epics, which evolved out of an oral tradition, that oral tradition was remarkably reliable about the configuration of the Bronze Age Troy and other details that can be tested by archaeologists. Those who depend upon oral transmission may in fact be especially careful about accuracy. It is also true, it hardly need be said, that those testifying here do not see themselves as writing about a mythological figure, such as Attis or Osiris, or even about a figure from the very distant past, but probably historical, such as Moses. The Jesus we are considering here is claimed to be a historical figure in the ordinary sense, known in Nazareth, famous in Jerusalem. Except for Paul, who never met him, those who wrote about him claim to have known him as a historical figure, indeed one within living memory.

Then the question becomes, Why did the narratives begin to be written down, starting around A.D. 65. with Mark? The reason is made clear by Paul in his first Letter to the Corinthians, chapter 15, a very important document: "For what I received I passed to you as of first importance: that Christ died for our sins according to the Scriptures, that he was buried, and that he was raised on the third day according to the Scriptures, *and that he appeared to Peter, and then to the Twelve. After that, he appeared to more than five hundred of the brothers at the same time, most of whom are still living, though some have fallen asleep* (1 Corinthians 15:3–6; emphasis added). Paul here is employing two modes of argument. Perhaps most saliently for us, he is speaking historically and knows how to establish a historical fact: the testimony of supposed witnesses, that is, the five hun-

dred people who witnessed the astonishing events, centrally, the reap-
pearance of Jesus after his execution. Of these five hundred, most, he
carefully notes, are still alive. That is, if the account he offers now is false,
they can refute it. And this is a public letter. But he also says that some of
the witnesses have died. Of course, none of the Gospel narratives we
have existed at the time of this letter. But we see here why the narratives
had to be written: the witnesses are dying off.

But Paul also argues that "Christ died for our sins, as in the scriptures." Here his appeal is to prophecy, which indeed would have had
weight with a scripturally attuned audience. By "scriptures" here Paul
makes reference to passages in the Prophets that can be read as foresee-
ing the events he is discussing. His readers in Corinth would have in
mind the Suffering Servant of Isaiah 52–53, for example, who was "de-
spised and rejected by men, a man of sorrows . . . pierced for our transgressions . . . Crushed for our iniquity." Or Hosea 6:2, "After two days
he will revive us, on the third day he will restore us, that we may live in
his presence." The idea of redemptive death is carried forward into the
Gospel narratives. Paul thus reminds the Corinthians that Jesus as Christ
is the fulfillment of the prophetic tradition, and he is clear about what is
at stake. As he writes in 1 Corinthians 15, "And if Christ has not been
raised, our preaching is useless and so is your faith."

As to these passages from Isaiah and Hosea, it is not absurd to think
that men having profound insight might foresee what welcome might
await a prophet with such a spiritually renovative message as that of
Jesus. As we have seen in the *Republic,* Plato thought that if a prisoner in
the Cave escaped into the light and then returned to free one of the
others he would be killed.

But for the modern reader Paul's historical argument here is no
doubt the more weighty. Of course, assessing these historical claims, we
cannot exclude a possible conspiracy to deceive, or perhaps self-hypnosis
or mass delusion regarding these events, especially the risen Jesus.

Yet we know that many of those early Christians, including Paul
himself, were willing to forfeit their lives based upon the truth of the
claims that Paul sets forth. Ordinarily such testimony about an event in

the ancient world would be strong if not conclusive evidence. But we must consider David Hume's famous argument that the resurrection of Jesus was improbable to a degree that amounted to virtual impossibility. About that it can be said that an argument from probability is not easily conducted as regards a unique event. And further, that Hume is really arguing that the Resurrection did not occur because the cosmos is the kind of place where it could not occur. But if it did occur, then it could occur, and the cosmos is the kind of place in which it could occur.

Paul in that passage from Corinthians gives us the answer to why the four narratives were written down thirty or more years after the events. They were written down because although most of the five hundred witnesses are still alive, some have already died, and the rest will die soon. Unless it is written down, the presumed history will be lost or mangled in oral transmission.

Often in these narratives one comes upon a detail that seems to bring us unmistakably close to those ancient events. We feel that we are there. In chapter 8 of John, for example, we have the familiar account of the woman guilty of adultery. According to the law she must be executed by stoning. But something intrudes into the brief narrative that can only be there because it happened. The narrative is very brief:

> The teachers of the law and the Pharisees brought in a woman caught in adultery. They made her stand before the group and said to Jesus, "Teacher, this woman was caught in the act of adultery. In the Law Moses commanded us to stone such a woman. Now what do you say?" They were using this question as a trap, in order to have a basis for accusing him.
>
> But Jesus bent down and started to write on the ground with his finger. When they kept on questioning him, he straightened up and said to them, "If any one of you is without sin, let him be the first to throw a stone at her." Again he stooped down and wrote on the ground. (John 8:3–8)

His twice stooping down and writing on the ground seems to have nothing to do with the rest of this brief narrative. This detail must be there because he actually did this, the account coming down through oral tradition or from some lost written source. This is a mysterious touch of truth in the narrative because, for reasons we cannot discern, he stooped down and seemed to write something on the ground.

These preliminaries about historicity over with, the question arises as to what these narratives are about. This is no different from asking the question, What is the *Iliad* about? Or, What is the *Symposium* about? Not at all surprisingly, the answer to a very considerable degree is set forth in Jesus' famous Sermon on the Mount. For convenience here I will stick with the most complete account given of it in Matthew, chapters 5–12, and it is a remarkable document indeed.

Why a sermon delivered from a "mount"? Jesus, we are told, led his disciples and followers to an elevated piece of ground in or near Jerusalem. The text suggests why he chose this mount. He means to do nothing less than engage in a dialogue with Moses, who handed down the Law on Mount Sinai. Jesus' sermon means to internalize the teaching of Moses and selected prophets, stretching back over many centuries.

The intellectual journey we are about to undertake here is similar in many ways to the journey Socrates-Plato undertook in relation to Homer. Jesus intends to internalize the Law and thus move it in the direction of inner purity or holiness. The idea of holiness is a difficult one. In his classic work *The Idea of the Holy*, Rudolf Otto argued that the holy is not transferable into any other categories but rather has a radical separateness about it.[12] It is awe-inspiring and can both attract and repel. I hazard the idea that holiness seems to amount to a mental condition of radical simplicity but concede, as Rudolf Otto said, that it is very difficult for words to define. Jesus will have to do his best with words and then embody the idea in action. Nevertheless, the idea of the holy, the goal of spiritual aspiration, is an idea—along with the aspiration to cognition in Socrates—that has decisively shaped the Western mind. Perhaps the best definition of holiness comes in the totality of the four Gospel narratives.

We see that when Jesus ascends the piece of high ground to give his sermon, it is his followers who accompany him, while a larger crowd gathers at some distance. Biblical scholars tell us that when he reached his location on the Mount he almost certainly sat in a cross-legged position, the ceremonial stance of one about to speak in prophetic terms.

We notice at the outset he speaks only to his followers, who are near him. Very likely they have heard many of his points before. The crowd meanwhile keeps its distance. Yet after he has given his Sermon, and what a sermon it is, the crowd has come forward, closer to him. The conclusion of the narrative about this event (Matthew 7–8) gives their reaction: "When Jesus finished saying these things the crowds were amazed at his teaching because he taught as one who had authority, and not as their teachers of the Law." The crowd certainly has understood the point of the Sermon, that Jesus' interpretation of the Law moves it from external behavior to the inner disposition of the soul. The response here of the crowd also suggests the power of his interpretation to affect people beyond the immediate circle of his followers. "When he came down from the mountainside large crowds followed him." Historically considered, this is momentous.

The core of the Sermon is established in the second part, called the "antitheses," which follows upon the introductory "blessings" or Beatitudes. In these antitheses Jesus talks back over the centuries, primarily to M , the great Lawgiver, intending to internalize or "perfect" his teaching. Each of the antitheses has the structure, "You have heard . . . " or "It has been said. . . . But I tell you . . . " In each case what they have heard or what has been said is a teaching either of Moses or the Prophets, who are part of the sacred Mosaic tradition. Jesus' reiterated point is that good behavior is not enough. What he does is turn the older teaching inward in a spectacular way, "amazing" the crowd, turn it inward with such intensity that it revolutionizes the inner life of the individual who follows the new teaching.

Thus Jesus cites one of Moses' Commandments handed down centuries before at Sinai: "You have heard it said to the people long ago, 'Do not commit murder.' But I tell you that anyone who is angry with his brother will be subject to judgment" (21–22).

This is an extraordinary proposition. Who among his listeners has not experienced anger? Achilles felt rage at Agamemnon. Moses was often furious. Is it possible that Achilles should not have felt anger over Agamemnon's insult or that Moses should not have been outraged over the worship of the Golden Calf? But there is no doubt about it, Jesus is drastically escalating Moses' Commandment and proposing, to say the very least, a special state of mind.

"You have heard that it was said, 'Do not commit adultery.' But I tell you that anyone who looks at a woman with lust has already committed adultery in his heart" (27–28). This is a religious guided missile launched at Moses from another mountain. Are we to take seriously the idea that we should strive for a state of mind that will not even entertain the possibility of committing a lustful infidelity? Jesus wants not only good behavior but a radical purification of being. These are very strange things to think about as we move into the twenty-first century.

As we have just seen, Jesus changes Moses' commandment "Thou shalt not commit murder" by saying that you shall not even feel anger at someone who has committed an outrage. But what are you supposed to feel about him if you are advancing toward the state of mind Jesus is recommending? Apparently you are not to feel anger at the person but only sorrow or pity toward someone who has thus deformed his own soul to the extent that he has committed the outrage.

But suppose off at the edge, if you were forced to it, you had to draw your sword? Suppose the man from Samaria, traveling along the dangerous road to Jericho, had arrived fifteen minutes earlier, not when the man was lying beaten by the side of the road but while the thieves were doing their brutal work. Surely the Samaritan should have intervened. But it seems likely the thieves would have stood and fought him, fought perhaps both him and their erstwhile victim. The Samaritan might have been obliged to kill them if he could.

But could he kill them without experiencing anger, kill them while experiencing the inward love and profound sorrow that Jesus seems to be recommending? It is interesting to try to imagine what the response of a figure like Achilles from the older epic world would be to this teaching, or the response of David on the field before Goliath.

Just how serious is Jesus about lust when he says in his Sermon, "If your right eye offends you, gouge it out and throw it away"? That is, rather than damage your soul through lust. Much biblical commentary interprets this as rhetorical hyperbole. I don't think so. He is of course saying, "Avoid temptation." But, off at the edge, he means what he says. If what you see prompts invasive sexual feeling, then get rid of the eye. In other words, let nothing stand between you and the ideal perfection of your soul. Thus Sir Thomas More, who was famously tempted by luxurious clothes, wore a hair shirt beneath them to remind him of his failure. Short of gouging out an eye, I suppose one could pray or enter a monastery. Augustine would wrestle with this problem.

We begin to grasp Jesus' goal for all of us: the condition of holiness in which the inner self is so disciplined, so perfect, that no stain can possibly adhere to it. Surely this is why it is so difficult, though not impossible, for a rich man to enter the kingdom of heaven.

Plainly, there is no need for the taking of oaths if your inner assent is so absolute that deviation from it would be unthinkable. If insulted or punched, you are to turn the other cheek—but of course not from fear or some other low emotion. You do so out of spiritual strength, which pities the half-man capable of insulting or hitting you.

As for the Ten Commandments, which remain basic for Jesus, it is not terribly difficult to go through life without committing murder, stealing, committing adultery, bearing false witness, and so on. What Jesus is proposing is something far more demanding, even savagely demanding. The question may be unanswerable as to whether it is more demanding than the intellectual and physical disciplines required at Plato's Academy. To put it another way, Moses requires only a Pass degree, Jesus a First.

In the Sermon there is a very deep and mysterious antithesis that goes as follows: "You have heard it said, 'Love your neighbor and hate your enemy.' But I tell you, 'Love your enemies and pray for those who persecute you, that you may be sons of your Father in Heaven.'" Just

what can that last mean, "sons of your Father in Heaven"? It is a metaphor he uses at important moments.

If we work within the texts always present to Jesus, and which indeed
constitute his conceptual world, we of course meet God first in Genesis 1,
at the beginning. I offer the speculation that the God we meet there
loved his Creation, every part of it, even the serpent—"saw that it was
good"—even though it kept falling away from him. Might it not be that
the state of perfect holiness that Jesus asks for in his Sermon on the
Mount resembles the mind of God encountered in Genesis? It is possible
to understand the metaphor "sons of the Father" to mean that one
should understand—more than understand, "know"—the state of mind
of God in Genesis and participate in it. Love of this kind is cosmic in
character. Perhaps the God of Genesis loved even Sodom and Gomorrah, somewhat as Shakespeare must have loved Iago and Edmund in
order to have the plays at all. Like the Ancient Mariner, we are to learn
to love the sea serpents.

To be sure, looked at from the point of view of ordinary human life,
full of the undercurrent buzz of ambition, pride, envy, lust, anger, greed,
and all the rest, such an ideal of holiness must have a terrible aspect,
seem "inhuman," "strange."

But from the point of view of Jesus, men of ordinary human virtue,
such as the rabbis in the Temple, are "whited sepulchres," whitewashed
tombs. He is very far from saying that they are bad men. In fact their
behavior very likely was exemplary. But this is only appearance. They
resemble a tomb painted white on the outside but within holding a
rotting corpse. The Sermon on the Mount wants the whiteness to go all
the way through. From the point of view of perfection, the "whited
sepulchres" are also a "generation of vipers."

In these accounts there are various ways of expressing Jesus' closeness
to or identity with the God of Genesis. The narrative of John begins by
identifying him with the Logos of Greek philosophy. And Jesus himself in
a remarkable linguistic moment indicates that he is on extremely intimate terms with God. In the Lord's Prayer ("Our Father, who art in

Heaven . . . ,"), Jesus scandalously uses the word *abba* for "Father." *Abba*, grammatically, is a familiar vocative, but that does not tell the whole story. It is also a childish usage, the first word an infant might use, somewhat like "dada," which evolves into "daddy." That Jesus here uses *abba* to address the majestic *Jaweh*, the transcendent Other, the Creator maximus, is astonishing and revealing. "Most astonishing of all," writes John Murray Cuddihy, "is the fact that, in teaching his disciples the Lord's Prayer, Jesus authorizes them to repeat the word *abba* after him. 'He gives them a share in his sonship and empowers them, as his disciples, to speak with their heavenly Father in just such a familiar, trusting way as a child would with his father.'" This language must have been scandalous within first-century Judaism.[13]

At some point the reader of these narratives will want to step back and ask just what this man Jesus would be like if we met him, right here and right now. I think Plato has given us a very clear impression of Socrates. But we should ask ourselves whether these narratives, carefully considered, communicate a sense of the immediate presence of Jesus. Perhaps we would find his inner unshakable serenity strange, even scary. We would certainly be struck by what are his instantaneous perceptions. Thus he can look at the rich young man and see—from his fancy clothes? from his bearing?—that his wealth is too important to him. The rich young man is worshipping a false god, is preferring the lower to the higher. Wealth in its place is all right, but not the worship of wealth. Jesus tells the young man to get rid of his wealth, not for the sake of the poor but for his own sake. No wonder the young man goes away "sad." Whatever stands in the way of the soul's turning toward holiness must be "plucked out." In the narratives, Peter in many ways is the least impressive of the twelve disciples, yet he seems to be Jesus' favorite, even though he is slow of wit and slow of foot and denies Jesus under pressure. What does Jesus see in him? Perhaps he has noticed the directness and simplicity of Peter's belief in him: "As Jesus walked beside the Sea of Galilee, he saw Simon [Peter] and his brother Andrew casting a net into the lake, for they were fishermen. 'Come, follow me,' Jesus said, 'and I will make you fishers of men.' At once they left their nets and followed him" (Matthew 4:18–20). Though Peter has many flaws and can be weak, he too has special perceptions and Jesus surely notices this.

The mention of Peter brings up another point. It is notable that not one of the twelve disciples seems to come even close to achieving the condition of holiness urged in the Sermon on the Mount, at least up to the conclusion of these narratives. Yet their wills, except for Judas's, do incline toward him, and in that sense they do "follow" him. Connected with this, I think, is the strong undercurrent of pity and forgiveness in these narratives, a strange music that often comes to the surface. The Prodigal Son is clearly a rotten young man, yet he somehow receives special, even unfair, forgiveness. If Mary Magdalene is indeed a fallen woman, still it is she who discovers the empty tomb. The parable of the mustard seed may have a psychological dimension, holiness growing slowly and from the tiniest of seeds. Indeed, so far as I can tell, everything in these narratives radiates from the ideal of holiness, the pearl of infinite price. There is a passage of great importance to consider in this connection, describing the so-called Transfiguration: "After six days [no doubt alluding to the six days of the Creation] Jesus took with him Peter, James and John the brother of James, and led them up on a mountain [of course, a mountain] by themselves. There he was transformed before them. His face shone like the sun, and his clothes became as white as the light. [We remember that Moses' face had similarly shone when he came down from Sinai.] Just then, there appeared Moses [Who else?] and Elijah, talking with Jesus" (Matthew 17:1–3). The imagery in this vision-ary scene comes prominently from the Creation poem at the beginning of Genesis and also from the Mount Sinai experience in Exodus, and from that Mount where, in his Sermon, Jesus entered into a momentous discussion with Moses and the Prophets. This Transfiguration passage may be read as claiming that the energy of God at the Creation is now irradiating Jesus, making his face shine "like the sun" on the third day. Turning his clothes white as light is probably the original light—"Let there be light"—of Genesis. We might, in considering this passage, think back to that scene before the battle at Potideia when Socrates, after standing for two days in a trance, awakens to pray to the sun. Socrates, standing there before battle, one must assume is approaching or has arrived at a vision of the Logos, the Form of the Cosmos, beyond all appearances. Jesus in this Transfiguration may have experienced oneness with the mind of God in Genesis.

But how could Jesus have claimed, after his drastic internalization of Moses' and the prophets' teaching in the Sermon on the Mount, that he had come not to repeal the old Law but to fulfill it? Here we should consider, as C. S. Lewis does in his *Reflections on the Psalms,* the following quotations:

> Thou shalt not hate thy brother in thy heart.
> Thou shalt not avenge or bear any grudge against the children of thy people, but shalt love thy neighbor as thyself.
> If thou seest the donkey of him that hateth thee lying under the burden . . . Thou shalt surely help him.
> If to meet with thine enemy's ox or his donkey going astray, Thou shalt surely bring it back to him.
> Rejoice not when thine enemy falleth, and let not thy heart be glad when he stumbleth.
> If thine enemy hunger, give bread.[14]

Without being able to locate these statements, anyone would say that they "sound like" the New Testament. In fact, except for the last one, they are all from the Hebrew Bible, the first four from Proverbs, the fifth from Leviticus. The last comes from Paul and is based on Proverbs 25:21.

The point here is this. The New Testament is drenched in the culture and the formulations of the Hebrew Bible. Biblical scholars have assembled many pages of sentences and phrases taken from the Hebrew Bible and made part of the New Testament. The mentality of Jesus, Paul, their circle and their followers was inhabited by Hebrew scripture, and we may be certain that when the young Jesus disputed with the rabbis in the Temple in Jerusalem he matched them citation for citation.

Indeed, it could be argued that the Hebrew Bible, taken as a whole, expresses a complete religious experience. Just about everything is there: the primacy of the one God, the vicissitudes of the spiritual quest, human sin and heroism, the Promised Land, the celebration of holiness. What Jesus does in his Sermon on the Mount is concentrate the theme of holiness that can be found in the Hebrew Bible, concentrate it to a sharp point and, as he says, "fulfill" it. It could be argued that the Hebrew Bible in its deep structure yearns for fulfillment in such a hero as this, who embodies the triumph of holiness in word and act. Even the greatest of the early figures, Abraham, for example, or Moses, was flawed. Isaiah, the greatest of the Prophets, was a voice of lament and longing.

Here it is useful to think again of Socrates. As presented by Plato, Socrates does embody the goal of the central tradition in Greek thought beginning with Homer, in whose striving for excellence, *areté*, we see the germ of the perfect Forms. Socrates internalizes the heroic and refines it into philosophy. There is no hero comparable to Socrates in the Hebrew Bible, no one who is the perfect exemplar, the point toward which everything has tended. It is possible to speculate that Jesus saw himself, among much else, as the last and greatest of the Prophets and the fulfillment of the Hebrew spiritual quest. This is certainly how Matthew sees him. It is worth noting here that though Jesus has internalized the Law and the Prophets, and urges others to do so, he never rejects viable religious institutions such as the great Temple or the local synagogues, never rejects them as such, and indeed seems to presuppose them. There is no indication that when he commissions Peter to be the "rock" on which he founds his church that he has anything different in mind as far as outward form goes from the familiar institutions of Jerusalem. Since the Sermon on the Mount, and indeed everything else he does and says, is about holiness, I think we can infer that he considers such familiar institutions to be valid if their guiding principle is holiness, however imperfect such institutions may be in their actual practice.

Jesus' early teachers, however, and the rabbis in the Temple, could not have been charmed by his implication that he understood the Law better than they did, let alone his idea that he knew how to perfect it.

Indeed, at times he says almost explicitly that he himself is, actually, the perfection of the Law. Nevertheless, it is also true that he is exhaustively traditional in his references to Scripture, and it is Scripture indeed that forms the rhetorical basis for his remarkable eloquence. It is worth reflecting that, considering the narratives about Jesus purely as literature and thinking about other great works, such as those by Shakespeare, Dante, and Dostoyevsky, one realizes that great as they undoubtedly are, none has the power possessed by Jesus actually to change lives. Jesus' power, and Paul's prose sometimes has this too, draws deeply from the prose of the Hebrew Bible. To carry this idea one step forward, I suggest that Jesus seems to "live within" the established biblical texts, as if they constituted his universe. They certainly are probative for him and his followers. I feel comfortable in asserting that Jesus was so thoroughly in command of scripture that he could cull from it and pull together in a synthesis exhortations and clues from the Hebrew Bible so as to produce a direct communication of the state of holiness he embodied and sought to produce in others. He would have been the last person to think that there is some sort of chasm between the Hebrew Bible and what would emerge as the New Testament. In his great prayer, he connects holiness with the ancient God of the Creation, "Hallowed be thy name," reaching back through the Psalms, the Prophets, Moses, and the patriarchs to that Creation. The places touched by God are holy: Horeb, Sinai, the Ark of the Covenant. The narratives explicitly connect Jesus himself with this theme: "The Holy One of God (Mark 1:24), "therefore the child to be born will be called holy, the Son of God" (Luke 1:35), "you are the holy one" (John 6:69). In Acts he is called "the Holy and Righteous One" (3:14). When we consider the passages about the young Jesus' disputes with the great rabbis in the Temple, it seems clear that very early in his life Jesus was an adept handler of scriptural texts and thought he had seen into their depths, seen what they ultimately mean with respect to the mind of God as that began revealing itself beginning with the Creation in Genesis. If, as Paul later wrote, we see God as through a glass darkly, it is possible that Jesus, the textual adept, thought he saw the

face of God clearly in the living scriptural tradition, more clearly than it
had been seen in Moses and the Law.

Did the mind of Jesus live, in a phrase I have used, "solely in these texts,"
that is, did he constitute his universe through his deep reading of scripture? Did the texts and actuality completely coincide for him?

   In an attempt to answer such questions, let us consider finally here,
his famous and climactic words while dying on the cross. These words
are sublimely textual. When fully understood, they seem inevitable.
They are, that is, what he, this man we have met in the narratives, would
say. At that moment he was in almost inconceivable agony; had been
scourged with the Roman flagrum, a leather whip with lead weights
sewn into it; had been nailed to the cross with spikes through his wrists
and feet; and was so positioned that he was dying of asphyxiation as he
tried to breathe. Yet in our narrative he cites, as he has done so often, the
Hebrew Bible and—one wants to say of course—transforms it. He may
even tell a sort of cosmic joke. I have not seen the following point, and it
is an important one, made in the commentary.

   The key texts are Psalms 22 and 23. We see that Jesus, at least as
reported here, makes use of both of them. Not incidentally, both Psalms
are traditionally attributed to King David, an ancestor of Jesus. First, he
cites the opening line of Psalm 22, crying out: "My God, my God, why
hast thou forsaken me?" In saying this, he looks back to David as he
earlier had looked back to Moses. Having transformed Moses, he now is
about to transform David.

   Having quoted that line of despair and emptiness from Psalm 22, he
deliberately and I would say triumphantly skips the rest of that Psalm—
and says nothing. But the silence speaks. Everyone present at that moment knows that Psalm 23 comes next, perhaps the greatest of the
Psalms. He makes those followers fill in the silence, if only mentally,
with what comes next. Psalm 23 is vibrating there in the air around
him: "The Lord is my shepherd . . . Though I walk through the Valley
of the Shadow of Death, I will fear no evil, for Thou art with me."

Because he himself does not say this, he makes them think it and turns it into *their* prayer.

He certainly knew at that moment that he was in the Valley of the Shadow of Death, but in the silence that surrounds him his unspoken words take on tremendous power. He is not only "in" the valley, but is "walking" in it. Since in fact he is nailed to a cross, the verb "walking" has more than a touch of cosmic humor about it. And he is not only "walking," he is "walking through" it. Loud in his silence, these words become a declaration of triumph, even of cosmic insouciance. In that moment of complete vulnerability he exhibits not weakness but almost unthinkable strength, and through thus remaking Psalms 22 and 23 reinterprets them in terms of this moment, here, now. And through the authority of the 22–23 sequence makes his witnesses share in the reinterpretation.

At that moment, while we ourselves speak into his silence, he is powerfully creative even while dying. He had spoken back over the many centuries to Moses and the Prophets, and now he speaks with David. He has re-created Psalms 22 and 23 in ways that David could not have imagined, and made them, perhaps, the greatest of the Psalms through his reimagining of them, turned them into a prayer with a new meaning.

Considered purely as a poet, Jesus has topped himself, completed the Sermon on the Mount, and gone beyond his earlier "Our Father." He has beaten his rich Parables and even his many existential dramas along the way. Nailed to the cross and dying, he has with a lordly ease turned that moment of tragedy into a permanent triumph.

CHAPTER FIVE

Paul: Universal Synthesis

Paul (formerly Saul) of Tarsus stands at the center of a mighty transformation, the coming together of biblical tradition and Greek philosophy. Needless to say, he did not accomplish this alone, but he was the energizing figure amid powerfully converging currents of thought. He is not so dramatic a figure as either Socrates or Jesus; how could he be? And what comes down to us about him is much more fragmentary. Yet he is the major figure there at what, without exaggeration, can be called the birth of the Western mind, shaping events and shaped by them.

Four preconditions made possible the astonishingly rapid spread of Christianity beyond Palestine and throughout the Mediterranean world. These were: (1) biblical tradition and the reported events of Jesus' life and death; (2) the spread of the Greek language and Greek philosophy throughout the Near East in the wake of the conquests of Alexander the Great; (3) the international civilization of the Roman Empire with its laws, roads, military power, and stability; and (4) the universal claims of the monotheist Creation account in Genesis and implicit in the narratives about Jesus.

For those Jews in and around Jerusalem who accepted the oral accounts of Jesus' life, death, and resurrection, the question posed was: "What does it all mean?" They had the historical burden of clarifying the meaning for themselves and others. Events do not speak for themselves. A Judaizing account of Jesus would place him in the tradition of the major Prophets and would try to see him as the Redeemer foreseen

earlier in the biblical tradition. For Hellenizing Jews, Jesus became intelligible through the lens of Greek philosophy.[1]

Clearly, what both the Judaizing and Hellenizing Jews sought was a
context of meaning in which to locate what they understood to have
happened. Thus both understandings, Prophetic and Greek, were in the
broadest sense philosophical, shared ways of talking about presumed
actualities.

The drama of Paul's mind consists of the effort, surprisingly successful, to speak both philosophical languages, occasionally both at the same
time, but more often one or the other depending upon his audience.
That is to say, Paul attempted to effect in his own mind a synthesis
between Athens and Jerusalem. If that claim can be sustained, it is fair to
say that he presided over the birth of the Western mind.

Born near the beginning of the first century, Paul lived at about the
same time as Jesus, though apparently they never met. Tarsus, his birthplace in what is now southern Turkey, was a lively commercial and intellectual center at a considerable distance from Jerusalem. There is some
evidence that Jesus did speak in the important synagogue in Tarsus. But
however that may be, Paul became preeminent among the many who
carried the basic narrative of Jesus throughout the then-known world.
He and his colleagues were able to take advantage of the excellent
Roman roads and local shipping and enjoyed the relative order of the
empire as maintained by its laws and secular power. Thus they traveled
easily through the cities of the entire region, from Jerusalem up through
Asia Minor and over through Athens to Rome. Astonishingly energetic,
Paul established churches in one city after another and supervised their
activities through repeated visits and his important correspondence.
Restlessly, he looked beyond Jerusalem to Damascus, Corinth, Antioch,
Ephesus, Tyre, Sidon, Athens. After Athens he planned to travel to the
imperial province of Spain, completing the arc from Jerusalem around
to the Pillars of Hercules at Gibraltar. Around A.D. 65, however, he met
his fate in Rome, beheaded by Nero's authorities. It was left to others to
carry the message throughout the rest of the Roman Empire.

Greek philosophy, writes Werner Jaeger, was "the decisive event in the development of the Christian mission and its expansion in and beyond Palestine. [This expansion] was preceded by three centuries of worldwide expansion of Greek civilization."[2] By "worldwide" Jaeger means the Eurasian world, the eastward limits of which were defined by the conquests of Alexander the Great (356–323 B.C.). There had been an important Greek presence in Asia Minor at least since the Trojan War; and the tenth chapter of Genesis mentions the Sea People, perhaps from Crete and the Greek islands. The influence of Hellenic culture, however, expanded enormously in the wake of the fourth-century conquests of Alexander. Tutored as a youth by Aristotle, he ascended the throne of Macedon after the murder of his father Philip, raised a formidable army, and, consciously patterning himself after Achilles, conquered the Persian Empire and, on his way, destroyed the great city of Persepolis. He invaded India and subdued both Egypt and Arabia and established some seventy cities as centers of Greek learning, preeminent among them the appropriately named Alexandria, which became a center of Greek intellectual life and was influential throughout the entire region.

Tarsus, where Paul was born, was a cosmopolitan city known for its Greek and Jewish intellectual life. As already pointed out, Paul was a contemporary of Jesus but, and I want to stress this here, also a contemporary of Philo of Alexandria. A major figure, Philo was simultaneously a religious Jew and also a Hellenizing philosopher, interpreting the Pentateuch allegorically as expressing the highest human wisdom as also found in Greek philosophy.

Surely the chronological conjunction of Jesus, Paul, and Philo during the first century has a dramatically symbolic equality. Paul, a rabbi, a Pharisee (the strictest tendency in current Judaism), a Hellenizing Jew, a beneficiary of the Roman order, and then a Christian convert, pulled together in his own being the most powerful and apparently contradictory themes of his own historical moment and embodied the immense conjunction of Athens and Jerusalem that was emerging during the first century.

I have mentioned the sketchy evidence that Jesus may actually have addressed the intellectually active synagogue in Tarsus. Paul also addressed it, though apparently not at the same time. It is tantalizing to think that they might have met, but on this the evidence is silent. The reputation of Jesus as active in the region, however, is confirmed by the Roman poet Lucian, who mentions Jesus as introducing a new *telete*, or way-of-being, into the world.[3]

The four narratives we have about Jesus, written in Greek, were compiled from earlier material, certainly oral, some perhaps written. In using the Greek language, they could not avoid inheriting Greek ways of looking at the world, Greek metaphors, connotations, nuances. Despite this firm inheritance, it is striking that these four narratives do not resemble any previous literary forms from the ancient world. The *Mosead* has clear epic roots in the archaic Near East. These do not. Unprecedented in form, and making unprecedented claims, they are without doubt the most influential pieces of writing in human history.

In contrast, Paul's own Letters, and his public addresses in Acts, derive from established Greek literary forms. So does the narrative of Acts itself, a "small epic" in the classical mold. When Paul spoke on his lengthy journeys, he spoke in Greek. It seems safe to say that there was a strong tug throughout the intellectual life of the region away from orthodox Judaism and in the direction of a Hellenistic way of seeing the world.

The fourth and last narrative, John's, conspicuously Hellenizes. It was probably written somewhat later than A.D. 85, or some twenty years after Paul's execution in Rome. Its introductory verses, a bravura performance and a sort of introductory poem, and of course like all of the New Testament, written in Greek, uses centrally the Greek word *Logos* (Word) to describe Jesus. A Greek-speaking audience, whether Jewish or Gentile, acquainted with Platonic or Stoic thought would recognize the Logos as familiar philosophical territory.

But in John, the use of the term *Logos* reaches in two directions. Within the Hebrew Bible, the term *Word* has deep roots, going back to Genesis 1. The Word was God's creative presence through which the universe came into being: "And God said . . ." Within this "Word" tradition, John affirms that in Jesus the Word in that sense was uniquely present to mankind, a creative Word bringing new life.

Yet of course John wrote in Greek, potentially for an audience well aware of Greek meanings. In Stoic and Platonic philosophy, the term *Logos* means "universal unifying pattern." John thus brings together Jerusalem and Athens. His double use of the term *Logos* made the meaning of Jesus Christ intelligible to both Judaic and Greek traditions.

When John says that the universal pattern is completed by Jesus, which would be incomplete without him, he addresses the vexatious problem of evil, which appears in Genesis 1: If God is both good and all powerful, then how do we explain the serpent, the universal perception of evil? If Jesus Christ is part of the underlying pattern of the universe, the problem is solved. He becomes the second Adam, God's own self-sacrifice, redeeming the original Fall and potentially all subsequent deformations of the human will.

But John's cultural pun on the term *Logos-Word* is not finally Greek. He does not approach his Logos through Greek philosophy. In John there is no geometry or dialectical analysis. He writes in Greek, but he is not a philosopher. His reality is particular and historical, in the Hebrew tradition. His conception of the Logos as God's creating "Word" may not be very far from the Logos of Greek philosophy, but it is not the same thing. Nevertheless, he was bringing Athens and Jerusalem closer.

In such a verse as Matthew 2:28, Jesus speaks in a way that might, it seems to me, belong to either the Greek or the Hebrew tradition: "All was given to me by my father, and no one knows the son except the father, and no one knows the father except the son, and anyone to whom the son wishes to reveal it." From that it is but a short step, if a step at all, to John 8:58: "Then the Jews said to him, 'you are not yet fifty years old, and you have seen Abraham?' Jesus said to them, 'Truly, I tell you, I am from before Abraham was born.' " What we see here in slightly differing modalities are attempts to speak about Jesus in terms within the range of both the Greek and the Hebrew traditions of intelligibility.

Thus when we listen to that opening chapter of John we stand at a great crossroads of history: "In the beginning was the Logos [Word] and the Word was with God. Everything came about through him, and without him not one thing came about. . . . And the Word became flesh and lived among us." It is certainly difficult to know what any reader unacquainted with the modes of Greek thought and Hebrew biblical tradition would make of all this. John is saying very clearly, however, that Jesus is to be understood in terms both of the Hebrew Wisdom (Word) tradition and the Greek (Logos) philosophy.

The author of Acts was well aware of the historic symbolism of Paul's arrival in Athens. The entire episode, well developed in chapter 17, epitomizes Paul's mission as apostle to the Gentiles, reaching out beyond Palestine to the cities of the Roman Empire and building on the existing foundation of that advanced civilization. Acts is philosophical history, reminiscent in important ways of Thucydides. It was intended as a continuation of the narrative of Luke and recounts the experiences of the earliest witnesses, their efforts to understand what had happened, and their debates about how to act upon their new knowledge. As in Thucydides, the speeches of the main characters are probably epitomes rather than attempted transcripts; that is, they are based upon history but so framed as to communicate the essence of what the speaker would have said in that situation.

The Areopagus at which Paul speaks in chapter 17 refers to the Hill of Ares, northwest of the Acropolis, and also to the Council, which met there. This was a legal body that heard individual cases and had general oversight regarding the laws of the city. There is no indication here that Paul is on trial, but the author has arranged the scene so as to recall the trial of Socrates before the Athenian jury. Perhaps we are even meant to compare Paul favorably with Socrates.

As he walked through the streets of Athens, as recounted at the beginning of chapter 17, Paul would have found monotheism already an important part of the intellectual atmosphere of the city. When he says that he found the Athenians a "god-fearing" people, he knew that the Athenians would recognize a quotation from Sophocles' *Oedipus at Colonus*. Paul's intention throughout his visit to Athens is to build his

Christian message on already existing cultural assumptions. As Werner Jaeger writes, monotheistic ideas had crept into the old [polytheistic] faith via a philosophic discussion that had been going on for centuries and had even reached the ears of the common man.[4]

During the fifth century B.C., Athens had been the most powerful of the Greek cities, a regional power able to defeat Persia. At the same time, it was the intellectual and artistic capital of the Hellenic world. Its military dominance came to an end with the war against Sparta in 404, but its intellectual supremacy remained. It joined a conspiracy against Roman hegemony in 88 B.C. and was captured and subordinated to imperial rule. It remained a center of learning, a university city to which wealthy Romans sent their sons to absorb Greek culture. The author of Acts comments sardonically on this in chapter 17: "All the Athenians and their visitors from abroad spent their time on nothing except saying or learning something new."

When Paul arrived in Athens, he first spoke at the synagogue to Christianizing Jews and to the merely curious, as was his practice on entering a new city. To such an audience, speaking in Greek, he undoubtedly placed Jesus in the tradition of the Redeemer foreseen by the Prophets. From that perspective, Paul's mission beyond Palestine—his universalism—went back through the biblical tradition to the first chapter of Genesis and its universal monotheistic God. When he went on to give his momentous address at the Areopagus, however, he not only spoke in Greek but almost as a Greek philosopher.

In the organization of Acts as a classical miniepic or *Pauliad,* this is the pivotal moment, the breakout of Christianity into the intellectual capital of the wider Greco-Roman world. "That was the decisive moment in the encounter of Greeks and Christians," writes Werner Jaeger. "The future of Christianity as a world religion depended on it. The author of Acts saw this clearly when he let the apostle Paul visit Athens, the intellectual center of the classical Greek world and the symbol of its historical tradition, and preach on that venerable spot, the Areopagus, to an audience of Stoic and Epicurean philosophers, about the

Unknown God. He quotes the verse of a Greek poet, 'We are his off-spring'; his arguments are largely Stoic and calculated to convince an educated philosophical mind."[5]

The scene in Acts 17 is so dramatic and so important historically that quotation at some length is justified. "In Athens, while Paul was awaiting them, his spirits were exasperated within him as he saw the city was full of idols. And he would have discussions with the Jews and the worshippers in the synagogue and in the marketplace every day with anyone he happened to meet. And some of the Stoic and Epicurean philosophers encountered him" (16–18). In a few sentences the author communicates a sense of Athens as a lively center of religious and philosophical activity, with old pagan sculpture, a sizable Jewish population, and philosophical discussion going on in the streets and in the crowded marketplace. The Stoics and Epicurean philosophers invite him to make his case at the Areopagus. "Then Paul, standing in the middle of the Areopagus, said: 'Gentlemen of Athens, I perceive that you are in every way more god-fearing than others; for as I went about and observed your sanctuaries I even found an altar inscribed To the Unknown God' " (22–23). Paul, of course, has come to fill this empty space with something concrete and definite. In 1 Corinthians 15, he has placed Jesus as the culmination of Hebrew prophecy. Now he will interpret him as completing the journey, filling in that blank space, of Greek thought. He is at once referring to Greek philosophy and indicating its limits. "What you worship, without knowing what it is, this is what I proclaim to you. God, who made the world and everything in it, being Lord of heaven and earth, does not live in hand-built temples, nor, as one who needs anything, is ministered to by human hands, since he himself gave life and breath and everything to all. And out of one [Adam] he made every nation of men to live on every face of the earth" (23–26). Paul then begins to rise to rhetorical heights he will achieve also in his Epistles. "Being then as we are the offspring of God, we ought not to believe that divinity is like gold or silver or stone, the carving of art and the thought of man" (29). Speaking on the Hill of Ares, within sight of the Parthenon, Paul admits that Jerusalem cannot match the spectacular artistic achievements of Athens. Nor can it match

Plato and Aristotle, the "thought of man." Paul knows that he is moving beyond that, as he appeals to the resurrection of Jesus. There is a marvelous coda to this chapter 17 narrative: "When they heard about the resurrection from the dead, some scoffed but some said: 'We will listen to you again concerning this matter.' So Paul went from their midst; but some men attached themselves to him and believed, among them Dionysius the Areopagite and his wife, who was named Damaris, and some others with them" (32–34). That is the end of chapter 17. The next chapter begins, "After that he left Athens and went to Corinth." There is a fine inevitability about that. Paul, full of an astonishing energy, is always moving on. In his own person, during that first century, he himself is Athens and Jerusalem.

One wonders, lingeringly, about those two Greeks, Dionysius and his wife Damaris. For just that moment they are pulled into the focus of world history, and then they disappear (unless, with Dante and others, we identify this Dionysius with "pseudo-Dionysius").

Paul of Tarsus, as he acts within history, is an extraordinary figure. He possessed powers of mind and will, education and eloquence, that made his convulsive conversion matters of universal history. To give only a few examples, a passage from Paul's Epistle to the Romans precipitated Augustine's conversion. Both Origen and Aquinas wrote lengthy commentaries on this Epistle, and it was central to Martin Luther's doctrine of salvation by faith. When he was still an obscure German monk, Luther wrote to the famous Erasmus to say that he should pay more attention to Paul. John Calvin and John Wesley were specifically indebted to Romans for central teachings in the mass movements they launched. With an Epistle of some five thousand words, Paul could have that effect. He thus is one of the most important converts in history, along with a very few other momentous figures, Augustine certainly, and the Emperor Constantine for his political effect. Virtually all that we know of Paul comes from Acts and his Epistles, which are only fragments of the enormous amount he wrote. These original sources are surrounded by centuries of scholarly interpretation and learned conjecture.

The Epistles themselves were written in response to particular occasions, Paul settling disputes, arguing about doctrine, denouncing his opponents, and also making eloquent contributions to thought. To many readers, no doubt because of the heat of his arguments, Paul remains an unsympathetic figure. Yet one can show from the same documents his capacity for friendship, personal loyalty, and affection.

We have some hints that Paul was not physically attractive, though we do not know in what respect. Surprisingly, there is evidence that he was not a compelling public speaker but relied mainly on cogency. He was most effective with the written word, in which he had an intensity that came from his own religious experience on the road to Damascus. More than Peter or any of the other original disciples, Paul had the power to shape the debates of the future.

Before his experience on the road to Damascus, he had been well educated in the teachings of Judaism, and as an adult he had aligned himself with its strictest tendency, the Pharisees. As we have seen, he had a considerable knowledge of Greek philosophy, and his style often shows the influence of the Greek translation of the Hebrew Bible. Initially he was hostile to the nascent Christianity around him and harassed it enthusiastically. He was a successful artisan and supported himself in the important regional craft of tent-making.

Chapter 9 of Acts describes his violent emotional experience while journeying to Damascus. According to this account, he experienced a blinding light and fell to the ground. He heard Jesus speak to him, asking why he was persecuting him. Jesus told the now-blinded Paul to go to Damascus and await instructions. Since those traveling with Paul saw no light and heard no conversation we can assume that his experience was entirely internal to Paul. Some have conjectured that Paul had an epileptic fit, but because he seems to have had no such fits before or after, this idea can be discarded.

In Damascus, Jesus appeared to a disciple named Ananias and told him to go to Paul and instruct him to "carry my name before the Gentiles and their kings and before the people of Israel" (9:15). Thus

Paul becomes the prime instrument at that time for the universalization of Christianity outside the boundaries of Palestine and outside Judaism. The convulsive character of Paul's experience on the road to Damascus doubtless reflects his own emotional intensity.

In his subsequent accounts, Paul is quite specific about what the experience amounted to. What he felt was a conviction that he had, so to speak, been invaded and occupied by Jesus. He felt a new personality, that of Jesus, growing within his old personality and displacing it. For example, he writes to the Christians in Rome: "But you are not in the flesh but in the Spirit if the Spirit of God lives in you. One who does not have the Spirit of Christ is not his. But if Christ is in you, your body is a dead thing because of sin, but your spirit is life because of righteousness. But the Spirit of him who raised Christ Jesus from the dead will make your mortal bodies live through his Spirit that dwells in you" (Romans 8:9–11). I think we must conclude that before the Damascus experience, even while Paul was thoroughly contained within Judaism, and indeed was a strict interpreter of the Mosaic Law, he nevertheless had been powerfully impressed by what he knew about Jesus. The four narratives we have had, of course, not been written yet; but the oral tradition must have been very strong. There probably were written collections of say-ings of Jesus and perhaps, as some scholars think, a "Q" narrative (*Quelle* means "original" in German) on which the four Gospels were based. I myself would infer that Paul was aware of some or all of this earliest material, that it germinated in his mind and at last produced the drastic reaction on the road to Damascus. Once he had changed his mind as regards the validity of Jesus, his powerful mind worked with the facts as he now understood them. Echoes of Jesus are frequent in his Epistles, which are earlier than any written material we have about Jesus, and Paul's insights flash out like lightning amid the swirling clouds of local controversies.

It would be diversionary here to discuss at length even the main themes of Paul's thought as they occur in Acts and in the Epistles, which, in any case, are the subject of vast commentary. The unshakable foundation of Paul's thought is that Jesus did in fact rise from the dead. Paul would admit to no equivocation on that point. Jesus was not a legendary figure lost in time long past but a contemporary of Paul himself. Paul had talked with many people who had known Jesus. As Paul writes so precisely in 1 Corinthians 15, Jesus had been seen after his resurrection by the original twelve and then by five hundred, only some of whom are now dead. And Paul declares flatly, "And if Christ has not been raised, our preaching is useless and so is our faith" (1 Corinthians 15:14). Arthur Darby Nock puts the matter precisely:

> The belief that Jesus did in fact rise from death is the basis of the faith of the Christian community. The Church is from the beginning not a band of men honoring the memory of a founder who had passed from contact with them (like the followers of Epicurus), but a corporate body which feels itself animated by the Spirit of One whose rising is the guarantee that He lives and will come again, and which regards the period between that rising and that coming as a transitory phase of history between the old order and the new. . . . The simple explanation of the tradition which the first Christians bequeathed is that it represents their impression of what had happened.[6]

That is Paul's unshakable premise. Another basic premise is that Jesus is God. This of course represents a startling break with both Judaism and with fifth-century Greek philosophy, as in Socrates, Plato, and Aristotle. For both Judaism and Greek philosophy, God is utterly and finally other. In that sense, though he tried to establish continuities with both traditions, Paul also contradicted them. On this point he was insistent. "Your attitude," he wrote to the Philippians, "should be that of Christ Jesus, who being in very nature God. . . . And every tongue confesses that Jesus Christ is Lord, to the glory of God the father" (2:5–11). This is an enormous jump from the abstraction of the Greek philosophers' god and the entire otherness of Yahweh. Paul, trying to find a language for what he thinks has happened in the narrative about Jesus, becomes the first theologian of the West. The word *theologian* means "one who talks about God." Under the pressure of what he understands to have happened, Paul's language tends to shiver between the language of the Greek philosophers and the language of the Hebrew prophetic tradition. He says of Jesus, "All things have been created through him and for him. And he is before all things and all things come together in him" (Colossians 1:16). That is Paul of Tarsus, a new Christian, coming close to philosophizing in Greek, characterizing Jesus in terms of Logos philosophy.

Yet finally Paul was more Jew than Greek. In his Epistle to the Romans, the last letter he wrote before his imprisonment in Rome, he achieves the most coherent as well as the most serene statement of his thought. Here his appeal is not to Greek philosophy but to the Hebrew Bible as his preferred way of speaking about final realities. Thus in Romans 5:12–14: "Therefore, just as sin came into the world through one man, and through sin death, so also death went about among all men, because all sinned. Before there was the Law there was sin in the world, but when there was no Law it was not reckoned as sin. But death was king from Adam until Moses, even over those who did not sin after the example of the transgression of Adam, who is the type of what was to come."

For all his passion, Paul managed to be an adept practical diplomat, settling one controversy here, another there, often surprisingly open to compromise. Some of these compromises sound ludicrous today, such as the one over the circumcision of Gentile converts. When Paul established that Gentiles did not have to be circumcised he was setting aside an important part of the Mosaic Law, under which the circumcision rite signifies that the creative-reproductive power ultimately derives from God and not from the individual. Circumcision was a rebuke to the notion of human autonomy. For Paul to set this aside for Gentiles was serious and caused a storm against him. Yet Paul had two considerations. He thought, based upon his own experience, that when a person had been "inhabited" by Jesus, the primacy of God went as a certain consequence. It is easy to see why many considered this a dangerous teaching. An individual might well claim to have been inhabited by Jesus and therefore to be free from all normative and sacred considerations.

Paul's answer, not satisfactory to all, was that a person so inhabited by Jesus would be more, not less, obedient and righteous than someone following the Law as external obedience. Paul, always a practical man, also no doubt found that the prospect of circumcision did not enhance his appeal among prospective male Gentile converts. The success of his universal mission required that the ancient Judaic rite be marginalized.

The many disputes Paul had to deal with are interesting and sometimes amusing, but in his Epistles Paul often rises to an eloquence that lends powerful support to his claim to theological authority. These extraordinary passages owe a great deal to the language of the Greek translation of the Hebrew Bible, with which Paul obviously was thoroughly familiar; and they may also owe much to the language of Jesus himself as it came down to Paul through the oral or written tradition. When Paul speaks in his prophetic voice, he undoubtedly thinks that Jesus is speaking through him:

> If I speak in the tongues of men and of angels, but have not love, I am only a resounding gong or tinkling cymbal. If I have the gift of prophecy and can fathom all mysteries and all knowledge, and if I have a faith that can move mountains, but have not love, I am nothing. If I give all I possess to the poor and surrender my body to the flames, but have not love, I am nothing. Love is patient, love is kind. It does not envy, it does not boast, it is not proud. It is not rude, it is not self-seeking, it is not easily angered, it keeps no record of wrongs. Love does not delight in evil but rejoices with the truth. It always protects, always trusts, always hopes, always perseveres. Love never fails. But where there are prophecies, they will cease; where there are tongues, they will be stilled; where there is knowledge, it will pass away. For we know in part and we prophecy in part, but when perfection comes, the imperfect disappears. When I was a child, I thought like a child. When I became a man, I put away childish things. Now we see as in a glass darkly, but then we shall see face to face. Now I know in part; then I shall know fully, even as I am fully known. And now these three remain: faith, hope and love. But the greatest of these is love. (1 Corinthians 13)

Jesus himself was eloquent. Paul here matches him in defining holiness, in which love of God—love as God loves: *agape*—radiates out to the world. Perhaps not surprisingly here, Paul combines the voice of the Prophets with the voice of Greek philosophy and with the Platonic theory of knowledge. His metaphor of "seeing through a glass darkly" probably derives from Plato, the transitory "childish" things of the world standing at great remove from the ultimately real.

When Paul wrote his summarizing Epistle to the Romans he of course did not know that he would be beheaded in Rome. He is eager to move on to the capital of the empire, knowing its importance to his mission: "But now that there is no more place for me to work in these regions, and since I have been longing for many years to see you, I plan to do so when I go to Spain. I hope to visit you while passing through and to have you assist me on my journey there, after I have enjoyed your company for a while. . . . I urge you, brethren, by our Lord Jesus Christ and by the love of the Spirit, to join with me in my struggle by praying to God for me" (Romans 15:23–24, 30).

The precise circumstances of Paul's death are unknown. The author of Acts, writing after Paul's death, seems to compare Paul to Socrates as he describes that important address at the Areopagus, a traditional scene of Athenian trials. If that is the intention of this famous scene, and I think it is, the author means to imply that, like Socrates, Paul died for the truth, though a truth of a different kind.

Arthur Darby Nock provides a brief summary of what we know and can surmise about the death of Paul.[7] Essentially, Paul was imprisoned in Rome as a "troublemaker." His crime under Roman law was *maiestas*, or "high treason," but this could be and often was interpreted very broadly. The Roman state was tolerant in some ways but did not look with favor on public disturbances of any kind. Paul, we know, was a constant source of excitement and contention during his travels and even stirred up riots. His house arrest in Rome seems to have something to do with court politics, perhaps involving Poppaea, Nero's mistress and later his wife. We know from the last sentences of Acts that Paul was under a version of house arrest for about two years: "For two whole years Paul stayed there in his own rented house and welcomed all who came to see him. Boldly and without hindrance he preached the kingdom of God and taught about the Lord Jesus Christ" (Acts 27:30).

We do not know why the Roman authorities finally decided to put an end to him. A reasonable guess is that his talk about a "lord" Jesus and of some sort of "kingdom" sounded to them like political subversion, a questioning, or worse, of the emperor's sovereignty. Very likely, the Roman judges did not know what to make of him, gave up trying, and ordered him beheaded. It remained for other missionaries to move out along the paved Roman roads to the imperial provinces of Spain and Gaul, and then to other lands that would eventually become Europe.

The lasting importance of Paul lies in both the substance and the form of his thought. In substance many of the central themes of the Western mind are especially prominent. Paul has at once a powerful sense of transcendence and a nearly overwhelming sense of human imperfection. He wishes to be the architect of the just community, but he knows he is working with fallible human material. His mind rises to *agape* (divine love) but is remarkably strong in *philia* (friendship; the Greek *philia* is much stronger than its English translation). In his Greek aspect he looks back to philosophy, while as a Jew he is rooted in Scripture, pulled in one direction toward generalization and clarification and in another toward particularity and mystery. When you trace Western thought back along its many roads you find Paul standing there at a moment of strategic crystallization. Read Augustine, Dante, Luther, Shakespeare, Milton, Swift, Dostoyevsky—you are aware of Paul. When you think of the recurrent Western impulse to build an international order, you may again think of Paul.

If Paul is important in substance he is at least equally important in overall form. He brought Athens and Jerusalem together, sought to see them as one coherent whole, yet there persisted in him a tension that was inherent in the things themselves and would remain at the center of the Western mind. This tension can be characterized in many ways. Clearly there must be tension between the Greek and the biblical ways of seeing the world, between the Greek tendency toward generalization and clarity and the Hebrew tendency toward history, unpredictability, and awe. There must be tension between the cosmic pattern of the philosophers and the irreducible singularity of Jesus of Nazareth. Werner Jaeger is correct when he offers this summary: "The merging of the Christian religion with the Greek intellectual heritage made people realize that both traditions had much in common when they were viewed from the higher vantage point of the Greek idea of *paideia* or education, which offered a unique general denominator for both. We have found the idea of such a merger as early as Paul's speech in Athens in Acts."[8]

That is good, but it is not quite good enough. Athens and Jerusalem may indeed become a synthesis, be held in balance, especially in an educational curriculum such as Jaeger describes, but under pressure they can pull apart—as in the great quarrel between Erasmus and Luther, Erasmus stressing Latin culture and Luther sin and Christian holiness. They need not pull entirely apart, but a tension persists, energetically and creatively, a tension that acts and reacts within history. Which is to say that the mind of the West was born amid tension and contradiction and draws strength from refusing to be either-or but rather both-and, both Greek and Jew. Upon reflection we can see that in many areas of experience an entity draws strength from the effort to contain its contradictions.

Thus, in the first century, there was the difficult idea of the man-God, the Logos-as-Jesus, the One God of Genesis actually walking the streets of Jerusalem, the Alpha and Omega pulled together, extreme generalization and extreme particularity, the different ways of knowing, Greek and Hebrew, fused, Athens and Jerusalem. Paul knows all of this, knows contradictory things and tries to move beyond the contradictions. He knows that Jesus was a particular man from Nazareth, in fact a man about his own age. He also sees him as universal and timeless, present before the beginning. It is in his overwhelming experience on the road to Damascus that he moves from either-or to both-and.

Paul is a colossal figure. Yet he remains more elusive in history than either Socrates or Jesus. The great artists of the Renaissance left us few portraits of Paul on canvas or in marble. We have a great many representations of Moses, Jesus, Mary, David, annunciations, martyrdoms, but around Paul there obtains a kind of silence. We do not know what he looked like, even in a traditional sense or conventional representation.

Yet in its taut and heroically managed polarities his mind was powerful and shaping. A civilization that begins by managing these polarities can surely manage the polarized truths of Voltaire and Dostoyevsky, Montaigne and Dante, can wonder with the physicists whether reality is like a mathematical equation or with the poets like a mysterious poem. It can handle the polarities of freedom and order, self and society, reason and love. The civilization that derives from Athens and Jerusalem is sometimes dangerously active within those polarities, but active nevertheless. It can hold in balance Shakespeare and Goethe, Prospero and Faust, Rousseau and Augustine. It not only maintains contradictions but is energized by them. To put it another way, its contradictions talk amongst one another. They challenge and are answered. When Montaigne's vision comes into conflict with that of Dante, it receives a strong rejoinder. Virgil's Aeneas, Goethe's Faust, and Conrad's Marlow have different things to say about empire. Cervantes, Molière, and Swift debated illusion, madness, and heroism. If the philosophers of the Enlightenment thought God remote or nonexistent, Dostoyevsky thought Raskolnikov knew him intimately. The irregularities of history and the quest for holiness, on the one hand, and the drive for generalization and scientific truth, on the other, express different agendas but neither displaces the other; they remain in ever-shifting tension.

When Columbus sailed, he had three very different motivations: (1) religious: spread the Christian message; (2) scientific: navigation and exploration; and (3) economic: access to the riches of the East. Milton affirmed simultaneously "Things unattempted yet in prose and rhyme" and Raphael's advice to Adam that he "be lowly wise: / Think only what concerns thee and thy being." Goethe's Faust is stretched between heroic striving and the desire to say to the delicious moment, "Verweile doch, du bist so schön" (Linger awhile, you are so fair).[9] Perhaps it is not too much to say that in the powerful mind of Paul, stretched between Jerusalem and Athens, there began to emerge the essential form of the Western mind, which is dialectical, and also many of its central themes.

PART 2

Explorations

DESCRIBING THE FORMATION OF THE ATHENS-Jerusalem dialectic has been the job of the first part of this book, which brought us as far as Paul and touched upon the important debate between Clement and Origen, who were open to classical learning, and Tertullian, who led the party opposing it. My argument here is that the Athens-Jerusalem dialectic is unique to Western civilization and that the shifting balance within that dialectic, resulting from tensions in the mind and heart, underlies the restlessness and the achievement of that civilization: the glory of its science; the depth of its insights; the special character of its art; its development, uniquely, of the theory and practice of representative government; and its often tormented pressing of questions about ultimate meaning, the destiny of man and the nature of Being. Down that road we have had heroic exploratory thought, whether expressed in discourse, music, science, literature, or visual art. And it is not too much to say that the science and philosophy of the West are now approaching the status of global universals, at least in the advanced nations. Western science is universal. There is no other science, and assertions to the contrary by multiculturalists and others are bogus. The theorems of Newton and Einstein are as valid in China or Africa as they are in New York or Paris. Representative government attempts to solve the ancient political problem of the one, the few, and the many (monarchy, aristocracy, democracy), and it may, with local modifications, be the only legitimate form of government in the world today, or at least among the advanced nations. It is also a uniquely Western development. About aesthetic achievements there will always be differences of opinion. Very great works of art can spring from such cultures, for example, as that of Homer. Yet it would be very difficult to gainsay the distinctiveness and grandeur of the Western achievements in the arts from Homer through the present.

Christopher Columbus, and in this he is typical of many of the great navigators, held in balance three principal motives that impelled him westward. As navigator, his motive was scientific. He believed the globe to be smaller than it actually is and also somewhat pear-shaped. In testing those theories, he was an empiricist. He also put to the test his theory that he could reach Asia by sailing westward.

In addition, he was a Christian, with a flagship named the *Santa Maria,* and he was sincere in his desire to bring religious truth as he understood it to whatever pagan peoples he might meet. Finally, his motives were economic. Islamic military power lay across the land routes to the east, and sailing to the west might find another route for trade and profit. This combination of motives represents an excellent example of the Athens-Jerusalem paradigm and the energies it generated in a man of the late fifteenth century.

Perhaps it need not be said that such profound sources of energy, cognitive and spiritual, in the West have sometimes issued in ghastly deformations. The Inquisition was a cruel deformation of religious zeal mixed with nascent nationalism. Under the Nazis, an extreme version of nationalism turned murderous, the high culture of nineteenth-century Germany tragically issuing in this. As Homer and Milton knew, the highest things are often the most vulnerable, the great Achilles plunging to the moral depths and Milton's Satan demonstrating that spiritual disaster could consume even the greatest of the archangels. Massacres and high crimes are virtually universal. Indeed, they are frequent in Asia, Africa, and elsewhere. The crimes of the West are not unique, but its achievements are.

The brief explorations that follow focus upon Augustine, Dante, Shakespeare, Molière, Voltaire, and two novelists— Dostoyevsky and F. Scott Fitzgerald. They seek to illuminate the works themselves and also to explore the operations in them, direct or indirect, of the Athens and Jerusalem paradigm. Of course a great many other works could be pressed into service, but I have already touched on Homer in part I, and by virtually universal agreement Dante and Shakespeare along with Homer constitute the three greatest poets in the Western tradition. The stature of Molière, Voltaire, and Dostoyevsky is secure, and I make a case for *The Great Gatsby*. I must add that although all of these works possess great centrality to their respective historical periods, I by no means suggest that any single work could approach full representation of all important aspects of a given period.

There exist many useful book lists, some extensive, some abbreviated. Recently, as a visiting professor at a small college in Massachusetts, I taught an experimental seminar in which we read and discussed the following: the *Iliad, Symposium, Apology, Crito, Phaedo,* Exodus, Matthew, John, Acts, *Inferno, Hamlet, The Tempest.* This selection is reflected in part 1 of this book and an abbreviated version of part 2. I believe a lot was accomplished with an abbreviated list in a single course.

Recently, a friend of mine who is a professor of classics and an expert in Latin and Greek, told me that he found it almost impossible to teach either Homer's *Iliad* or Plato's *Republic* to today's undergraduates. He evidently found it impossibly difficult to communicate to them the reasons why he had devoted so much of his life to those two books. Maybe he had forgotten why. Perhaps he was professionally occupied with the small points that get argued in the professional journals. But there comes a time when the connection must be made between text and life, between a book and what the Greeks called *paideia*, the shaping of a person, education.

It goes without saying that, though I have had professional experience with all of the books here, I do not hesitate to recommend them to students, educated readers, or my academic colleagues. All these authors are heroes of mine, heroes of intellect, art, and spirit. When I speak of them, it will be without any trace of academic authority. In the classroom, as in my writing, I aspire to transparency: let the work shine through all discussion, as its author surely hoped.

What follow here are explorations. It may seem strange that the modern poet Hart Crane saw Columbus as a personal alter ego, a visionary explorer like himself. Crane, in my view, might have chosen any of the great writers discussed here in part 1, or any to be discussed in part 2. Certainly many other books could have been chosen, but none of those included here could, I think, be omitted. There are highways and there are byways and the Western mind is always a work in progress. In the large sense, however, and as argued here, it has achieved permanent dialectical form, a creative tension existing over time. I have cited here the German philosopher Herman Cohen: "Plato and the Prophets are the most important sources of modern culture." And I will quote here T. S. Eliot: "Fare forward, voyager."

CHAPTER SIX

Augustine Chooses Jerusalem

In the *Confessions,* written during his middle years, Augustine (A.D. 354–430) searched deeply into the inner life, and in this pursuit he exemplified the pursuit of inner perfection demanded by the Sermon on the Mount. He came to Christianity, however, chiefly through the Platonic tradition, which was most immediately expressed for him by Cicero and Plotinus. He also considered that the truth about the cosmos is to be found in the operations of mind. This inner exploration, which Augustine shared with many of his contemporaries but of which he is the master, marks an important shift from the temper of the classical Roman world toward the medieval sensibility being born within it, and it certainly prefigures Dante, whose immense epic poem consists entirely of the internal journey of a mind toward perfection.

A second theme of the *Confessions,* which will be touched on in this brief discussion of Augustine, is the extreme difficulty Augustine experienced in this inner journey. This took the form for him of both knowing and willing the good. For the Platonic tradition, to know the good is to will it. In his own experience Augustine found that this was not true, that the will was frail compared with desire and that the will needed help. Augustine was not obsessed with sex, as is popularly thought. What perplexed him was that when he had decided to give up sexual love, his will would not follow. He had been faithful to a single concubine for fifteen years, and she had borne him a much-loved son whom they named Adeodatus or "gift of God." But when he willed celibacy and a contemplative pursuit of truth, he found these impossible. The defect of the human will is at the center of the *Confessions*. Paul's experience on the road to Damascus was sudden and overwhelming. Augustine's experience of his own defective will was equally radical. He believed that it took direct divine intervention to overcome the defect. This strand of religious experience, of utter dependence upon God's freely given grace, descends from Paul and is important in Augustine, Luther, Wesley, and beyond.

His *Confessions,* therefore, are not "confessions" about scandalous personal behavior, as is often supposed, but testimony about his inner experience and about God's grace.[1] By the time he wrote the *Confessions* (397–401) Augustine, who had been an important professor of rhetoric (based in literature and philosophy) at the university in Carthage (Tunis), believed that the truth about the cosmos lay in the depths of one's being, that there is such a thing as Wisdom, which one may achieve but which ultimately provides modes of access to the mind of God. One can approach it through great effort and self-discipline, but for those particularly beset by a defective will the approach requires divine grace. As he writes in the *Confessions:* "Men go to gape at mountain peaks, at the bottomless tides of the seas, the broad sweep of rivers, the encircling ocean and the motion of the stars: and yet they leave themselves unnoticed: they do not marvel at themselves."[2]

Augustine's basic proposition is that the mind is our clue to the nature of the cosmos because the mind is the only entity we can fully explore from within. Everything else is external to us and, as far as experience is concerned, opaque. It is man's tragedy that he flees outward into this external world. God is an intellectual premise, deducible by reason, but more important, God is "deeper than inmost being."

Remembering that the *Confessions* were written long after he first went to the university in Carthage as a student and must therefore evaluate his experience from a new perspective, that of a bishop and Christian ascetic, we have to discount to a degree his depiction of the famous city. At the start of book 3 he announces, "To Carthage then I came, where a cauldron of shameful loves seethed and sounded about me on every side."[3]

Yet there is abundant evidence that as a student he very much enjoyed that great city.[4] The Romans had fought three devastating Punic wars with Carthage, finally annihilating it in the middle of the second century B.C. Rebuilding it completely, they had turned it into the capital of their North African empire. It had a magnificent harbor lined by a colonnade, its principal avenues were lined with trees, and in and around the university it had a lively intellectual life. Augustine was fascinated by its bookstalls, theaters, music, and generally high level of culture and was drawn, we learn, to the skeleton of a huge whale large enough to hold twelve men. The palace of the Roman proconsul stood on an elevation overlooking the city, and to the south, for hundreds of miles, extended the Roman African empire.

It is important to know, however, that Augustine, first a student, then a professor at the great university in Carthage, then elevated to the post of court orator in Milan, and finally a Christian convert and ascetic, did become a hardworking bishop at the city of Hippo Regius in North Africa, then a seaport second only to Carthage. Such men as Saint Anthony had led their followers into the desert to contemplate that special silence that was vital to Augustine, but Augustine did not end as a desert father or a cloistered monk. In the many years that remained to him following the *Confessions* he produced a quantity of philosophical writing that is so vast that scholars believe he must have dictated to multiple scribes. He also preached an enormous number of daily sermons, only a fraction of which have survived, not to mention conducting a polemical correspondence with the combative scholar Jerome, who was translating the Bible into Latin in the Holy Land. We should think of him during these years dressed not in the familiar regalia of a bishop, a later development, as Wills points out, but in the gray garb of a monk.

Augustine's journey, however, was difficult. Socrates (and Cicero) had taught that to know the good, especially the highest good, is also to choose it. Augustine was blocked at that moment of choice. He found that the human heart, his in particular, is bent toward sin. Let us take a single famous passage in the *Confessions* in which Augustine reflects, long after, upon an experience from his boyhood, at a time just before he left to continue his studies at the university in Carthage. Augustine remains idle in his home town of Thagaste and commits an act, relatively trivial in itself but indicative of a will bent toward gratuitous evil. It is a moment of great resonance that haunts him in retrospect, and I find that it haunts readers today as well.

> In a garden nearby to our vineyard there was a pear tree, loaded with fruit that was desirable neither in appearance nor in taste. Late one night—to which hour according to our pestilential custom, we had kept up our street games—a group of very bad youngsters set out to shake down and rob this tree. We took great loads of fruit from it, not for our own eating, but rather to throw it to the pigs; even if we did eat a little of it, we did this to do what pleased us for the reason that it was forbidden.
>
> Behold my heart, O Lord, behold my heart upon which you had mercy in the depths of the pit. Behold, now let my heart tell you what it looked for there, that I should be evil without purpose and that there should be no cause for my evil but evil itself. Foul was the evil, and I loved it. I loved to go down to death. I loved my fault, not that for which I did the fault, but I loved the fault itself. Base in soul was I, and I leaped down from your firm clasp even toward complete destruction, and I sought nothing from the shameful deed but shame itself.[5]

Augustine understands that he chose transgression for the sake of transgression itself, a gratuitous act. In retrospect he sees the relevance of the story of the Fall in Genesis 1 and Adam's willingness to follow Eve in rebellion. He thus associates himself with the original Fall, the pattern and essence of all future transgressions. In retrospect he sees the relevance of the entire Genesis narrative as applicable to his own behavior and inner reflection.

From his professorship at Carthage, Augustine proceeded to Milan, now no longer a professorial tutor accepting fees from students but a "court orator" in that northern city, which was also the site of the emperor's court and a good place to continue his philosophical work. There he fell in with a congenial group of young men, Neoplatonists, who were drawn to Ambrose, bishop of Milan. A Roman aristocrat, influential at court, and a powerful thinker, Ambrose delivered sermons on biblical interpretation that had become famous. Among other things, Ambrose rendered palatable the passages in the Hebrew Bible most offensive to high classical taste by interpreting them as moral and religious allegories. The classicist Augustine, expert in Virgil, Cicero, and other polished Roman authors, had seen the Hebrew scriptures as stylistically low. Ambrose helped him to see their luminous core.

As is rare for figures in the ancient world, we have a good idea of what Ambrose actually looked like. A mosaic exists that depicts him as a frail man holding a codex of the Scriptures. He has a high forehead, a long, melancholy face, and large eyes.[6] In a passage of great historical significance in the *Confessions,* Augustine tells us that sometimes he came upon Ambrose reading and was surprised by what he saw.

"When he read, his eyes moved down the pages and his heart sought out their meaning, while his voice and tongue remained silent. Often when we were present—for no one was forbidden to entry, and it was not his custom to have whoever came announced to him—we saw him reading to himself, and never otherwise. After sitting for a long time in silence—who would dare to annoy a man so occupied?—we would go away."[7]

Augustine is surprised that while reading Ambrose does not move his lips or make sounds, as would an educated Roman like himself. Augustine and the other professors taught literature as oratory, focused outward to the forum, senate, or law court. The goal was external and public. Augustine included this passage in the *Confessions,* I think, because he sensed that it reflected a momentous shift, away from the public world and toward the depths of the mind. Augustine doubtless saw this as part of his own story.

Often the best way to approach a book that has the shape of a voyage is to understand the point toward which that voyage is headed. It is even possible to read the *Confessions* as a counter-*Aeneid,* another "Mediterranean voyage" that displaces key elements and ends very differently for Augustine-Aeneas. In the *Confessions,* Augustine's mother, Monica, a Christian though not learned, is intense, has an implacable will, and is a powerful emotional force driving Augustine's voyage. In the pattern of the *Confessions* it seems inevitable that the great moment, when it comes at the end of book 9 and essentially concludes the autobiographical material, should be a moment of spiritual union with Monica. Not surprisingly the first experience of genuine serenity in the *Confessions* occurs here in this extraordinary passage, so powerful and so psychologically rich that it should be quoted here at some length. Planning to return to Africa from Italy, Augustine and Monica have come down to Ostia, the seaport for Rome at the mouth of the Tiber. Augustine has come a long way to reach this point and this sense of Christianity, but reach it he has:

> With the approach of that day on which she was to depart from this life. . . . She and I stood leaning out from a certain window, where we could look into the garden within the house we had taken at Ostia on the Tiber, where, removed from crowds, we were resting up, after the hardships of a long journey, in preparation for the voyage. We were alone, conversing together most tenderly, "forgetting those things that are behind, and stretching forth to those that are to come. . . ."
>
> When our discourse had been brought to the point that the highest delight of fleshly senses, in the brightest corporeal light, when set against the sweetness of that life seemed unworthy not merely of comparison with it, but even of remembrance, then, raising ourselves up with a more ardent love to the Selfsame, we proceeded step by step through all bodily things up to that heaven whence shine the sun and the moon and the stars down upon the earth. We ascended higher yet by inward thought and discourse and admiration of your works, and we came to our own minds. We transcended them, so that we attained to the region that never fails. . . .
>
> Therefore we said: if for any man the tumult of the flesh falls silent, and the images of earth, and of the waters, and of the air; silent the heavens, silent for him the very soul itself by not thinking upon him-

self, silent in his dreams and all imagined appearances, and every tongue and every sign; and if all things that come to be through change should become wholly silent. . . . And God alone speaks, not through such things but through Himself, so that we hear his Word, not uttered by a tongue of flesh, nor by an angel's voice, nor by sound of thunder, nor by the riddle of a similitude, but by himself whom we love in these things, himself we hear without their aid—even as we then reached out and in swift thought attained to that eternal wisdom which abides over all things. . . . When shall this be? When "we shall rise again, but we shall not all be changed."[8]

Here Augustine deploys the great resources of the Ciceronian periodic sentence, as well as the other technical skills of the professor of rhetoric; and there can hardly be a doubt that Dante drew on this passage for the sweep and the imagery of his *Paradiso*. Let us be aware that Monica herself did not and could not have expressed herself in such gorgeous terms in describing the ascent of a Christianized platonic ladder of love. As Augustine says at the end, "Such things I said, although not in this manner and in these words." He means that he experiences the moment in such terms and that she understood it in her own way.

A great deal might be said of this passage, about the garden within the house into which they gaze, about the river Tiber flowing down to the sea, and about the various voyages the passage has in mind. I have placed quotation marks around two biblical quotations among the several that Augustine weaves into this passage, both from Paul: Philippians and Corinthians i. By this point in the *Confessions* it is clear that Augustine has learned to read the Bible in such a way that he hears the voice of God in it. It is also evident that the Christian experience described in this passage is of a highly Platonized sort, though the citation from Corinthians has to do with the Resurrection. Augustine gives a great deal of credit for his conversion to Neoplatonist friends, such as Simplicianus and Theodore, though it seems clear that Monica is a powerful presence as well, though scarcely a philosopher.

Five days after this conversation at Ostia, if "conversation" is the word for it, Monica dies and, not caring where she is interred, is buried there at Ostia, far from her home in Thagaste. Much later, medieval pilgrims copied the verse epitaph above her tomb. A pilgrim from northern France named Walter was allowed to take home a body part as a relic. In summer 1945, two boys playing in a courtyard beside the church of St. Aurea in Ostia began to dig a hole for a wooden post for soccer. They disturbed an old fragment of marble on which was part of the original inscription for Monica.[9]

Augustine's conversion as described in the *Confessions* was not a sudden thing, although the moment of decision is highly dramatic. He is aware of his powerful sexuality, aware of gratuitous sin, as in the pear tree and other episodes. He hears about the conversion of a Roman named Victorinus, prominent enough to have his statue in the Forum, but when he tries to make up his mind to emulate Victorinus, he feels as if "sleep" is descending upon him. Although in pursuit of serenity and inner perfection he has often pleaded for chastity and has heeded the inner voice he now hears by sending his longtime concubine off to Africa, he has not been able to overcome his sexual habit and free his will.

Here it is important to remember that the idea of rejecting worldly distractions was not unique to Christianity. The Platonists, the Stoics, and indeed Cicero all counseled ascetic discipline. Worldly pleasures, marriage and children, holding public office, all were impediments more or less fatal to the philosophical pursuit of wisdom. Augustine remains too beset by his passions to follow either the classical philosophers or the apparently serene example of Victorinus.

Much more pertinent to Augustine's inner life than Victorinus was his close friend Alypius, a lawyer, whose story he tells in book 6 of the *Confessions*. Alypius cannot understand Augustine's turmoil over sex, but he himself has an impediment of his own—his attraction to the violence of the Coliseum. He could not stay away, even though he wanted to, from the lethal human combat, fights among men and animals and among animals, the more exotic the better. At Carthage he had managed to control himself, but when he followed Augustine to Rome his friends hooked him again. He resists, but they drag him to the Coliseum.

He says he will close his ears and eyes. He fails, as Augustine describes in another famous passage: "He fell more miserably than did that gladiator at whose fall the shout was raised. The shout entered him through his ears and opened his eyes. . . . As he saw that blood, he drank in the savageness at the same time. He did not turn away, but fixed his sight on it, and drank in madness without knowing it. He took delight in that evil struggle, and he became drunk on blood and pleasure. He was no longer the man who entered there, but only one of the crowd that he had joined."[10] For neither Augustine nor Alypius are reason and will sufficient to overcome the power of the turbulent attractions of the world.

The account of Augustine's moment of decision constitutes a brilliant mininarrative within the larger narrative of the *Confessions*. It comes at the end of book 8. It thus pairs with and prepares for the great scene of serenity with Monica at the end of book 9.

This mininarrative begins with another chance encounter that affects Augustine deeply, and which he certainly understands is not due to chance. While he and Alypius are sharing a house in Milan as guests of the absent owner, a man named Ponticianus shows up and casually picks up a book lying on a gaming table. He finds it to be a volume of Paul's Epistles. Ponticianus, a public official and a Christian, tells Augustine and Alypius about other officials who had become Christians. Augustine begins to reflect upon his own failed struggles.

The decisive moment occurs in a garden attached to the house, and the details of the narrative are important. That it is a garden has numerous resonances in this narrative. It anticipates the garden into which he and Monica gaze during their "conversation" in Ostia. It also looks back to that pear tree in book 2, a scene of gratuitous sin. The present garden contains its own tree, a fig, and it of course recalls the original garden and the Fall, and the fig leaves with which Adam and Eve covered their nakedness. The sentences that introduce this garden, in Milan, have a quality of anticipatory serenity: "Attached to our lodging there was a little garden; we had the use of it, as of the whole house, for our host, the owner of the house, did not live in it."[11] This contrasts with the tumult of emotion that is boiling within Augustine: "The tumult within my breast hurried me out into it, where no one would stop the raging combat I had entered into against myself. . . . I rushed then into the garden and Alypius followed in my steps."[12] Augustine's torment persists until he hears the voice of a child from a nearby house: "a voice like that of a boy or girl, I know not which, repeating over and over, 'Take up and read, take up and read.' Instantly, with altered countenance, I began to think intently whether children made use of any such chant for some kind of game, but I could not recall hearing it anywhere."[13]

Augustine knows from his familiarity with the Bible how much a single phrase can mean: "Sell what you have . . . and follow me." There the rich young man's besetting sin is pride in wealth. So Augustine takes up and reads the volume that has been lying on the gaming table: "I hurried back to the spot where Alypius was sitting, for I had put there the volume of the apostle when I got up and left him. I snatched it up, opened it, and read in silence the chapter on which my eyes fell: 'Not in rioting and drunkenness, not in sensuality and impurities, not in strife and envying, but put you on the Lord Jesus Christ, and make not provision for the flesh and its concupiscence.' "[14] No doubt Augustine had read that passage many times before. No doubt many other passages in Paul's Letters would have "spoken" to him similarly, because his resistance has resembled that of Paul before the experience on the road to Damascus. Augustine tells us: "No further wished I to read, nor was there desire to do so. Instantly, in truth, at the end of this sentence, as if before a peaceful light streaming into my heart, all the dark shadows of doubt fled away."[15] He and Alypius go to Monica nearby, and, of course, she "rejoiced." This powerful account prepares for the climactic scene with Monica at Ostia at the end of book 9.

Augustine's account of his experience in the garden is densely textured with biblical allusions, some of which I have already noted. Its fig tree recalls the clothing made for Adam and Eve after the Fall, hiding their sexuality. The voice that asks him to read is that of a child, neither boy nor girl, sexless, and, as it were, free from Augustine's sexual torments. One thinks of Eliot's somehow angelic "children in the apple tree."[16] That the book he picks up is Paul's Epistles speaks to his condition. That it lies on a "gaming table" has considerable significance: truth is not a matter of chance but of deep understanding.

This episode in the *Confessions* is a beautiful, consummate piece of narrative. Dante in his own epic of the inner life will make good use of it and much else in the *Confessions,* as when, for example, Francesca da Rimini in Canto V of the *Inferno,* who has been seduced by a courtly romance and commits adultery with Paolo (ironically reminding us of Paul?), also says, "That day we read no further."[17]

CHAPTER SEVEN

Dante, Rome (Athens), Jerusalem, and *Amor*

Along with Homer and Shakespeare, Dante is more than a major poet. By consensus, by our inspection, and by the measure of centuries of commentary, he is, with Homer and Shakespeare, one of the three greatest poets in the Western tradition. A poet such as this seems always to rise out of a rich cultural matrix. Homer had his context in the epic tradition of the Near East. Shakespeare had Chaucer, the medieval festival drama, the sacred stage, and his surrounding example of the Elizabethan theater. We can take account of the poetic and other cultural material available to Dante in the fourteenth century; but what he did with that material could not possibly have been anticipated. Keats said that when he first read George Chapman's Elizabethan translation of Homer he was astonished by something entirely new. He felt "like some watcher of the skies / When a new planet swims into his ken."[1] Keats must have known that, brilliant as he himself was, he would not achieve anything like that. T. S. Eliot placed Dante and Shakespeare together as the supreme poets of the "modern," as he called it, era; meaning postclassical, and Eliot made good use of both Dante and Shakespeare in his own poetry.

Dante himself was not overcome by modesty. Within his poem he gives abundant indication that he is convinced that he is writing the greatest poem of all time; indeed, he suggests that it is on a plane with divine revelation. Yet the *Divine Comedy* is such an extraordinary achievement that such claims do not seem absurd.

Indeed, with the exception of the Bible the *Divine Comedy* has been commented upon more than any other work in Western literature, and by a very wide margin. Discussion is a measure of importance and respect. Shakespeare comes next, and among his plays *Hamlet* has provoked the most commentary. In the seven hundred years since it was written, the *Divine Comedy* has been translated into dozens of languages, including Japanese.

If we step back and look at Dante's epic in its larger context, we see that his intellectual project was to bring together three powerful traditions. He attempted on a vast scale a renewed synthesis of the Athens-Jerusalem tension—bringing together such polarities as epic and scripture, Virgil and Augustine, Cicero and Aquinas—and then added a spectacular third element, the so-called religion of Love, the religion of *Amor* which had become powerful very suddenly in the eleventh century, first in the south of France, then spreading throughout Europe.

Giving epic form to the project of interiorizing the heroic and making it the ideal of inner perfection, Dante added a third element, the ideal woman, as messenger of God—which would have been astonishing to Virgil or Paul—and wrote an epic about a man's journey through the inner world of human possibility. The apotheosis of the ideal woman arose suddenly in Provence and Aquitaine during the eleventh century out of causes still mysterious. Its enormous influence on Western civilization can be understood when one compares the position of women in the West today with their position in Asia or Africa. Something that happened in the south of France in the eleventh century led to this enormous difference.

Here a personal note is called for. The three best essays I know of about Dante are all by poets: George Santayana in 1910, T. S. Eliot in 1929, and Mark Van Doren in 1946.[2] That these were poets of very different scale is obvious. But they were drawn to Dante by what must strike any reader, that is, his language. Whether in Italian or in translation, that language is startlingly clear, hard-edged, concrete. Dante's world is emphatically there, and his hold on it never loosens. Yet this language can concentrate Dante's images to the point where they become charged with significances that go far beyond that recognizable concrete world. Any poet wants to charge language with meaning. Dante could do this to an exceptional degree in a passage of even a few lines, and an unusual amount of this survives in any good translation.

To the special qualities of his language he added a remarkably firm overall architecture. His vast epic poem, with its hundred cantos, with its three large subordinate parts, or "kingdoms" as he called them, is so firmly designed that everything in it seems to have a reason for being there. Anything subtracted would leave a gap. The poem is as tightly organized as a short lyric. It is astonishing to think of a human mind holding such a vast design together while at the same time perfecting the myriad details.

These are some of the important reasons why the *Divine Comedy* has been so highly esteemed: texture, architecture, seriousness, and reach. The *Divine Comedy*, as T. S. Eliot said, "is a complete scale of the depths and heights of human emotion."[3] Yet he also celebrates Shakespeare: "Shakespeare understands a greater extent and variety of human life than Dante; but . . . Dante understands deeper degrees of degradation and higher degrees of exaltation." He adds: "And a further wisdom is reached when we see clearly that this indicates the equality of the two men."[4]

The Dark Wood

Any reader, whether in the original or in translation, will see at once the special clarity and directness of Dante's language. "In the middle of the journey of our life I came to myself within a dark wood where the straight way was lost."[5] This is apparently simple but reaches for wider meaning. We can all imagine what being lost in a dark wood might be like. Such a wood appears in legend and folklore as well as in high culture. Ludwig Wittgenstein has remarked that all philosophy begins with the recognition, "I am lost." Dante's grand yet modest opening lines gesture toward all of this, including high philosophy. His wood is specific, yet it is also in the middle of "our" life and therefore a common experience. A little later in this opening, the lake and the pass are similarly both specific and general, and the "straight way" that was "lost" has biblical overtones.

Robert Frost used Dante's method and competed with him in his fine poem "Birches," in which he uses Dante but also draws back from him.

> It's when I'm weary of considerations,
> And life is too much like a pathless wood
> Where your face burns and tickles with the cobwebs
> Broken across it, and one eye is weeping
> From a twig's having lashed across it open.

Frost proceeds to define himself through Dante and against Dante. He says he would like to swing on a birch tree up but only toward heaven, not into heaven, and then return to earth. Dante's wood is universal enough for Frost to use, and then challenge Dante:

> I'd like to get away from earth awhile
> And then come back to it and begin over.
> May no fate wilfully misunderstand me
> And half grant what I wish and snatch me away
> Not to return. Earth's the right place for love:
> I don't know where it's likely to go better.
> I'd like to go by climbing a birch tree,
> And climb black branches up a snow-white trunk
> *Toward* heaven, till the tree could bear no more,
> But dipped its top and set me down again.
> That would be good both going and coming back.
> One could do worse than be a swinger of birches.[6]

Placing himself against Dante here, no Paradiso for him, Frost also writes with a Dantean clarity, yet everything in his poem is a metaphor. He is lost in Dante's wood, but he would rise only "toward heaven." He asserts, but carefully does not know, that "earth's the right place for love." He merely does not know "where it's likely to go better."

Frost's poem is strong as it uses Dante and draws from his strength, even if to distance itself from him and even while using Dante's method.

In Frost, as in Dante, everything in the foreground is real and also has further meaning. "In the middle of the journey of our life I came to myself within a dark wood where the straight way was lost."

The phrase "I came to myself" seems simple enough, but really it is not. Of course it is commonplace to reassess, take thought, during one's middle years. This can be a period of confusion and crisis. Just so the narrator comes to himself and realizes that he is lost. But he comes to himself, it may be by dreaming, because in a dream he can discover the inner truth that has been hidden in his waking life. Just what the "dark wood" might be we do not yet know. When the action begins he does not wake up; the dark wood and everything in it become part of a dream that goes on for a hundred cantos. He lost his ordinary life and found the "straight way" to his real life, that is, to holiness.

The figure "Dante" in the poem, who undergoes these visionary experiences, is not the poet Dante who is writing the poem. "Dante," sometimes called "the pilgrim," must undergo the experiences; but it is the poet who tells the tale. This pilgrim's exploration of all the possibilities of the inner life will be the subject of the poem, though pilgrim and author draw close at the end. The pilgrim encounters everything from the foulest degradation to the intensities of holiness.

In that seeming dreamscape of the opening scene, with its lake, its pass, and the menacing leopard, wolf, and lion, the pilgrim plausibly despairs of escape from the dark wood when assistance arrives in the form of one whom he has known in the past but not heeded lately, "who through long silence seemed hoarse."[7] This turns out to be Virgil, who instructs him that he must take "another road"—a long and difficult one. That is, before he can understand holiness, he must be educated in its antitheses. Paul and Augustine are near at hand here, unseen, though the present guide is to be his beloved but long neglected, or not fully understood, Virgil.

The friendship between the pilgrims Dante and Virgil, which continues through much of the poem, is one of the very fine things in literature: " 'Are thou that Virgil, that fountain which pours forth so rich a stream of speech?' I answered him, my brow covered with shame. 'O glory and light of other poets, let the long study and great love that has made me search thy volume avail me. Thou art my master and my author.' "[8] The pilgrim's long journey with Virgil is subtle and dramatic. It is marked by love and deep courtesy, and by advancing wisdom on the part of the pilgrim Dante. Virgil is no two-dimensional figure. He knows a great deal, though not everything. But first of all, and important here, is the point that Dante cannot make the journey alone and unaided. He needs a guide, Virgil, but also many other guides and among them and most important, Beatrice. But along the way he needs the major insights of his civilization: poets, philosophers, astronomers, mathematicians, theologians, scientists, biblical narratives and interpretations—Aristotle, Paul, Cicero, Boethius, Augustine, Ptolemy, Thomas, Statius, the Provençal poets; the list is seemingly endless. The power of Dante to assimilate this rich tradition or traditions is one of the many startling things about the *Divine Comedy*. To put it another way, since his subject is the world, the universe, and he finally reaches beyond the universe, he must put everything knowable into this comprehensive poem. Although the *Divine Comedy* is one hundred cantos in length, he can accomplish this only by concentration rather than extension; only concentration permits him to try to do it at all.

From Virgil, the pilgrim Dante soon learns that he must take the long journey down into the depth of human deformation before he can ascend to the heights of vision. In the *Aeneid,* Virgil brought Aeneas to the underworld, where his dead father, Anchises, showed him the future of Rome, culminating in the reign of the emperor Augustus. The journey to be taken by the pilgrim Dante, however, is quite different. No doubt shaped by his own experience, which surely includes many readings of Augustine's *Confessions,* Dante knows that his pilgrim must visit not the dreary Hades of Virgil and the other ancient epics, but must receive a full education in evil before beginning to move up and beyond it. As the basis for his analysis of the vices and their opposites, Dante relies on Aristotle's *Ethics,* Cicero, Thomas, and others, but he assimilates them so thoroughly that you do not need to know they are there in order to experience their effects within the narrative.

Along the way, there will be various kinds of competition between Dante and Virgil. He will write a Hell much more impressive than Virgil's Hades. In Hades Aeneas heard from Anchises about his destiny and the future of Rome; in the Paradiso, Dante hears from his relative Cacciaguida that he will write the *Divine Comedy* and be the instructor of mankind. This perhaps friendly competition is familiar in the epic tradition, a sort of Olympic Games of poetry; and especially with Dante and Virgil it also expresses the relationship between teacher and student, Virgil and Dante.

Virgil and Beatrice

Virgil and Beatrice are the two poles of energy between which the *Divine Comedy* moves. Virgil first appears in Canto I, sent by Beatrice to lead Dante out of the dark wood by "another road." He stays with Dante through Hell and then up the mountain of Purgatory until the wisdom he possesses, impressive though it is, can aid Dante no further. In Canto XXX of the Purgatorio, an increasingly uncertain Virgil bids his pupil a poignant farewell. This wisest of ancient poets knows about suffering, about history and loss, knows about one form of destiny, and knows about unsatisfied longing for something more, but he cannot lead Dante one more step toward his destination.

The Virgil of the *Divine Comedy* is not to be identified with such abstract qualities as "reason" or "worldliness." He is Virgil, Publius Maro Virgilius, born in 70 B.C., dying in 19 B.C., the great poet Dante knew by reading him with special intensity, much as Virgil himself had read Homer. As rendered here, he is charged, like the *Aeneid*, with delicate and powerful emotion. His portrait also amounts to an extended estimate of his poetry and a commentary on it by Dante.

Throughout, their relationship is one of very great mutual respect, though with Virgil as teacher to a superior student. Dante's Virgil is a great Roman gentleman, as he surely was at the court of his patron the emperor Augustus. In his courtesy toward his student, he is also the ideal educator. As they move on together he often explains, as a teacher must, but he would rather lead Dante to the edge of discovery and allow him to reach understanding by himself. He gracefully resists the professorial temptation to talk too much, but when he does speak he makes his words count. There are hints early on that this student may well surpass his master, the ideal but always poignant goal between teacher and student.

The poet Dante, as distinguished from the pilgrim in the narrative, understands his position in relation to Virgil's *Aeneid*. Aeneas carried his Trojan household gods to Italy. In a comparable *translatio*, the *Aeneid* passes the Greek epic tradition to Dante but suffuses it with the Roman ideal of international empire, *imperium sine fine* as Virgil wrote. In that Roman idea Dante's own idea of empire gestated, as well as successive later ideals of Europe as a unique, even unified, civilization.

In Canto IV of the Inferno, the pilgrim Dante and Virgil come upon the great writers of the ancient world, "neither sad nor joyful," in the mildly pleasant fields of Limbo. Preeminent are Homer, Ovid, Horace, and Lucan. "The good master began: 'Mark him there with sword in hand who comes before these as their lord; he is Homer, the sovereign poet.'"[9] The pilgrim Dante, echoing his master Virgil, sees Homer as "that lord of loftiest song who flies like an eagle above the rest."[10]

These are handsome compliments from both Virgil and the pilgrim. But it is Virgil, not Dante, who calls Homer sovereign. Dante sees Homer standing "above the rest," but this does not include Virgil. Obviously, for the poet Dante, it is Virgil who is the sovereign poet, Virgil the master of the pilgrim but whom he eventually will surpass. Virgil is the sovereign poet until the *Divine Comedy* displaces him.

This moment in the Inferno is complex and very important. Virgil's relation to Homer here epitomizes the relation of Rome to Athens: intellectually and artistically derivative but adding to, and conditioning everything by it, the idea of successful empire. As Richard Jenkyns has written, "The whole of Roman literature was written under the shadow of Greece; from the Greeks the Roman poets derived their genres, metres, mythology, figures of speech. . . . Horace is proud to tell us that he has shown Archilochus and Alcaeus to Rome; Propertius proclaims himself the Roman Callimacus."[11]

Although half as long as either the *Iliad* or the *Odyssey*, the *Aeneid* rewrites the action of both. In the first six books, journeying from ruined Troy to Carthage, Aeneas experiences adventures like those of Odysseus. When he recounts them to Queen Dido, he resembles Odysseus at the court of Alcinoüs. The last six books render Aeneas as a warrior, significantly more like Hector than Achilles, fighting to establish rather than destroy a city. Virgil takes over scores of Homer's incidents, giving them to Aeneas, but he consciously recasts them, using allusion and contrast to establish differentiated and often very subtle meanings distinct from Homer's. He is dependent upon Homer as Rome is dependent upon the mind of Greece. Homer is indeed Virgil's, but not Dante's, sovereign poet. In his life of Virgil, Suetonius records that critics of Virgil accused him of plagiarizing Homer, but this is to miss the point of the dependence, which involved transformation. In fact, the transformation was Virgil's point. By making Homer a continuous presence in the *Aeneid*, Virgil invited, and dared, comparison and so directed attention to the multiple and important differences.

History, as it appears in Virgil, is scarcely present in the *Iliad* and *Odyssey*. There are genealogies, legends, and myths, but Homeric time focuses on the sharpness of the present moment. That is why we remember his scenes with such exceptional clarity. But the *Aeneid* is soaked in awareness of the long reaches of time. Chronos is the real god here. For that reason the present moment tends to be marked by vagueness, tenebrous darkness, as if already dissolving in the flux of time.[12] Aeneas has seen the distant future of Rome in the long celebratory but also sad vision vouchsafed in the underworld by his father, Anchises. He has fully accepted his mission as his destiny and his duty. He bears the enormous burden of knowing that the future of civilization depends upon him. Homer's heroes had no such knowledge. Aeneas is made humble and solemn by the extraordinary weight of his responsibility. He bears that responsibility, and therefore the *Aeneid* is suffused in sorrow, tears everywhere: over the ruin of Troy, the deaths of Creusa, father Anchises, helmsman Palinurus, Queen Dido of Carthage, who kills herself when Aeneas abandons her (and memorably turns from him in the under-

world with a face of stone). Nisus and Euryalus die, and finally, Turnus
the warrior dies, whose death ends the poem and is necessary to the
Rome of the future. When Turnus dies as the second Achilles, Aeneas
and duty become historically necessary and are here celebrated as the
Roman heroic model. Individualistic *areté* gives way to imperial destiny.
Aeneas becomes a Roman consul before the post existed. Not surprisingly, the *Aeneid* was an important part of the nineteenth-century curriculum in British schools, ideal for those who would serve the empire.

But duty is cruel to the individual. What matters to him must be
subsumed to the greater idea of empire. The things we remember in
Homer are vivid and immediate scenes. What we mainly remember in
Virgil are elegiac lines that resonate with sadness, the greatest among
many, but essentially untranslatable, being about the "tears at the heart
of things," the word "things" embracing everything (*sunt lachrimae rerum,
et mentem mortalia tangunt*).

Achilles dies at the end of the *Aeneid,* translated by Virgil into Turnus,
a local chieftain like Achilles. Aeneas hesitates at the moment of the
sword thrust. Achilles would have had no such scruple. But then

> He sank his blade in fury in Turnus' chest,
> Then all the body slackened in death's chill,
> And with a groan for that indignity
> His spirit fled into the gloom below.[13]

With that sword thrust, Rome's future is secure, and Virgil expresses
a morality that goes beyond Homer's pursuit of *areté.* Aeneas becomes
not Achilles but Hector and reverses the decision of the *Iliad.* Hector, the
man of family and the City, not only Troy but the idea of the city, lost to
Achilles, the destroyer of cities in the *Iliad.* Now dutiful Achilles / Hector
plunges his sword into Turnus, the second Achilles, and Virgil rewrites
Homer in favor of civilization, though as ever with the qualification of
Virgilian sadness.

Indeed, throughout it is all a very hard thing for Aeneas. Civilization here has its discontents. But when his will wavers before duty, the
Sibyl orders him forward with this stern rebuke: "We squander hours in

weeping" (*Nos flendo ducimus horas*). In other words, as in the military everywhere, "Shape up, and get on with it."[14]

Dante heard the excruciatingly sad music at the heart of the *Aeneid*, sad but never rebellious. Yet Virgil's praise for the Roman Empire of Augustus is undoubtedly sincere, as indeed it should have been. The empire was the greatest political construction his world had seen, and it rose as an idea above what were undoubtedly his mundane experiences at the imperial court. Dante was fully aware of the dark question at the heart of the *Aeneid:* "Was it all worth it?" Indeed, therefore, "Is human history worth it?" Virgil, a noble and tragic Stoic, answers, "It has to be worth it, because that is all there is." Not far off here, are the Stoical *Meditations* of the emperor Marcus Aurelius (A.D. 161–180).

When T. S. Eliot located Virgil in terms of sensibility, he did so exactly as Dante had done: Virgil has "a significant, an exact place, at the end of the pre-Christian and at the beginning of the Christian world. Virgil looks both ways; he makes a liaison between the old world and the new." As a student and professor in Carthage, Augustine, not surprisingly, meditated on Queen Dido of that city as an example of unappeasable longing. Eliot also calls attention to the revolutionary difference in meaning between Virgil and Dante with respect to two words: *lume* (light) and *amor* (love).[15]

In the *Divine Comedy* the displacement of Virgil by Beatrice in Canto XXX of the Purgatorio comes with a sense of inevitability, which is a tribute to the development that has gone before. Virgil will retire with his unfulfilled longings to the pleasant fields of Limbo and to the other great writers and philosophers of the ancient world; they knew no more than Virgil did, if as much. (Dante of course is unaware of the ecstasy of cognition in Socrates and Plato.) Beatrice brings into the poem another kind of human destiny, one that Virgil could not have known because it had not been discovered.

For Dante, Beatrice is the culmination of the European literature of the religion of Love, mysterious in its eleventh-century origins. As C. S. Lewis writes in *The Allegory of Love:* "[The religion of *Amor*] effected a change which has left no corner of our ethics, our imagination, or our daily life untouched, and [the eleventh-century troubadour poets] erected impassable barriers between us and the classical past or the Oriental present. Eros in the ancient world could be merrily pleasant, or coarse, or humorous, or comfortably affectionate. It could veer dangerously toward insanity. What neither the classical world nor the non-Western world imagined was ideal love in the form apparently invented in the small courts of southern France and celebrated by the eleventh century poets writing in Provençal."[16] C. S. Lewis is far from alone in considering this a moral revolution, perhaps even a modification of human nature, comparable to that effected a thousand years earlier by Christianity.

The reasons for this revolution in consciousness during the eleventh century remain mysterious. Scholarly attempts to connect it with Islam, with the adoration of the Virgin, with Platonism, or with the extirpated religion of the Albigenses have largely failed. The religion of *Amor* seems just to have appeared all of a sudden.

The basic plot, as spread by the wandering troubadour poets, is simple enough. The desired lady is inaccessible, perhaps because of her high station in the local castle, perhaps because she has been confined in its tower while her husband is off to a war or on a crusade. To attract her attention and favor, the lover (poet, knight, courtier) perfects his manners (courtesy). He composes delicate and ingenious songs for her, their poetic skill reflecting his admiration, his lovesickness, his melancholy. His goal, his only reward, can be her "favor" (perhaps a smile of recognition, maybe even a handkerchief or garter). Historians have shrewdly said that this love in many ways resembles the feeling of a medieval vassal toward his lord. In the religion of Love, the lover is the lady's servant and even her prisoner. She alone can smile upon him and release him from his prison of longing.

Beginning in the eleventh century, poets produced an extraordinarily rich body of verse based upon this plot. Their metrical forms powerfully influenced the mainstream of the Western lyric, and continue to do so, especially in technical invention. Viewed in that light, the *Divine Comedy* is at once indebted to the classical epic (Virgil), and it is also the greatest of the troubadour love poems. Beatrice, the inaccessible but beloved lady, is in the tallest of all towers, that is, heaven, beyond time. Her liege lord is not off on a crusade, but fully in residence as God. She sends Virgil to the pilgrim Dante as a go-between, and Dante later sings for her his great song, the *Divine Comedy*. The "favor" he wins from her is not a smile or a garter. It is spiritual purification and a vision of God.

It is not surprising that many of Dante's love-poet colleagues appear in the *Divine Comedy*, and of course there is a good deal of astute conversation about poetry. They include Cavalcanti, Pier della Vigna, Brunetto Latini, Bonagiunta, Guinizelli, and Arnaut Daniel. Here we have another poetic competition. Dante claimed to be writing a better epic than Virgil. Now he claims to be writing a greater love poem than all these fine poets. It is clear that Dante wins both contests.

What Beatrice revealed to Dante was, as Santayana says, the "secret of the universe."[17] That is, she revealed that the universe must be such that it could produce a Beatrice, the miraculous young girl Dante much earlier encountered in the streets of Florence. The historical Beatrice Portinari was born in 1266 and died at the age of twenty-five. She was the daughter of a prominent Florentine citizen and married a banker, Simone dei Bardi. In his *La Vita Nuova* (approximately 1294), an elaborate combination of love poetry and prose commentary, Dante describes his emotions when he met her and also their major consequences. Just how historical all of this is we cannot say, but it seems probable that Dante did have a remarkable experience connected with her. According to *La Vita Nuova*, he saw her in the street when she was eight and he nine and was struck by her angelic beauty. He subsequently sees her several times, and though they never speak, his emotions deepen. The divine has passed before him in visible form. Once, because of gossip, Beatrice snubs him and, crushed, he sends her a poem. He falls ill, sees her once more, and hears of her death at twenty-five. Again he is devastated. *La Vita Nuova* ends with a famous pledge, which reads in part as follows: "After writing this sonnet, it was given unto me to behold a very wonderful vision; wherein I saw things which determined me that I would say nothing further of this most blessed one, until such time as I could discourse more worthily concerning her. And to this end I labor all I can; as she well knoweth."[18] In fact, he spent fourteen years amassing the vast knowledge and developing the skills that made the *Divine Comedy* possible. Nevertheless, and while Beatrice was still alive, he married Gemma Donati and had four children. The special and intense emotion central to the religion of Love was not associated with marriage.

The emotions Dante says he experienced in connection with Beatrice may be rare but they are not unique. William James deals with them at length in *Varieties of Religious Experience*. Indeed, pertinent here are several roughly similar experiences we know T. S. Eliot had, one when he was close to the age of Dante as he first glimpsed Beatrice. Spending a boyhood summer with his family at Cape Ann, north of Boston, Eliot, then ten, was exploring rock pools on the shore when, peering down through the water in one of them, he saw a sea anemone for the first time. This was an experience, he remembered with characteristic understatement, "not so simple, for an exceptional child, as it looks."[19] In his essay on Dante originally published in 1930, Eliot includes a section on *La Vita Nuova* in which he offers the informed opinion that the experience Dante claimed to have had at the age of nine very likely occurred even earlier. I suppose we can infer that Eliot himself had had such numinous experiences earlier than the one at the rock pool. In *T. S. Eliot: An Imperfect Life,* Lyndall Gordon shows how such transcendent moments are central to Eliot's poetry, shaping both it and his life. For his poetry, of course, the example of Dante is of enormous importance.

There is one final point to make here about Beatrice in the *Divine Comedy*. She is the unattainable lady of the troubadour religion of Love, but in the vast architecture of the poem she is also, astonishingly, Christ. She does not play the role of intercessor, such as might have been the case with the saints or with Mary. She is not the pilgrim's advocate. She sternly rebukes him and is very severe about his failings. It is she who leads him to God. The theological identity here of Beatrice and Christ is

startling and radical. It must be read as the climax of the searing criticism Dante makes throughout the poem of the institutional church in
his time.

Damnation

The modern reader, as I know from considerable experience with students, is likely to be repelled by Dante's Hell. Yet a bit of reflection can be
clarifying. In a commonsense way, everyone knows that such things as
gluttony, sloth, envy, rage, lust, and so forth can damage one's relation to
the world, even ruin it. Each of these excesses, however, is the distortion
of something that is intrinsically good, as gluttony in connection with
food or drink is a distortion of a decent enjoyment of them. Sloth is a
distortion of relaxation, rage of a justified anger, lust of a decent enjoyment of the body, and so forth.

The souls in Dante's Inferno are not placed there by some external
agency, throwing them into jail against their wills. In fact they go will-
ingly to the location in Hell appropriate for them. They had chosen their
Hell while still alive. Their wills never turned against their choice. Dante
often speaks in his poem of the "sweet world" and gives many examples
of it in his similes. Those in Hell lost this sweet world while they were in it
through the distortions of their actual choices, their defective wills. In
external appearance, while in the world, they might have been handsome or fair, and prosperous and powerful, but internally they had
turned away from the sweet world and also from the highest good. Their
destiny in Hell, as Santayana says, "is just what their passion, if left to
itself, would have chosen. It is what passion stops at, and would gladly
prolong forever."[20] In Hell, to put it another way, they achieve the ideal
form of what they had willed all along without ceasing to will it. Thus the
sullen have "lazy smoke" in their hearts. Farinata, like the Epicurean
poet Lucretius, believed that the soul dies with the body. In Hell he rises
out of his flaming tomb, "upright with breast and countenance, as if he
entertained great scorn of Hell."[21] Although Farinata's heresy has been
disproved by his presence here, he nevertheless still insists on believing it,

even though his soul is alive in Hell. His denial and his aristocratic scorn are memorable.

Dante sees the choice of Hell as tragic. This is especially true of those figures who retain qualities of greatness even in Hell. They have been, though great, undone by a tragic excess that they could not or did not control through a will directed by reality. This is especially true of the three figures I will examine briefly here, Francesca da Rimini, Brunetto Latini, and Ulysses. Each had superb qualities—heroic, intelligent, or sensitive—yet each chose against reason, willed against the sweet world and of course the higher good.

Even if one assents to this account of Dante's Hell, however, their condition in Hell may seem excessively severe. That is because Dante sees each soul from the perspective of what might have been. Viewing them from the great distance of the Paradiso, and through the lens of perfection, Dante the poet—not the pilgrim—sees how far they have fallen and what they have lost. The pilgrim on his journey suffers sometimes with the damned, weeps, even faints, often feels great regret, but the poet who oversees the journey does so from the perspective that can view the world as "the little threshing floor that makes us fierce." The poet Dante, who tells the story, has already been there on that "threshing floor." He has also seen perfection through the eyes of Beatrice. His Hell has depths because his world now has heights; he wants his pilgrim, along with his reader, to see things from those heights.

Very early in the poem, Dante must show that he recognizes that goodness and greatness do exist in the total absence of such heights. After all, he is talking about things unknown to the classical literature and thought that mean so much to him. Thus, in a poem about states of mind, he must deal with his beloved Virgil, as well as with Homer and the other great classical spirits.

Let us return for a moment to Canto IV, where the pilgrim, in the company of Virgil, meets the famous writers of the ancient world. He and Virgil find them just inside the gates of Hell, inhabiting a pleasant green field. There is no pain here but also no exaltation, at least as Dante understands it. The word *honorable* echoes through these passages. It is both commendatory and limiting. They were "honorable," but no more than that. The pilgrim asks Virgil, "who are these who have such honor that it sets them apart from the rest?" The canto continues: "And he said to me: 'Their honorable fame, which resounds in thy life above, gains favor in Heaven which thus advances them.' At that moment I heard a voice: 'Honor the lofty poet! His shade returns which left us.' When the voice had paused and there was silence I saw four great shades coming to us; their looks were neither sad nor joyful."[22]

Meeting there and honoring both the pilgrim and his guide Virgil are Homer, Horace, Ovid, and Lucan. Homer is called "an eagle above the rest." The whole episode is marked by exquisite courtesy. They welcome "Dante" the pilgrim as a "sixth among them." Yet along with their virtues of honor and courtesy, the *Divine Comedy* places and judges them. They are neither sad nor joyful. They and the other ancients have "grave and slow-moving eyes and looks of great authority." They speak "seldom and with gentle voices."[23] Dante, as I have said, does not seem aware of the ecstatic cognition of the platonic tradition. Perhaps he thinks that Augustine has settled that question in his critique of the unaided will. Yet his judgment of his great predecessors here seems to me precise and exquisite. He thinks that in the unaided world, despite all his reverence for its great masters, the new state of mind he most highly values was simply not available. It is something new in culture, known through Christianity to be sure, but coordinately in the new and powerful religion of Love. It will take Dante's pilgrim a long time to achieve this state of mind, but those ancients with their grave eyes and voices will never achieve it.

Francesca da Rimini

In Canto V the pilgrim meets Francesca, one of the most famous and appealing figures in the vast panoply of the *Divine Comedy*. She exists in a very different psychological world from that of the classical authors in Limbo. Dante needs a bravura performance here and delivers it. Francesca and her lover Paolo succumbed to carnal passion and committed adultery; their case was a cause célèbre when Dante wrote his poem. Both were married and had children, and both were murdered by Francesca's outraged husband.

In the overall scheme of the *Divine Comedy*, it is notable how gently Dante deals with illicit love, especially within the context of the religion of Love. Paolo and Francesca are close within the entrance of Hell, are pitiful, but suffer no physical pain. In Dante their warm passion is far better than the icy fate, far below, of the cold of heart, the liars and traitors. In the *Purgatorio*, similarly, the carnal sinners are not so far from the top of the mountain, closer than most to God. Thus the love poets Guido Guinizelli and Arnaut Daniel are far up toward the peak, the restored earthly Paradise. Dante is somewhat gentle with the erotic sensibility, even when it leads to errors.

Francesca's situation here reflects the choice she made during life. She and Paolo are blown and buffeted by winds, "borne on," "driven." Dante thus represents the power of unrestrained passions. Before the winds the lovers are almost helpless, as they were when alive. "Abandon yourself," commented George Santayana, "to a love that is nothing but love, and you are in Hell already."[24] The religion of Love, Dante might have said, can elevate you but also possess you.

Dante develops a beautiful simile involving birds to represent this spiritual condition. We first see the cloud of lovers from a distance: "As in the cold season their wings bear the starlings along in a broad dense flock, so does that blast the wicked spirits. Hither, thither, downward, upward it drives them; no hope ever comforts them, not to say of rest, but of less pain."[25] The simile represents the lovers seen from afar, the lesser along with the greater; but soon the pilgrim is aware of the great lovers: "And as the cranes go chanting their songs, making themselves a long line in the air."[26] Here we see Achilles, Helen, Semiramis, the legendary lascivious queen of Assyria, Dido, who killed herself when abandoned by Aeneas, Cleopatra, Paris, and Tristan.

The first poetic note struck regarding Paolo and Francesca is poignantly elegiac. The pilgrim says to Virgil: "Poet, I would speak with these two who go together and seem so light upon the wind."[27] The pilgrim, the spiritual lover of Beatrice, is strongly drawn to this couple. Now the simile switches from starlings and cranes to doves: "As doves, summoned by desire, come with wings posed and motionless to the sweet nest, borne by their will through the air, so these left the troop where Dido is, coming through the malignant air, such force had my loving call."[28] Only the words "malignant air" remind us that this is Hell. Otherwise the lines are sweet, lyrical, courtly.

When we first hear Francesca, Dante provides her with poetry of a special tenderness. She tells the pilgrim that she was born in Ravenna, "where the Po, with streams that join it, comes down to rest."[29] This is a beautiful line, but ends with "rest," which she now must desire but cannot experience. In what follows that word, Francesca tells the pilgrim in a very few lines why she cannot rest. The word *love* (*amor*) echoes through the passage. As she explains it, her love was not a coarse passion but one steeped in delicacy and sentiment. Yet intermixed there are sinister notes. This passion "seized" her with such power that "it does not leave me yet." Paolo was himself seized by such passion for her fair body. When at Dante's request Francesca tells the story of her seduction, the short passage is one of the greatest in literature:

> There is no greater pain than to recall the happy time in misery, and this thy teacher knows; but if thou hast so great desire to know our love's first root, I shall tell as one may that weeps in telling. We read one day of Lancelot, how love constrained him. We were alone, and had no misgiving. Many times that reading drew our eyes together and changed colour in our faces, but one point alone it was that mastered us. When we read that the longed-for smile was kissed by so great a lover, he who never shall be parted from me, all trembling, kissed my mouth. A Galeotto was the book and he that wrote it; that day we read no further.[30]

The famous line "that day we read no further," as already noted, very likely echoes Augustine's line in the *Confessions* after he reads the decisive passage in Paul that led him to abandon concupiscence: "No further wished I to read."[31]

For Paolo and Francesca, the book—and they have read it only in part—helps turn them decisively away from God. In Augustine, as we have just seen, the effect of an Epistle of Paul is precisely the opposite. Dante is concerned here with the effect of books both good and bad, and he is certain that literature does have an effect on both character and morals, though he surely knows that literature has many other aspects. The debate about this goes on through Cervantes and is particularly intense in our own debates about fictional obscenity and violence.

As Francesca tells her story, and Paolo weeps nearby (does "Paul" weep for them?), the pilgrim Dante falls unconscious; he, after all, has been the author of *La Vita Nuova* and a devotee of the religion of *Amor* and sees its dangers in Francesca. Her story literally "knocks him out."

The fundamental emotion in Canto V is one of deep sympathy and elegiac pity for the vicissitudes of eros, but there is also judgment. Francesca throughout is defensive but defiant. She thinks that, swept by emotion, she could have done no other, that their passion blew them away like their present winds. She thinks that her husband, who killed both of them with his sabre, belongs in the deeper Hell of Cain, among the violent against kinsmen.

Still, the judgment here against her is strong. Passion unrestrained by reason becomes a demon, driving those possessed by it restlessly on. To spend eternity in the arms of a lover, or even weeks, cannot be bliss. As is evident in her own account, Francesca's will never rejected the choice she made, and her punishment is self-punishment.

When she says that the book they were reading was a "Galeotto," she is referring to a widely read French romance, *Lancelot of the Lake,* in which one Galehault (Galeotto) acts as a go-between for Lancelot and Queen Guinevere, the wife of King Arthur. If, instead of reading no more that day, they had in fact read further, they would have found that the adultery of Lancelot and Guinevere and the incest of Arthur wrecked Arthur's court and that Arthur and his son Mordred killed each other. In Francesca's life, according to Boccaccio, the affair with the married Paolo continued, her husband found out, surprised them, and killed both. Sexual anarchy leads to disaster. The pilgrim Dante may faint with sympathy, may have shared emotions like those she describes, but the poet's judgment is unyielding.

Brunetto Latini

In this portrait of Dante's revered and beloved mentor Brunetto Latini, we have another divided response to a figure whose apparent greatness is distorted by inner torment. The pilgrim experiences the tragedy, while the poet expresses the inevitable judgment.

Paolo and Francesca were among the incontinent and passionate. Much farther down in Hell, in Canto XV, the pilgrim and Virgil meet the violent against God, nature, and art. Standing on a bank with Virgil, the pilgrim Dante sees a "troop of souls" approaching. They are naked, scorched, and must keep moving to avoid a rain of fire. The ground on which they move is hot sand. In a celebrated simile, Dante writes that "each looked at us as men look at one another under a new moon at dusk, and they puckered their brows at us like an old tailor on the eye of his needle."[32] As these souls move along in haste below, one of them catches the pilgrim Dante by the hem of his garment and exclaims, "How marvellous!" The pilgrim's response registers his surprise at seeing this man here: "Are you père Ser Brunetto?"[33]

During his life, Brunetto Latini had been a dignified public man in Florence, a special mentor to Dante and a famous author, chief among whose works was an encyclopaedia in French entitled the *Treasure*. For the pilgrim to meet Ser Brunetto here, naked, stepping quickly on this hot sand, is the equivalent of seeing a respectable citizen lurching out of a bawdy house. Again the theme returns: in the Inferno, the inner reality of an individual can be very different from the outward appearance during life. That Brunetto Latini is here as a homosexual can scarcely be in doubt. Although the term is not mentioned in the canto, neither was the specific flaw mentioned in the episodes of Francesca or Ulysses. Yet everything in Brunetto's portrait conduces to that conclusion. Although it has never been questioned until recently, commentary has always assumed homosexuality to be the issue here, and in their new Oxford edition of the Inferno, Ronald Martinez and Robert M. Durling appear to have settled the matter.[34]

Here, as usual, Dante concretizes Brunetto's inner condition, the goal toward which his will has turned and never turned back. The hot sands are infertile and express the torment of childlessness. The showers of fiery rain express the burning of sterile lust. The restless motion of the tormented souls suggests the restless unfulfillment of their sexuality. As the pilgrim Dante and Brunetto move along conversing—Brunetto must keep moving—the pilgrim is torn between affection and reverence for his mentor and his pity over his condition and the inner truth it represents. His words to Brunetto reflect these conflicting emotions: "In my memory is fixed, and now goes to my heart, the dear and kind paternal image of you when many a time in the world you taught me how man makes himself immortal."[35] The ironies here are multiple and searing. Brunetto seemed "paternal." He could never have been a father. He taught Dante how man makes himself immortal, presumably through his instruction in literature and philosophy. But Brunetto could never become immortal through offspring since he was homosexual. The title of Brunetto's most notable works, the *Treasure,* a kind of encyclopedia, and also the *Little Treasure,* an allegorical journey in Italian verse, which may have suggested Dante's poem, taken together may have taught Dante how to "make himself immortal." Still, Brunetto's memory will live, not through children and not through such dignified literary work, which will be forgotten, but through the *Divine Comedy,* in which his former pupil immortalizes him in this painful revelation of his inner reality. And still one more irony. The inspiring teacher, Brunetto Latini, foresees future greatness for the pilgrim Dante, but his own work will be a footnote.

Adding to this tragic portrait is Brunetto's self-loathing, his disgust at being seen in this company: "And he said to me: 'Of some it is well to know; of the rest I would be more creditable to be silent. . . . Know in a word that they were all clerks and great and famous scholars, defiled in the world by one and the same sin. Priscian goes on with that wretched crowd, and Francesco d'Accorso, and if thou hast a craving for such scurf, him thou mightest see there that was translated by the Servant of the Servants from the Arno to the Bacchiaglione, where he left his sin-stained nerves.' "³⁶ This refers to a bishop of scandalous life, an ally of Dante's detested Pope Boniface VIII.

The canto ends with one of Dante's magnificent poetic moments, perfectly expressing the pilgrim's divided feelings about Brunetto as both an apparent winner and an actual loser. Dante's simile here draws upon an annual footrace held at Verona, in which the victor received a roll of green cloth. He sees Ser Brunetto move quickly along the hot sand with the others: "Then he turned about and seemed like one of those that run for the green cloth in the field at Verona, and he seemed not the loser among them but the winner."³⁷ The repetition of the word "seemed" here is powerful. During his life in the world, Brunetto "seemed" a winner, but in truth he was a loser. The green cloth that was the prize contrasts with the hot sand on which Brunetto moves and its greenness may suggest fertility. He did not really run in the "field at Verona" but, in his inner life, ran on these baking sands.

Ulysses

Ulysses (Odysseus) is one of the most famous characters in literature. In depicting him, Virgil competed with Homer, and in Canto XXVI Dante competes with both, though primarily with Virgil. When Dante met the great writers of the ancient world in the Limbo in Canto IV, he was a "sixth among them," but he clearly associated himself with Homer and Virgil as an epic poet. When he created his own portrait of Ulysses, he had many things in mind, among them a challenge for poetic primacy. Ulysses is the only major Homeric figure to speak in the *Divine Comedy*, and Dante has him tell his story at greater length than any other figure in the poem.

For Homer and the Greek tradition, Ulysses was a great hero, not only a formidable warrior but a clever one, a "man of many devices." He demonstrates his tactical agility many times in the *Odyssey*. Virgil's view of Ulysses is entirely negative. He is the deceitful Greek who at night stole the statue of Pallas Athena from Troy—she was the tutelary goddess of the city—and then devised the stratagem of the Trojan horse that led to the city's destruction. Of course the destruction of Troy was necessary if Aeneas was to found Rome, but for Virgil, poet of the Civilized City, that in no way excused Ulysses or ennobled his behavior.

In all of this, Dante follows Virgil, but he is also powerfully drawn to the adventurous side of Ulysses, depicts in him the virtues he admires, and makes him heroic whereas in Virgil he is not (and certainly he is not in Shakespeare's *Troilus and Cressida*). Here, as in his treatment of Francesca and Brunetto, a powerfully sympathetic portrait coexists with stern judgment.

When the pilgrim Dante and Virgil come upon Ulysses in Hell, they find him inside a double flame, the lesser half of which contains his fellow conspirator Diomed. The flame externalizes the fiery spirit within them, though Ulysses' flame is the larger, suggesting greater energy, intellect, daring, but also destructiveness, as in the final fire that consumed Troy. The tongue of the flame also suggests Ulysses' eloquence, soon to be exhibited here, which can be spectacularly fatal.

As Dante reconceives the story, Ulysses did not return home to Ithaca and his family but left Circe's island with a remnant of his crew and sailed westward to the Pillars of Hercules, or the Straits of Gibraltar. According to legend, Hercules had split one mountain in half, creating two mountains facing one another at the straits. Ulysses sailed through them and out into the Atlantic Ocean, turned southward, passed the equator, and in five months reached the southern Pacific, where, in view of the tallest mountain he had ever seen, his ship was overwhelmed by a storm and sank, killing everyone aboard.

Traditionally, the Pillars of Hercules represented the limit of the known world. The Southern Hemisphere was thought to be merely a vast ocean without land. Yet in Dante's day a few explorers ventured into the Atlantic, notable among them the Vivaldi brothers in 1291. They sailed into the Atlantic and were lost. Thus it is possible to see in Dante's treatment of Ulysses a tension between the traditional sense of limits and a new impulse toward testing those limits through an always risky exploration. Yet Dante himself, in his practice as a poet, is an adventurer, an explorer, venturing where no poet has gone. Like his Ulysses, he is avid for knowledge. He often compares his poem to a journey by sea. Yet he is unlike Ulysses in that he knows where he is going and in his complete confidence as a navigator. Given Dante's complex relationship to his Ulysses, it is not surprising that the pilgrim "bends toward [the flame] with desire" to hear Ulysses' story from within it.

The structure of Canto XXVI is unique in that so much of it is given to Ulysses' speech about his final voyage. In fact, it is a sort of mini-epic, Dante competing with Virgil; yet it is short enough and good enough for quotation here. Ulysses' account is "flung forth" proudly from the flame, and he proceeds as if no one would dare interrupt him.

> When I parted from Circe, who held me more than a year near Gaeta before Aeneas so named it, not fondness for a son, nor duty to an aged father, nor the love I owed Penelope which should have gladdened her, could conquer within me the passion I had to gain experience of the world and of the vices and worth of men; and I put forth on the ocean deep with but one ship and with that little company which had not deserted me. The one shore and the other I saw as far as Spain, as far as Morocco, and Sardinia and the other islands which that sea bathes round. I and my companions were old and slow when we came to that narrow outlet where Hercules set up his landmarks so that men should not pass beyond. On my right hand I left Seville, on the other had already left Ceuta. "O brothers," I said, "who through a hundred thousand perils have reached the west, to this so brief vigil of the senses that remains to us choose not to deny experience, in the sun's track, of the unpeopled world. Take thought of the seed from which you spring. You were not born to live as brutes, but to follow virtue and knowledge." My companions I made so eager for the road with these brief words that then I could hardly have held them back, and with our poop turned to the morning we made of the oars wings for the mad flight, always gaining on the left. Night then saw all the stars of the other pole and ours so low that it did not rise from the ocean floor. Five times the light had been rekindled and as often quenched on the moon's underside since we had entered on the deep passage, when there appeared to us a mountain, dim by distance, and

it seemed to me of such a height as I had never seen before. We were filled with gladness, and so it turned to lamentation, for from the new land a storm rose and struck the forepart of the ship. Three times it whirled her round with all the waters, the fourth time lifted the poop aloft and plunged the prow below, as One willed, until the sea closed over us.[38]

"No one of his age was more deeply moved than Dante by the passion to know all that is knowable," said Benedetto Croce, "and nowhere else has he given such noble expression to that passion to know all that is knowable as in the great figure of Ulysses."[39] That is true, but it is only part of the truth. Ulysses himself knew that part: "Choose not to deny experience. . . . You were not born to live as brutes, but to follow virtue and knowledge."[40] In a passage Dante almost certainly knew, Cicero had said the same thing: "So great is our innate love of learning and of knowledge that no one can doubt that man's nature is strongly attracted to these things even without the lure of any profit."[41]

Yet Ulysses himself has second thoughts. In retrospect, he judges his voyage as a "mad flight" (*al folle volo*, line 125), and says that the ship went down "as One willed," or "as it pleased another" (*com'altrui piacque*).[42] Ulysses sees that something beyond himself and the practical disaster was wrong with his passion, despite the eloquence of his "brief words" to his crew.

There is indeed a good deal of self-condemnation implicit in his account itself: "Not fondness for a son nor duty to an aged father, not the love I owed Penelope which should have gladdened her, could conquer within me the passion I had to gain experience of the world and of the vices and virtues of men."[43] He has sacrificed some high values and strong human ties to his project, and the implication is present that he would sacrifice anything. There is irony in his desire to experience "the vices and virtues" of men. He has his own virtues, but he certainly has experienced his own vices. He has even thrust all prudence aside. Unlike Aeneas, who sailed with a fleet of ships to Italy, Ulysses has been reduced to one ship and most of his men have abandoned him. We need not think his ship small and vulnerable; it has many oarsmen and is seaworthy. But the risks were huge, sailing alone into the unknown.

Most commentators agree that Ulysses is in Hell because of his "crimes," as Virgil calls them, in connection with Troy. That is certainly part of it, but Ulysses is surely self-condemned here because he was a "false counsellor" with his "brief words" to his men, who then would not be restrained from going.

Of course, when he sees the mountain of Purgatory in the distance, he—as a man of the ancient world—fails to recognize it. Quite possibly Dante suggests by this that moral knowledge is more important than, though it does not exclude, other kinds of knowledge, such as exploration.

Dante's lines about the ship sinking have a beautiful cadence, "stern aloft . . . prow . . . down."[44] These lines echo a famous passage in Virgil's *Aeneid:* "A mighty toppling wave strikes astern. The helmsman is dashed out and hurled head foremost, but the ship is thrice upon the same spot whirled round by the wave and engulfed in the sea's devouring eddy" (book I, 14–17). Virgil, in eternity, must wonder whether the poet Dante has improved upon the *Aeneid.*

Dante's God

At the end of the *Divine Comedy* the pilgrim Dante, who now knows almost all of what Virgil can teach him—in the course of the journey the pilgrim and the poet draw closer together in wisdom—is rewarded by knowledge of God, the primal power that moves the stars and that made the universe. Dante, the greatest of the troubadour poets, must be rewarded by his lady in the tower for his love song to her with the ultimate favor, a vision of the ultimate truth that lies beyond the created universe.

The representation of God, who by definition is beyond the time-space continuum, is by definition an almost insoluble artistic problem. The Olympian gods in Homer did not present this problem because they had human form and live on Olympus. But representation has at its disposal only things we know from experience, that is, within the time-space continuum. Therefore the God who is beyond it can be represented in words or in art only by analogy. We concede the representation, understanding it to be an "as if." But there has been a competition among representations. In the Hebrew Bible, God speaks but remains concealed in such things as a cloud of smoke, a burning bush, a whirlwind, a pillar of fire, or mysterious representatives. In the New Testament Jesus is clearly human, has a birthplace and a known tomb. It is only through his words, acts, and what happens to him that the inference of divinity is made. In book 3 of *Paradise Lost*, Milton daringly brings God into his poem as a king on his throne surrounded by angelic courtiers, a king known mostly through his words. Milton's representation is similar to the representation of God by Michelangelo and other Renaissance painters. But most readers have considered it less satisfactory in epic poetry. Lyric poets have often indicated the presence of God through an experience of Light, but that is not sufficient for extended narrative. In his one-hundredth canto Dante offers his own representation in what must be the severest of all challenges to the art of epic poetry. Dante must deliver a representation of the God who was there before the beginning, what theologians call the premise of existence or the ground of Being—or, in grammatical representation, "the subject, of which everything else is predicate."

As the pilgrim Dante approaches the ever-brighter vision he thinks that all similes will fall short of expressing the steady increments of brightness, but the poet Dante's abilities prove equal to the task. The pilgrim stares into the light as long as he can and then begins by using the language of the geometer and the philosopher to express what he sees. Pythagoras, Euclid, Plato, and Aristotle are helping here. Then he uses the metaphor of a book: "In its depths I saw that it contained, bound in one volume, the scattered leaves of all the universe."[45] All commentary of which I am aware identifies this as "the book of nature," the wonder of which speaks to us of God. This was a familiar figure of speech. I suggest, however, that this book is also the *Divine Comedy* itself, a vast poem, indeed, but exhibiting a divine coherence and power to illuminate, a poem that knows everything and as a "book" is analogous to the universe. There is evidence in the poem that Dante believes it to be equal in revelatory power to scripture. It is an epic of universal grasp. Dante thinks that this poem is the "book" of the universe.

To express his sense of wonder, the poet, in a splendid piece of audacity, evokes the story of Jason and the Argonauts sailing in their quest for the Golden Fleece in the thirteenth century B.C., supposedly the first sea voyage, and which shocks the sea god Neptune when he sees the ship passing overhead: "A single moment makes for me greater oblivion than five and twenty centuries upon the enterprise that made Neptune wonder at the shadow of the Argo."[46] Even at his climactic moment of vision Dante thus does not lose his hold upon the classical world. He reaches back and then upward. Of course words are going to fail him ultimately: "Now my speech will come more short even of what I remember than an infant's who yet bathes his tongue at the breast."[47] Dante's Italian here actually imitates baby talk. Then he communicates insofar as words are able to tell what he saw. Dante believes that this is as close as it is possible to come to the vision Paul experiences on the road to Damascus and refused to describe. The point of this infant simile may be that "unless you be as children, you shall not enter into the kingdom of heaven."

> In the profound clear ground of the lofty light appeared to me three circles of three colors and of the same extent and the one seemed reflected by the other as rainbow by rainbow, and the third seemed fire breathed forth equally from the one and the other. . . . That circling which, thus begotten, appeared in thee as reflected light, when my eyes dwelt on it for a time, seemed to me, within it and in its own colour, painted with our likeness, for which my sight was wholly given to it. Like the geometer who sets all his mind to the squaring of the circle and for all his thinking does not discover the principle he needs, such was I at that strange sight. . . . Here power failed the high phantasy, but now my desire and will, like a wheel that spins with even motion, were revolved by the Love that moves the sun and the other stars.[48]

The term translated here as "phantasy," *fantasia*, means "the power by which the intellect represents what it sees." Thus the representation here is not a picture of the Godhead itself, but a representation, as close as Dante can come, to what he sees. His power "failed" because God, outside of time, is also beyond words.

As might be imagined, the commentary on this final vision is enormous, and recent scholarship has done much to trace it to medieval philosophy, which itself has roots in Aristotle and later Greeks. But even without such detailed scholarship, one is struck by the presence of philosophy and geometry here in Dante's long and complex metaphor. As it was written over the entrance to Plato's Academy, "Let no one ignorant of geometry enter here." The human face that somehow is infused into the circles represents the mystery of the Incarnation, and Dante cannot penetrate the mystery any more than he can square the circle. Yet the great circular spheres of the universe move, and Dante's desire and will move like two wheels that spin with even motion because of the impulses of Love from the Prime Mover of philosophy. In Dante's vision the geometers of Athens and the Incarnational teaching of Jerusalem are fused.

Mark Van Doren in his essay on the *Divine Comedy* notices that in Dante's three-line terza rima stanzas, beginning with "Within its depth I saw ingathered," each "tercet . . . is itself a folded rose, a periodic sentence of the fullest and deepest rapture."[49]

Paul would have understood Dante's fusion here of the Greek Logos with the human face, the mystery of the Incarnation. He had conceptualized the relationship of Jesus to God in exactly the same way, as did John in his first chapter. What Paul would have made of Dante's Beatrice I am not prepared to say.

About this final version in the *Divine Comedy* T. S. Eliot has written: "One can feel only awe at the power of the master who could thus at every moment realize the inapprehensible in visual images. And I do not know anywhere in poetry more authentic sign of greatness than the power of association in the last line [of the passage he is quoting], when the poet is speaking of the Divine vision, yet introduces the Argo passing over the wondering head of Neptune."[50]

That Dante's poem, taken in a large way, expresses a permanent human possibility cannot be doubted. Our sense of the noble and heroic has one source in Homer's world and poetry, but it is not confined to Homer's epics. The quest for spiritual perfection is a permanent part of the human experience, made so in the West by the Bible, Socrates and Plato, Augustine, the Provençal love poets, Dante, and many others. Shakespeare's plays can be read as a single long poem expressive of damnation, purgation, and, in the late comedies, salvation. T. S. Eliot, in his own sequence of poems, recreated the Dantean pattern in modern terms.

What remains a permanent possibility can never, by definition, be superseded. Eliot paid particular attention to that evocation of Jason, the Argonauts, and the god Neptune in the midst of Dante's divine vision but did not offer to explain why. Dante placed it there as part of his own refusal to let go of the past. In many of his similes, Dante himself is a voyager, like the first voyager Jason. Homer voyaged with Odysseus, Virgil with Aeneas, and Dante has a sense of all of them as his ancestors. In his great essay on Virgil, with which Dante would have agreed emphatically, Eliot made a large point: "We are all, so far as we inherit the civilization of Europe, citizens of the Roman Empire."[51]

CHAPTER EIGHT

Hamlet's Great Song

The Cambridge scholar E. M. W. Tillyard made an excellent point when he argued that William Shakespeare wrote the finest English epic poem, but that he did so in a sequence of five-act history plays rather than in the epic form familiar since Homer. Shakespeare, that is, brought the mind and energy of the English Renaissance to the Elizabethan stage, and his epic, which we could call the *Henriad*, consists of *Richard II, Henry IV* parts 1 and 2, and *Henry V.* The final play in the cycle actually begins with an invocation to the Muse in the epic manner: "O for a Muse of fire, that would ascend / The brightest heavens of invention."[1]

Yet out of everything Shakespeare wrote from first to last, if one had to choose a single work that is indispensable, that work would be *Hamlet.* Every great tragic actor beginning with Richard Burbage has wanted to play the prince, regarding that part as the pinnacle of theatrical aspiration. In their power and variety his important speeches may be compared to demanding arias. They are eloquent, memorable, testing the skills the actor can bring to the part. We listen to Prince Hamlet and as we do so what he says becomes the core of the play. It is his voice, not his deeds, that dominates the stage; his deeds, in comparison, seem erratic and questionable. Hamlet is a prince of words, rather than the real prince of Denmark. The great loss, the terror, we feel at the end of the play comes from the realization that his voice, that great song, is now stilled and that nothing like it will be heard again. Hamlet also knows this and says so as he dies: "The rest is silence." Not a hero of action, he says near the end that "the readiness is all." Yet it is not "all," and he waits passively on events. Finally he is borne "like" a soldier from the stage. He is no soldier, like his rough-hewn heroic father, and he is no soldier like the peremptory Norwegian Fortinbras.

Hamlet has been performed more often and had more written about it than any other play in the history of the theater. Almost every major critic in most of the European languages has felt the attraction of this play and the need to test himself on it, but with startlingly varied results. Goethe and Coleridge did not agree, and neither agreed with Samuel Johnson; Hazlitt and Swinburne viewed the play very differently, and none of them would have agreed with the drastic reservations of Matthew Arnold and T. S. Eliot, or with the Freudian interpretation proposed by Ernest Jones and brought forward in the strong 1948 Laurence Olivier film. No such wide differences of opinion exist regarding such other great tragedies as *Othello, King Lear, Macbeth,* or Sophocles' *Oedipus Rex.*

The opening moments of *Hamlet,* suffused with dubiety and dread, constitute a kind of masterly poem introducing the whole work. Here Shakespeare demonstrates how humble English words can be charged with a widening suggestiveness that provides the opening chords of the music that suffuses the whole. That Mel Gibson dropped this prologue from his film production was a startling miscalculation. When the play opens, two sentries, Bernardo and Francisco, are on the stage, but it is midnight and the battlements of the castle are murky. They cannot see each other, but perhaps Bernardo has glimpsed or sensed Francisco, whom he in fact is arriving on time to relieve. He shouts, "Who's there?"

At that point, we do not know that Bernardo is aware of the Ghost and thinks Francisco might be the apparition. Yet we sense the anxiety, even dread, in his two syllables. We do not know that the Ghost has already appeared twice, but silently. Seldom if ever have two ordinary words been charged with so much potential poetic meaning, setting in motion the dubiety and dread that pervade the entire play.

Francisco, the sentry who has been on duty, relieves the tension with ordinary military language: "Nay, answer me; stand and unfold your-self."[2] The world of common sense returns with the practical command. Perhaps Francisco lowers his pike. His action cuts through the dread, a polarity that reappears in the play all the way to the end and the appearance of young Fortinbras to calm the fury and order the chaos.

With grim irony, in view of the subject of the play, Bernardo replies with a satisfactory answer: "Long live the King." This is a fine touch of black humor. Now he knows he is not in the presence of the Ghost, and commonsense reality can return, though not for long.

At this point, we have heard only the first three lines of the play, and in the simplest language, yet a powerful poetic dynamic has been set in motion. To that opening question from Bernardo, "Who's there?" the rest of the play gives an extended answer, but the short answer would be "Everything," utterly evil depths and the glimpsed spiritual heights of the entire cosmos, from the darkest sin to the flights of angels. To all of this the Ghost will open wide the door. Mark Van Doren once remarked in class that the most important thing about this play is that it begins with a ghost. I take it that in this vatic remark he was referring to the entire opening scene, which in its opening presumes the Ghost's proximity and sounds the syllables of dread, setting the sinister tone of the entire play. "Who's there?" is an opening chord with many tonal variations. Outside the wall of the castle is menacing international warfare, while inside are the horrors the Ghost will begin to disclose: fratricide, regicide, usurpation, Machiavellian realpolitik, lust, incest, murderous plots, bottomless lies. Return to those first three lines:

BERNARDO: Who's there?
FRANCISCO: Nay, answer me; stand and unfold yourself.
BERNARDO: Long live the King!

The two men are, for a moment, reestablishing order. Shakespeare must have enjoyed that "Long live the King." It is not so conventional a phrase when one king has been murdered by his brother, who, in turn a king, will soon die as a result of his own plots. The Ghost will shortly appear to demand the execution of the regicide usurper by Prince Hamlet. The two sentries keep struggling to maintain the stability of their world.

> BERNARDO: Long live the King!
> FRANCISCO: Bernardo?
> BERNARDO: He.
> FRANCISCO: You come most carefully upon your hour.
> BERNARDO: 'Tis now struck twelve; get thee to bed, Francisco.
> FRANCISCO: For this relief much thanks; 'tis bitter cold, and I am sick at heart.

It is midnight indeed in Elsinore, and the darkness much more than physical. " 'Tis bitter cold, and I am sick at heart." On that dark note the great poem gets underway.

When the Ghost does appear and discloses to Hamlet the fact of the murder, demanding the execution of the murderer, now revealed as King Claudius, he also lays on him a charge that contains a very steep condition:

> But howsomever thou pursuest this act
> Taint not thy mind, nor let thy soul contrive
> Against thy mother aught. Leave her to heaven.[3]

Hamlet cannot yet be sure that this really is the Ghost of his father. It might be a deceiving spirit from hell. But what the Ghost charges here is later confirmed by Claudius's behavior in the play-within-the-play scene, and both Hamlet and we judge the Ghost to be authentic. But, importantly, the Ghost now is much more than the old king, the Achilles-like warrior who slaughtered the king of Norway with a weighted axe. The Ghost, evidently in purgatory, knows the Christian truth that even justified killing must be accomplished without "tainting" the interior life with anger, blood lust, and other stains. In other words, the Ghost now supplements the heroic demand for justice and revenge with the interior command of the Sermon on the Mount. This is surely one of the contradictions that tear at the heart of the prince, indeed perhaps the most powerful one.[4]

Yet Prince Hamlet, a highly educated university student at Wittenberg, also responds to the powerful intellectual currents of the sixteenth century and is pulled by them in many directions. Chaucer's Knight and Shakespeare's King Henry V were not aware of the towering aspirations of Pico della Mirandola in *On the Dignity of Man*, nor had they read Donne on suicide, or immersed themselves in Montaigne's skeptical aspect, or taken the humanist program in the classics at Wittenberg, or read Castiglione's *The Courtier*. Prince Hamlet had absorbed all of this and much more and had turned his mind toward intellectual possibility. That he could give such possibility immortal expression is a measure of how deeply it had affected him. A few examples here will have to suffice.

Throughout the play, Hamlet is a Christian: "Angels and ministers of grace defend us."[5] He knows that "There are more things in heaven and earth, Horatio,/Than are dreamt of in your philosophy."[6] Horatio, more an antique Roman than a Dane, is committed to the humanist program and is probably, at least superficially, a Senecan Stoic. Hamlet knows that there is "more." Yet he is a thorough classicist too, and in his first great soliloquy, in which he considers suicide, he uses his classics skillfully in referring to Hyperion (Apollo), Hercules, and Niobe.[7] His meditation on the possibility of suicide reflects a subject of common intellectual discussion in the late sixteenth century. "O that this too too solid flesh would melt,/Thaw and resolve itself into a dew!"[8] But "the Everlasting" has forbidden it. Still he returns to the subject, even while aware of the Ghost's evidence of an afterlife. He considers the nightmares that may await the suicide:

> For in that sleep of death what dreams may come
> When we have shuffled off this mortal coil
> Must give us pause.[9]

Hamlet shares the Jacobean sense that something is deeply wrong with the age: "The time is out of joint. O cursed spite,/That ever I was born to set it right."[10] Many have compared such sentiments with Donne's great *First Anniversary* (1611):

'Tis all in piece, all coherence gone,
All just supply, and all Relation.
Prince, Subject, Father, Sonne, are things forgot[11]

It is critical in Donne's poem, contributing strongly to this sense of foundations shaken, that the emerging science, especially astronomy, called into question the older model of the solar system. As Donne says in *The First Anniversary*, his "anatomy of the world," the new science "casts all in doubt." Mel Gibson in his production of the play had the happy inspiration of attributing to Hamlet a small scientific laboratory in the castle. Donne's sense of a world "out of joint" and in decay certainly applies to Hamlet's Elsinore.

Hamlet responds, also, to the idealism of such writers as Pico della Mirandola: "What a piece of work is man! How noble in reason! How infinite in faculties! In form and moving how express and admirable! In action how like an angel! In apprehension how like a god! The beauty of the world, the paragon of animals." But from that height he can drop immediately into a kind of nihilism: "Yet to me what is this quintessence of dust?"[12]

These intense polarities appear again and again in the prince. When he suddenly becomes aware of Polonius listening behind the arras in the scene that takes place in the queen's bedchamber, he quickly runs him through and kills him, supposing him to be the king. His tenderness comes to the fore: "Thou wretched, rash, intruding fool, farewell! / I took thee for thy better."[13] Yet a short time later: "I'll lug the guts into the neighbor room."[14] His sense of mortality, of its very carnality, as in the graveyard scene, can be obliterating: "That skull had a tongue in it and could sing once."[15] But when he learns the identity of a skull: "Alas, poor Yorick! I knew him, Horatio, a fellow of infinite jest. . . . Now get you to my lady's chamber, and tell her, let her paint an inch thick, to this favor she must come."[16] Hamlet is also well aware of the skepticism of Montaigne, especially of *The Apology for Raymond Sebond*, which was newly available to Shakespeare in the John Florio translation (1603). All of this tugs Hamlet away from the heroic ideal of justice urged by the Ghost, and also the ideal interiority of Christianity—"taint not thy mind"— urged by the Ghost, as well as away from the idealism of Pico della Mirandola and the ideal of the noble courtier as defined by Castiglione. To Ophelia, Hamlet was

> The courtier's, soldier's, scholar's, eye, tongue, sword;
> Th' expectancy and rose of the fair state,
> The glass of fashion and the mould of form . . .
> Now see that noble and most sovereign reason,
> Like sweet bells jangled, out of tune and harsh.[17]

In Prince Hamlet, Shakespeare clearly decided to express a wide range of poetic possibilities and make him the epitome of his age. The remarkable thing is that the prince does not become an anthology of great passages but remains a credible human being and even a credible genius. At times Hamlet reminds us to some degree of his heroic warrior father, and behind old King Hamlet there stands the ancient heroic tradition reaching back to Achilles, the killing machine who avenged Patroclus. Hamlet stays in practice as a swordsman. Yet Hamlet's skill with a rapier represents a civilized modification of his father's weighted battle axe, and Hamlet also belongs to the newer and more civilized world of Paris, with its falconry, tennis, and manners, and Wittenberg with its great university. Hamlet in Denmark, as Paul Cantor has written, stands geographically halfway between Norway and Christian civilized Europe: "To the north stands Norway, a yet untamed world of 'lawless resolutes.' Associated with the struggle of the elder Hamlet and the elder Fortinbras, Norway conjures up images of single-combat between martial heroes. It is presented in the play as a kind of Homeric realm surviving on the frontiers of modern civilization. . . . To the south of Denmark lies the heart of modern Europe, cultivated cities like Paris"[18] and Wittenberg.

An enormous amount has been written about the Renaissance and there is no intention here to attempt to summarize it. Something that could reasonably be called a Renaissance occurred in different places and at different times and involved new economic and social patterns, changes in architecture, painting, sculpture, philosophy, literature, and the decorative arts. In 1552 Rabelais epitomized this sense of the new: "Pantagruel jumped to his feet and took a look about him. 'Can you hear anything, comrades?' he asked. 'I seem to hear people talking in the air. But I can't see anything. Listen, listen . . . ' So as to miss nothing, some of us cupped the palms of our hands to the backs of our ears. The more keenly we listened, the more keenly we made out voices, until in the end we made out whole words."[19]

Of all the new developments in the Renaissance I would like to stress one in particular as it bears on Hamlet. This was the sense that the world could be viewed in profoundly different ways. Even though the Christian interpretation of the universe remained firmly in place, and indeed backed up by the law, for Shakespeare and his contemporaries other strong views existed and competed. They knew, for example, that Machiavelli had posited a universe without God and a "scientific" politics to match it. They admired Seneca's plays, and his Stoicism was much in the air. Luther, Calvin, and others had urged variant forms of Christianity. Montaigne's essays taught, to considerable effect, the ultimate reality in this world of natural process and change. Older conceptions of aristocratic honor were influential but were challenged by Shakespeare (in, for example, Falstaff) and Cervantes. Sheer will-to-power was an option, as in Marlowe, and bottomless nihilism, as in Shakespeare's Edmund. King Claudius is a thoroughgoing operational Machiavellian, although he does pray and does believe in God.

It seems plausible to argue that this newly expanded sense of alternative possibilities goes far to explain the emergence of such theater as that of Shakespeare. Shakespeare was intensely interested in experimenting with new ways of viewing the world and in seeing how they worked out in action. When he is writing at the top of his form, his characters have the quality of having existed before the play because Shakespeare had the ability to give them distinctive and memorable voices. He no doubt was an acute listener to the variety of voices and opinions in his great cosmopolitan city of London.

We can hear the voices of Shakespeare's characters, but no one has heard the voice of Shakespeare himself. Ben Jonson, his friend, called him "gentle Will," which may tell us a great deal about him. It is my opinion, however, and that of many others, that we can sense, if not quite hear, an overall Shakespearean voice or music. That voice, half-heard but growing more distinct in the late comedies, does communicate a moral ideal when the hellish storms that literally and figuratively accompany most of the major tragedies, and reach their climax on Lear's heath, finally have passed.[20]

As *Hamlet* reaches its conclusion, Hamlet's behavior has fulfilled neither of the commands given him by the Ghost at the beginning: "But howsoever thou pursue this act, / Taint not thy mind. . . . "[21] The prince certainly has not pursued revenge in any consistent way, and it is impossible to suppose that his mind, valuing Christian interiority, is serene and untainted by the anger, disgust, and despair that have occupied it. The Ghost has added: "nor let thy soul contrive / Against thy mother aught. Leave her to heaven."[22] Although Hamlet has not contrived directly against Gertrude, his fury against her is manifest, and in the bedroom scene he treats her cruelly. At the end of the play he has managed only to precipitate a wild catastrophe that spins out of everyone's control. Ophelia by now has gone passively to drown, Hamlet has killed her father and also Rosenkrantz and Guildenstern; finally the stage is littered with the bodies of Laertes, Claudius, Gertrude, and Hamlet himself. Hamlet had proclaimed that "the readiness is all," and that "There's a divinity that shapes our ends, / Rough-hew them how we will."[23] But as the catastrophe approaches he is a passive waiter on events brought about by others. Some commentators sense here a deeper Hamlet, now aware of providence; but if the catastrophe indeed is providential, then just about anything is providential and God does write straight in very crooked lines. I think we must interpret "the readiness is all" not as a maxim of general application but an expression of the limited stance of which Hamlet himself is capable. He will not himself decide. To decide would be to choose, and he will not choose. Torn in a great many directions intellectually, he has been unable to settle on a consistent principle of action. He is a swordsman, and if stung into action willing enough to kill. Sometimes he experiences heroic anger, but he is also a Christian who aspires to inner purity and heaven, which means avoiding rage and blood lust. King Henry V could at a much less exigent level effect a synthesis of the heroic and the Christian, could contain, in John Donne's famous phrase, the eagle and the dove, but Prince Hamlet cannot. He also has fully engaged most or even all of the contradictory possibilities of the Renaissance, from the lofty aspiration of Pico della Mirandola to bottomless skepticism, from the ideals of humanism to recurrent thoughts of suicide, from the intellectual reaches of Wittenberg to mocking cynicism and an awareness of the yawning grave. Because Hamlet was everything, he ran the risk of being nothing.

From the classical and humanist side of his mind, he might have reflected on the exemplary figure of Aeneas, the civilized and civilizing Trojan warrior, the dutiful founder of Rome. More like Hector than like Achilles, Aeneas at the end reluctantly plunges his sword into Turnus and goes on to found the civilized city. Hamlet could have seen Aeneas as a bridge extending outward from the barbaric-heroic toward the civilized conscience. From the Christian side of Hamlet's mind, bridges are also possible. If the Good Samaritan had come along the Jericho Road a few minutes earlier and interrupted the robbery, he might have had to draw his sword against the thieves; but if he adhered to the Sermon on the Mount, he would have killed the thieves while pitying them as sinners. Prince Hamlet is much more a man of intellect than King Henry V and he might have reasoned thus, but he did not. As Paul Cantor observes: "The conflict between the classical and Christian traditions has been central to Western civilization, and has provided the basis for its profoundest cultural achievements and its most deeply problematical moments. That Hamlet reflects these tensions, which reached their peak during the Renaissance, is one reason for the enduring power of the play."[24]

For the future of Denmark, the political results of Hamlet's behavior are dubious. He might have killed Claudius and succeeded him as king. But Claudius is an effective if Machiavellian king, and Hamlet succeeds only in distracting him and precipitating the destruction of his regime. Although the play achieves a sense of order at its end through the efficient presence of young Fortinbras, he has been depicted throughout as a military hothead, a sort of Hotspur who has narrowly been deflected by Claudius from invading Denmark and launched on a foolish invasion of Poland, which could have cost thousands of lives. What sort of regime he will bring Denmark remains very much up in the air.

There can be no doubt, despite all of this, that Hamlet is a tragic hero of major proportions, that when he dies something large goes out of the world. Yet his greatness lies not in anything he does, which is usually disastrous, but in what he is, and this in turn has much to do with what he says, immortally, and with what is said about him.

In spite of the wild carnage at its end, the play does come to an extraordinary verbal and dramatic conclusion, in which Shakespeare employs not only magnificent poetry but also martial music, military banners, and other impressive effects. Throughout the play, Horatio, Hamlet's fellow student at Wittenberg, has had a particular intellectual identity apart from his admirable steadfastness as Hamlet's friend. More an antique Roman than a Dane, as indeed his name suggests, he is a humanist scholar, a man of skeptical temper, and a Senecan Stoic.

It is less clear what Hamlet has brought home from Wittenberg, the university of Faust and Luther, but evidently it is a great deal. He is not a Senecan Stoic, not entirely a classical humanist, and he knows that there are more things in heaven and earth than are dreamed of in Horatio's philosophy. As the play itself has shown, there certainly are.

No doubt it is because of Horatio's firm friendship, but also because of a certain pedestrian quality in him, that Hamlet wants Horatio to "tell my story":

> O God! Horatio, what a wounded name,
> Things standing thus unknown, shall live behind me!
> If thou didst ever hold me in thy heart,
> Absent thee from felicity a while,
> And in this harsh world draw thy breath in pain
> To tell my story.[25]

At this point, startling things happen. One of them is that Horatio, throughout the play "good Horatio," Horatio the Roman Stoic, comes up with lines that, from him, are astonishing:

> Now cracks a noble heart. Good night, sweet Prince,
> And flights of angels sing thee to thy rest.[26]

That language is far beyond anything we have been led to expect from Horatio and certainly undreamed of in his philosophy. As Hamlet is dying, it is as if Hamlet's eloquence has been transferred at least for a moment to Horatio. His restricted Stoicism has broken open, his very personality seems changed. He even seems to bridge the classical-Christian contradiction with "noble heart" and "flights of angels." I hazard the idea that what Horatio has seen in Elsinore has cracked open his former universe and that he now sees cosmic heights after realizing the existence of the most foul depths.

Following those two astonishing lines, Shakespeare gives Horatio a third line, which is also marvelous where it is placed:

> Now cracks a noble heart. Good night, sweet Prince,
> And flights of angels sing thee to thy rest.
> What drum comes hither?[27]

The sound of the drum signals the approach of Fortinbras and his Norwegian army. He has been a presence on the fringes of the play, and he now strides on to the stage amid the chaos and begins to clean up the mess. Whether he will succeed in restoring good order to Denmark we cannot say, but with his drums, colors, cannon, and abundant energy it is possible that, simple warrior that he is, he will arrange things aright. Here ghosts and angels give way to the light of common day, the military presence, and the promise of Fortinbras. It is possible that the balance of the play now tilts away from conflict in the soul and toward the classical-heroic military basis of civilized order. The orders immediately issued by Fortinbras have an executive clarity and perhaps carry some guarantees about the future:

> Let four captains
> Bear Hamlet like a soldier from the stage.
> For he was likely, had he been put on,
> To have proved most royal; and for his passage
> The soldier's music and the rite of war
> Speak loudly for him.[28]

This martial music is important here dramatically, as indeed are the effects of sound throughout this final scene, even the clink of steel as Hamlet duels Laertes. (Lionel Trilling once remarked that the sound of steel comes as a relief amid the complexities and dubieties of the play.) As act 5 draws to a close, it is at least possible that the broken kingdom can be put back together again.

Earlier I argued that one aspect of the Renaissance was the intellectual availability of various and often incompatible ways of looking at the world: the traditional Christianity and the traditional Christian human-ism remain, but also present are the realpolitik of Machiavelli, the skepti-cism of Montaigne, the new stresses of Luther, the science of Bacon and Copernicus, the excitement of global exploration, and political utopian-ism. I said that the theater itself reflected this new and felt variety of possibilities, its varied characters often testing the possibilities in dra-matic action. Hamlet's mind is an extraordinary arena of exactly that expanded Renaissance possibility. If Shakespeare often distributed vari-ous possibilities among his characters, in Prince Hamlet he put as many of them as he plausibly could into a single character, making him articu-late them in unforgettable language and test them in action under dire circumstances. In that sense the poetry is the play, and all the action is stage business. That is why the great actors have aspired to play the prince, who spins at the center of the play like a multifaceted black diamond. In Prince Hamlet, Shakespeare contains all the contradictions within a matchless gentleman and scholar, what the age at court admired, as did most of the theater audience: the glass of fashion and the mould of form, a courtier, soldier, scholar—in that respect a figure like Sir Philip Sydney, a man out of Castiglione.

Ophelia loves him but cannot understand him and betrays him with Lilliputian plots. Indeed, how could Ophelia understand this strange young man whose mind could be expressed only by some of the greatest poetry? King Claudius, worldly as he is, remains baffled by Hamlet and considers him largely a dangerous nuisance. Gertrude, weak and malleable, cannot understand him either; and his closest friend Horatio may understand him only at the end of the play. When he dies and leaves behind the wreckage he has inherited but also caused, he continues to exist in his intensely remembered language. It has been said persuasively that Hamlet so loved the world that he was able to give complete expression to all of its possibilities. What Keats said of his Nightingale is also true of the prince: he poured forth his soul in an ecstasy of song. The stature of Prince Hamlet as a great tragic hero rests upon the fact that though in all practical terms he was a catastrophe—those bodies all over the stage—he nevertheless gave himself to and fully articulated the cosmos available to him in all of its splendor, horror, and multiple contradiction.

It would be diminishing to say that Hamlet is a superbly intelligent graduate student, though there would be some truth in that. It is his language that makes him a colossal figure, and when silence descends upon him it seems to enfold all of us. Mark Van Doren judged correctly when he wrote that Hamlet is one of the very few credible geniuses to be portrayed in literature: "Of the many statements he makes there is none which is made for its own sake and the sense that it would be true at another time or place. In any situation the relevant portion of the person speaks: the whole man never does, except in the play as a whole, which can be thought of as his body speaking, or rather, his life. He is that unique thing in literature, a credible genius."[29] That is exactly right.

Shakespeare made him the epitome of the rich intellectual values of the Renaissance and gave him the language in which to express them. We do know Socrates and Jesus through narrative, and they are certainly geniuses. Yet, as Van Doren says, such are very rare. If Napoleon was a genius, we have no narrative that can prove it. Perhaps Boswell's Johnson qualifies. Thomas Mann's Adrian Leverkuhn gets my vote. With Prince Hamlet, Shakespeare put a genius on the stage at the Globe Theater and into the mind of the West.

That is why the death of Hamlet when it comes is shocking and seems to make a major subtraction from the universe. A master spirit, a tragic *Übermensch*, he leaves an unfillable gap. He looked through a window in his mind and saw everything, and in the play was able to speak about what he saw. Of course he composed his own epitaph. His last words are, "The rest is silence."[30]

T. S. Eliot has said that Shakespeare's thirty-seven plays can be read as a single long poem.[31] If we so read them, the entire body of Shakespeare's work may be seen to have a deep structure of something like the *Divine Comedy* with *King Lear* representing the lowest depth of Hell, the late comedies an advance upon order and redemption, and *The Tempest* at least an antechamber to a Paradiso.[32] In this play Prospero, duke of Milan, has immersed himself in study to the exclusion of his duties as head of state. He is overthrown by his brother Antonio with the conspiratorial help of Alonso, king of Naples. Prospero and his infant daughter Miranda, put at sea in a small boat, drift to a magical island where the inhabitants are Ariel, a puckish spirit of the air, and Caliban, son of the witch Sycorax. A misshapen and smelly lout, Caliban is the lowest rung on the human ladder. Through his magic, Prospero makes both Ariel and Caliban his slaves.

In most editions the printed text of *The Tempest* is about half the length of *Hamlet*. This is because music, song, dance, and ritual constitute so much of the play. The entire play might be said to long for the pure harmonies of music, which the Elizabethan understood to reflect through all creation the principle of order, or the Logos. (See the role of music in the scene of Plato's death in chapter 3.) Indeed, action in this play slows almost to a stop. When properly performed and accompanied it is one of the most beautiful of all works of art. As its words move in the direction of music, silence descends finally after the benediction by Prospero in the form of an epilogue. It is possible that this was Shakespeare's farewell to the stage; but, even if that is not so, it does mark the end of the spiritual journey of his plays.

In act 1, Ariel sings two of Shakespeare's most beautiful songs, each of them adumbrating a major theme of the play: first, the love and marriage of Alonso's son Ferdinand and Prospero's now-grown daughter Miranda, and second, the transformation and redemption of Alonso himself, the conspirator against Prospero. Alonso, forgiven, returns to a "clear life." A moral order is restored that corresponds to the cosmic order.

Ariel's first song:

> Come unto these yellow sands
>   and then take hands:
> Curtsied when you have, and kiss'd,
>   the wild waves whist,
> Foot it featly here and there,
> And sweet sprites the burthen bear.[33]

Ferdinand asks: "Where should this music be? I'th' aire, or th'earth?" And Ariel's second song follows:

> Full fathom five thy father lies;
> Of his bones are coral made;
> Those are pearls that were his eyes;
> Nothing of him that doth fade,
> But doth suffer a sea change
> Into something rich and strange.
> Sea nymphs hourly ring his knell.[34]

The cosmic order penetrates the play through the sacramental structure that pervades the whole. Prospero, through his magical powers, has caused the ship bearing Alonso, Antonio, Ferdinand, and others to be (supposedly) sunk and wrecked near his island. This simulated storm is not the great storm of *King Lear*, and no one is hurt. It is a beneficent storm and the entrance to something rich and strange: Alonso's recovery of himself and a "clear life," and the marriage of Ferdinand and Miranda.

T. S. Eliot indicated the salvational and sacramental structure of the play when he strategically placed allusions to it in the midst of his *Waste Land*. These seem to possess a numinous quality:

> I remember
> Those are pearls that were his eyes.[35]

> Musing on the king my brother's wreck[36]

> A current under sea
> Picked his bones in whispers. As he rose and fell
> He passed the stages of his age and youth
> Entering the whirlpool.[37]

In the sacramental symbolism of *The Tempest*, the storm that supposedly wrecks the ship and drowns those on it in fact harms not a physical hair and is a baptism. Alonso partakes of other important sacraments: contrition, repentance, restitution, and amendment of life. Ferdinand and Miranda partake of the sacrament of marriage. Those in the play who remain sinners cannot partake in the "banquet," which is evidently the sacrament of Communion.

The sacramental order, reflective of the cosmic order, is restored; Ferdinand and Miranda foreseeably will enjoy the earthly reflection of that cosmic order: Ferdinand: "I hope / For quiet days, fair issue, and long life."[38] In the musical and dancing display, Juno reinforces this:

> Go with me
> To bless this twain, that they may prosperous be
> And honored in their issue.[39]

This ritual combination of words, music, and dancing naturally, and supernaturally, concludes with a graceful dance including agricultural reapers and nymphs. Among the many things to be noticed here is the

classical virtue of "honor"—and "honored in their issue." Shakespeare
rebuilds the classical-Christian synthesis throughout *The Tempest.*

He also acknowledges the pained cry of Christopher Marlowe's Dr.
Faustus when his debt to the devil comes due: Faustus screams, "I'll burn
my books,"[40] that is, his books of dark magic. Prospero, letting go, says,
"I'll drown my book."[41] Here there is all the difference between fire and
water, hell and divine order.

In *The Tempest,* however, the world remains the world. Antonio, the
usurping brother of Prospero and potential murderer of Prospero and
Miranda, is beyond or beneath the circle of regeneration, as is the lowly
Caliban. And when Miranda, overcome with happiness at the recon-
ciliations, exclaims,

> O wonder!
> How many goodly creatures are there here!
> How beauteous mankind is! O brave new world
> That has such people in it![42]

Prospero, who has seen the world, gently corrects her: "It is new to
thee."[43]

The epilogue, delivered in the character of Prospero, and almost
certainly spoken by the great actor Richard Burbage, is a beautiful coda
to the play, and quite possibly, though there are multiple possibilities,
also represents Shakespeare's own farewell:

> Now my charms are all o'erthrown . . .
> Unless I be relieved by prayer
> Which pierces so that it assaults
> Mercy itself and frees all faults.
> As you from crimes would pardon'd be,
> Let your indulgence set me free.[44]

CHAPTER NINE

The Indispensable Enlightenment: Molière and Voltaire

The period known as the Enlightenment, sometimes referred to as the Age of Reason (from about the middle of the seventeenth century to the end of the eighteenth), attempted something new and indispensable in human history. In its central thrust, it tried to shift the mind of the West away from Jerusalem and in the direction of Athens, away from a biblical understanding of human nature and history and toward philosophy (newly defined) and science. Some of its major thinkers considered that philosophy and science might, by themselves, give a fully adequate account of human nature, history, politics, and the universe itself. The power of this project, and its felt validity, had a profound effect on literature and the other arts, as we shall see in two very different but great and also representative authors, Molière and Voltaire.

When *Paradise Lost* was published in 1667, it struck most educated people as certainly a work of supreme genius, but also as a glorious anachronism, a sort of giant intruding into the drawing room or laboratory. Its vast sweep, its huge and often eccentric learning, its Baroque style, its epic claims, its basis in the story of Genesis 1—all of this seemed to educated opinion a work redolent of an older and slightly embarrassing time; for around the middle of the seventeenth century, a change took place that began to affect every department of educated culture. Of course the vast majority of people pursued their daily lives in the old ways, governed by necessity, the unfolding seasons, the liturgical calendar, birth, life, and death. In England and France, indeed, a change was underway even as Milton published *Paradise Lost*. He was closer in sensibility to Shakespeare, Marlowe, Michelangelo—in many ways he was essentially a Renaissance poet—than he was to his own contemporaries. I am going to offer some informed generalizations about this major shift in sensibility and thought, which continues to affect our lives in every minute of our existence, in full knowledge that such generalities, being such, will be challengeable and at least marginally inaccurate.

By the middle of the seventeenth century, Europe had become exhausted by more than a century of devastating warfare emerging out of the religious conflicts of the Reformation. The Peace of Westphalia in 1648 marks a decisive end to such warfare, though the matter was not settled in England until 1660 with the fall of the Puritan Commonwealth and the restoration of a more limited monarchy. In a realistic frame of mind, the wiser heads of Europe had come to realize that it was useless to try to settle religious disputes through warfare. The religious wars ended in a peace of exhaustion.

On another track, at the same time, the "new science" and the "new philosophy" had made exciting advances in an entirely different direction. In essence, they tried to kick free from previous controversies and rest things in general on a new basis. Bacon, Descartes, Leibnitz, Hobbes, Hume, and Locke are some of the major figures in a wide effort to reinvent philosophy. Experimental science and new technology, though only in their beginnings, held great promise. It seemed perfectly reasonable for an educated person to believe that a new world was being born out of the dusty and contentious wreckage of the old.

Since progress in science and philosophy rested on a new basis, that is, experiment and logic, it seemed plausible to suppose that progress in society might come from a similar rational understanding of human behavior in all of its aspects. Both government and society became objects of study in a new sense. In both Molière and Voltaire, the observing eye of the author takes up a position at a certain remove from society, indeed objectifies society. Such a stance often issued in critical conclu-

sions. Even profound critics of the Enlightenment, such as Jonathan
Swift, Samuel Johnson, and Edmund Burke were also part of it in thus
objectifying society and trying to see it whole. As Johnson famously said,
"I consider myself as acting a part in the great system of society."[1] Notice
the sense of distance in his phrase "acting a part." Molière, a supreme
artist, tends toward irony and comedy, Voltaire, scintillatingly brilliant,
toward savage scorn and tragic laughter.

Let us take the great John Locke as our representative philosopher.
His thought was decisive for a century and influential far beyond. He
began with the premise that if men would cease disputing about things
they could not prove, such as metaphysical ("deductive") propositions,
two major benefits would occur. First, the peace of society would not be
disturbed, as it had been in the recent past, by murderous discord about
unprovables, for example, religious differences; and, second, men could
"search out the *bounds* between opinion and knowledge, and examine by
what measures, in things whereof we have no certain knowledge, we
ought to regulate our assent and moderate our persuasion."[2] Here,
"certain knowledge" is empirical knowledge, the knowledge of the world
gained through the five senses, Everything else is "opinion." With this
sharp focus Lockian empiricism thus opened the world wide to precise
exploration and, implicitly, to human well-being. It downgraded or excluded much that had previously been thought to be knowledge. That is,
Locke sought to shift the focus of speculation and exclude much of what
previously had been considered the subject matter of philosophy, certainly, for example Plato, whom he would have considered a mere "man
of letters," and, of course, theology. Viewed in one way, Locke's philosophy was a peace treaty comparable to the Peace of Westphalia. And
Locke sought to settle a large range of issues on that basis. In his *Essay on
Human Understanding* (1690), he explored the conditions of human perception, outlined useful areas for investigation, and established categories for serious philosophy that remained prescriptive for at least the next
hundred years. In his *Two Treatises on Government* (1684–89), he attempted to outline the sanctions for and the limits of government, and

this retains considerable force today. In his *Letter Concerning Toleration* (1689), he advocated peaceful religious pluralism. In an essay with the remarkable title *The Reasonableness of Christianity* (1695), he reduced Christianity to commonsense morality and excluded miracles.

It is commonplace but also true to say that Locke was the architect in philosophical terms of the new English social, political, and religious settlement that was ratified in effect by the Glorious, or Bloodless, Revolution of 1688, and that established the supremacy of Parliament and the accepted worldview of a now prosperous England. It was in many ways an extraordinarily attractive worldview, confident, successful, constitutional. Its architecture, its literature, its music, its politeness reflected its sense of order and stability. Yet Locke certainly did narrow the traditional meaning of the word philosophy. He did this brilliantly because he had set out to do so. He defined what men of reason should reasonably concern themselves with. But what Plato, Socrates, Jesus, or Paul would have thought of his injunction that men ought not bother themselves with "matters beyond the reach of their capacities" can perhaps be imagined. One may add that wilder figures, such as Napoleon, and wilder theories of politics, as in Robespierre, excluded from the world of Lockian common sense, invariably came as a surprise to it.

Indeed, what Locke cautions against, and in his theory of knowledge excludes, may well concern the deepest of human matters, the ideas of good and evil, the nature of the universe, the ultimate bases of civilization, the goals of life. From the perspective of traditional philosophy, Locke was an "antiphilosopher." Again, he was so because that is what he set out to be. But beyond the limits he had productively set forth, the old questions of philosophy would be raised in a variety of forms.

The great project of the Enlightenment was concentrated in the major cities of Europe, mostly northern and western Europe—London, Edinburgh, Paris, Amsterdam, Geneva, Berlin, and Milan—and also in the derivative littoral of colonies on the Atlantic coast of North America. It accomplished great and one hopes lasting things. The critical intelligence was mobilized against superstition. Absurdities were scorned. Economic matters were examined critically, as by Adam Smith and David Ricardo. The principles of representative government were worked out by John Locke, Baron de Montesquieu, Thomas Jefferson, James Madison, and others, exemplified in British practice and in the American Constitution. Throughout the world today, such representative government appears to be the only legitimate form and the only form consistent with modernization. Other forms—tribal, various modes of third world despotism—are ugly and likely residual. The authoritarian capitalism of China is a problematical experiment. I think it beyond dispute today that anyone who becomes acquainted with a culture touched little or not at all by the Enlightenment experiences immediately the enormous difference it made. It is possible that this difference involved fundamental matters of human consciousness. The Enlightenment gave rise to a much more sustained critical reason and eventually no doubt to a more troubled and exigent consciousness.

In its own period of crystallization the new movement in thought and in educated culture had its critics, many of them profound; and it has had its critics ever since. Yet it is important to see that even its most trenchant critics, from Swift and Burke through Dostoyevsky, have had to put such criticism in terms laid down by the Enlightenment itself. That is, they have had to argue their case, not merely assume it, and appeal to fact, reason, and experience.

In his great and still often performed plays, Molière (Jean Baptiste Poquelin, 1622–73) dramatized a powerful and unsettling, and potentially revolutionary, impulse of the Enlightenment. In his dramas, society itself becomes highly problematic, not something given but perhaps arbitrary, and certainly often a joke. Society might be inherited and sanctified by religion. It might be humorous, absurd, or tragic. But it could be seen as something external to the individual self. From that perspective, though Molière never pressed the issue this far, society could become the object of rational analysis and consciously planned reform. In this Molière's great plays reach toward the intellectual heart of the

Enlightenment and express an enormous shift in the mind of the advanced nations of the West.

It is no doubt important to know that M. Poquelin rejected the security of a public office purchased by his father and became, instead of Poquelin, Molière, a total man of the theater as playwright, actor, and director. He was thoroughly acquainted with the dramatic traditions of Europe from classical drama to street theater and is the only playwright since the Renaissance who can bear comparison with Shakespeare. The French seventeenth century gave rise to three notable playwrights: Jean Baptiste Racine, Pierre Corneille, and Molière. Only Molière remains a fully alive force in literature and theater; his works continue to be widely translated, discussed, and very frequently are in production.

His durability is a matter both of style and substance. He developed a style of writing for the stage that is classical in the sense of being so pure and lucid that it is immune to time. It is as fresh and conversational today as it was in the seventeenth century. There is nothing about it that suggests another time and place. In his greatest plays he wrote comedy, but in them he also pressed against the boundaries of comedy in such a way that the plays moved in the direction of, and perhaps into, tragedy.

At the center of *Tartuffe*, *Don Juan*, and *The Misanthrope*, for example, we find a compelling individual it seems fair to call a monster (in *The Misanthrope*, two monsters). Characteristically, the monsters are enemies of important social norms. Tartuffe is a religious hypocrite of world-class standing who uses his smooth religious cant to advance his real interests, which are greed, lust, and power. Yet Molière is able to raise his hypocrisy to such a level that Tartuffe becomes a sort of cosmic champion of hypocrisy. We appreciate him as one of a kind, a work of art. His "religious" discourse is so fluent and temporarily so plausible that it deceives not only the other characters in the play but comes close to having the audience itself suspend its disbelief, appreciate his art, and nod with approval and even cheer him on to new heights of deception. Molière, master craftsman, delays the appearance of this monster until act 3, by which time the buildup has reached a pitch of high anticipation. But

Molière is up to the challenge he has constructed and delivers to us the great Tartuffe. Perhaps Tartuffe brings to mind such great flim-flam artists as Phineas T. Barnum and Houdini, whose art was so consummate that people enjoyed being taken in by it.

Not surprisingly, *Tartuffe* got Molière into trouble with the religious authorities. In its first version it was banned from public performance and was not brought to the stage again during Molière's lifetime. His depiction of hypocrisy cut too close to the bone of important ecclesiastical interests. He reasonably could have said that he was satirizing corruption and defending honest piety, but to dress a genius of deceit in ecclesiastical costume and bring him on the public stage no doubt seemed to have wider implications than a satire on religious abuses.

What kept Molière out of more serious trouble was the firm support of Louis XIV, the Sun King, who built Versailles as his capital and aspired to unify Europe under French hegemony. Like Augustus, and with Augustus in mind, Louis surrounded himself and decorated his court with artistic talent. Augustus had his Horace, Louis had his Boileau; Augustus had his Virgil, Louis had his great playwright. These and other important talents were the ornaments of empire and even to a degree its legitimation. The evidence is that Louis genuinely enjoyed the company and the works of his writers, painters, architects, and musicians. The friendliness of the court undoubtedly gave Molière and others some freedom to be daring. Without the protection of the Sun King, *Tartuffe* could easily have landed Molière in a dungeon.

The monster at the center of *Don Juan* is the legendary figure of voracious sexual appetites. Here again is a menace to society and its norms, and here again Molière touched a nerve. What Tartuffe was to hypocrisy, the Don was to the aristocratic amorous chase. To a monstrous degree the Don embodied what many aristocrats preoccupied themselves with throughout their supposedly adult lives. Molière in one aspect says: "You great men are hot on the chase. I now introduce you to the champion of what you are. Gentlemen, meet Don Juan!" Yet Don Juan is not a local and time-bound figure, a mere criticism of the aristocratic ethos. He has mythic stature, as Don Quixote, Hamlet, and Faust have mythic stature, embodying permanent extreme impulses within human experience.

The Don could have been treated as a comic, even grotesque figure, but Molière, as he always does, put in a complication. His sexually anarchic Don Juan is absolutely charming. His is the wit and charm that launches a thousand women. He knows what to say, and at the right time. The implication, of course, is that to launch a thousand women you need the thousand willing women, another smile at social convention.

The conclusion of this great play is, as it had to be, ambiguous. To bring the Don's sexual depredations to a close it takes what amounts to supernatural intervention. A lifeless statue moves and talks and kills the Don. Molière seems, one never knows, to be suggesting here that it will take something like a miracle to bring the enormous impulses of the Don and all the vast destructive impulses in human nature within bounds. It is possible that Molière means to suggest that behavior such as the Don's—and his thousand women—create their own negations, that there may be a sort of Sophoclean cosmic justice. No doubt Molière wanted his fashionable audiences, and wanted us, to leave the theater wondering.

Mozart was powerfully drawn to Molière's Don Juan and set it to music in his opera *Don Giovanni*. Prepared for rebuttal, when teaching Molière, I offer the opinion that *Don Giovanni* is not only the best opera ever written but also the best music ever written. The students, coming from Molière, listen to Mozart on CDs and notice how Mozart manages the distribution of the energies within the drama. The fact is, Mozart tilts in the Don's favor, the music moving in the direction of the Don's charm and physical energy. Mozart's Don is a gorgeous cobra, though a cobra nevertheless. In Mozart's treatment of Molière's play, the death of the Don is not justice but tragedy, despite the destruction he has caused. The struggle within Mozart seems to be whether his eighteenth-century musical forms can contain the anarchic heroism of the great Don. Here, we are well on the way to seeing the Don as a forerunner of the Byronic

Romantic hero. Mozart did not understand Molière's play wrongly, but
he flattened its ambiguity in the direction of Romantic energy.

By any estimate, Molière's *Misanthrope* (1666) is the climax of his art. We
are fortunate to have the very fine translation by the poet Richard
Wilbur, though other translations are adequate. Molière's French is so
lucid that it is a pleasure to translate, and Wilbur's rendering is a tribute
from one poet to another. Both Tartuffe and Don Juan are monsters of
different kinds, very difficult for society to deal with. In *The Misanthrope*,
Molière serves up two extraordinary monsters, Alceste and the beautiful
Célimène. Alceste has taken to heart the virtue of *sincerity*. Everyone
claims to believe in sincerity, and who cares to gainsay them? The difference is that Alceste really *does* believe in it and relentlessly practices it,
telling the truth as he sees it no matter what the consequences. Of course
his sincerity is outrageous and hilarious.

Unfortunately for Alceste, he has been overcome by love for the
beautiful Célimène. A great beauty and also a wit, she is the object of
every courtier's gaze. Utterly cynical, highly intelligent, she agrees with
Alceste's estimate of the shallowness of their polite society. But she is not
shallow. She treats her society as a stage that allows her to exhibit and
enjoy her own beauty and her brilliant wit. What she cannot stand is
Alceste's sincerity, his dark looks, his sullenness, his inopportune declara-
tions of love. She is fond of Alceste but cannot take seriously his hostility
to the society that is the circumstance of her luminous role.

Célimène may be Molière's own defense of that society, indeed of his
own role in it as an artist. She knows its shallowness; yet, an artist of her
kind, she uses the society and rises above it. She thinks that Alceste is
"honest" by his lights, or his darkness, but she does not think that with
Alceste she could still be Célimène.

All this gives rise to thoughts that are not explicitly stated in the play.
Could not this polite society be improved upon? Might not Célimène, in
a different setting, shine even more brightly? Those would be reformist
questions. But the answer to them might well be "no." Perhaps Célimène is a creature whose particular excellences require just *this* society.

As Talleyrand once remarked, no one knows how sweet life could be who was born after the French Revolution. Or, Alceste could reply, how awful. The comedy-tragedy central to this play is that the honest and gloomy Alceste is in love with the very flower of the society he hates, the beautiful, witty, brilliant Célimène. Molière is fully up to writing the two parts.

> ALCESTE: May I speak frankly, madame? Then I am very far from being pleased with how you behave. I begin to find it intolerable. I can see that we shall have to break off our relationship. Yes, it would be deceiving you to tell you anything else. We shall undoubtedly come to a breach sooner or later. Even if I gave you my word a thousand times over I shouldn't be able to stand by it.
> CÉLIMÈNE: So it seems you wished to see me home in order to scold me.[3]

Alceste here, and his hesitations show it, is defenseless against her. He is too much in love, and Célimène entirely sees through him. *She* may even be more sincere here than he thinks he is in his hostility toward society. Though she needs society as her metier, she is also penetrating enough to see the truth about it with great clarity. Her comments on her friends and admirers are often devastating:

> CLITANDRE: Now, what about Timante? Don't you think he's an admirable character?
> CÉLIMÈNE: The complete mystery man! He throws you a distracted glance in passing for he's always so busy though he has nothing to do. Any information he has to impart is accompanied by signs and grimaces—the fuss he makes is quite overwhelming. He's forever interrupting the conversation because he has some secret to whisper to you but there's never anything in it. He makes a sensation out of the merest trifle, and everything, even his "Good morning," has to be whispered in your ear.[4]

This has considerable universality. The acute intelligence of Célimène could be displayed today in any office in Washington or Beijing, New York or Calcutta. She operates magnificently within the world as she finds it. It may be that the particular Célimène described by Molière could reach her degree of perfection only in prerevolutionary France or something like it, but her type is universal.

Is Célimène a monster? She is a world-class hypocrite, yet tremendous as a monster. But so is Alceste. He is in love, sincerely, with the finest flower of the society he claims to detest. Alceste may be Molière's Prince Hamlet, caught in unbridgeable contradictions.

Molière ends this play in the only way, perhaps, it could end. Alceste decides to leave society and escape its hypocrisies through exile . . . somewhere. We sense that this may be a temporary mood, though the potentiality for suicide is not absent. If we are reminded of Hamlet, we may also be reminded of Gulliver's final derangement.

> ALCESTE: I mean to escape from this abyss of triumphant vice and search the world for some spot so remote that there one may be free to live as honor bids.[5]

It would be difficult to know how to deliver that line on stage. Should it be played comically, against Alceste? Of course there is no society on earth in which one can live as honor bids. Alceste could be played as a gloomy but comic buffoon. But not quite. The joke may be on us. He knows something about human society, and so does Célimène. His circumstance in society, and ours, may be tragic. After Alceste has spoken of going to live somewhere "as honor bids," Philinte says to Célimène: "Come, madame, let us go and do all we can to persuade him to give up this foolish plan."[6]

That line holds out the possibility that Alceste can be lured back into society, "corrupted," in his terms, taught to wear the inauthentic social mask. On the evidence presented in the play, this possibility is not excluded. Perhaps he needs this society, any society, in order to be Alceste. After all, he did love Célimène, that monster of social accommodation. Yet the same evidence, within the play, almost—almost!—justifies his disgust with society.

Clearly such monsters as Tartuffe and Don Juan are intolerable and, we agree, must be destroyed. But Alceste? Does telling the truth make him a monster? A society of brilliant, mordant Alcestes would be unendurable. As Erasmus argued long before in *The Praise of Folly*, the very circumstance of the individual in society generates falsehood. Yet if Alceste's truths violate the social peace, what do we think of a monster like Célimène, who glitteringly climbs to the top of the greasy pole?

The *Misanthrope* is a great but also representative product of the Enlightenment. It turns a critical gaze on the human circumstance within society, even as does *Gulliver's Travels*, though Molière does so with seeming equanimity. The *Misanthrope* renders society as in important ways external to us and, though our fate, also subject to critical analysis. The play opens up questions that are philosophical and psychological. Is Philinte, at the end, right?—that Alceste must be persuaded to return to society? He seems to speak with the voice of common sense, but does the play as a whole speak with that voice? Do we leave the theater thinking that Molière has said that we must live in society even if it is dominated by fools and crowned by the likes of Célimène? But, just as our inner Alceste gets the upper hand, we remember that Célimène is beautiful, witty, intelligent, perhaps even wise, and knows how to triumph within her social fate—as, indeed, did Molière.

Samuel Johnson and William Blake agreed on one thing. They both loathed Rousseau and Voltaire. "Mock on, mock on, Voltaire, Rousseau,"[7] wrote Blake, seeing the two men as negaters of the spirit, killers of vision. When Boswell asked Johnson whether Voltaire was as bad a man as Rousseau, he replied, "Why, Sir, it is difficult to settle the proportion of iniquity between them."[8] He considered them immoral and dangerous. When Edmund Burke visited his young son in Paris, he loathed the mocking wit of the *philosophes*, or intellectuals. Matthew Arnold said he would prefer an English boy from Eton to a French boy brought up on Voltaire. Auden wrote that Voltaire was "the cleverest of them all," as if to say, only "clever," that is, shallow. Voltaire has not exported well to England.

Yet there is a very great deal to praise in Voltaire. His famous wit has its roots in his anger that men are not more reasonable than they are and that his France had much more than its share of corruption and stupidity. No one was ever more deadly when sticking pins into balloons that deserved to be stuck. Voltaire made wit a positive force of intelligence, not lovable to be sure, but bracing. On any given day, do things not arise that make one think, "Voltaire, Françoise Marie Arouet, thou shouldst be living at this hour!"?

When he wrote *Candide* in 1758 Voltaire was at the pinnacle of his fame and intellectual reputation. He amounted to an international force. His tragedy *Oedipe* (1718), which no one reads today, enjoyed vast acclaim in Paris. His epic *La Henriade* (1724) is now pretty much dead, as far as anyone can discern, yet in its time it was widely compared with Homer and Virgil. *Sic transit gloria mundi*. Voltaire's great work of history, *The Century of Louis XIV,* compares very well with Gibbon on Rome and Hume on England. It is one of the (temporarily) lost great books. Voltaire produced a torrent of essays, novellas, and treatises attacking not just the present monarchy in France, but the entire system inseparable from the monarchy. Toward the end of his life, when he visited Paris his reception in the streets and in the salons became a celebration of intellect itself and a personal triumph for Voltaire, and his estate at Ferney had become a focus of intellectual pilgrimage.

The phrase that sticks to Voltaire is of course *écrasez l'infâme* (destroy the outrageous thing), by which Voltaire meant not only the Catholic church but the entire encrusted old order of the France of his time. Voltaire, however, was much less radical than that one phrase might imply. When he wrote *Candide,* Voltaire was living at Ferney, across the French border but near Geneva. *Candide* is a short and brilliant spoof, and for sheer enjoyment in reading no book excels it. Voltaire's wit sends electric charges through his lucid sentences, explosions going off in sentences that themselves achieve a brilliant simplicity: " 'I have seen worse,' replied Candide. 'But a wise man who has since had the misfortune to be hanged taught me that there is a marvellous propriety in such things; they are shadows in a beautiful picture.' "[9] Voltaire's wit brings "misfortune to be hanged" into discordant conjunction with "a beautiful picture," and destruction is achieved. In a sentence like this it does not matter that indeed there might be a marvelous propriety in the hanging, that is, justice. Voltaire's wit captures the field.

One thing of major importance must be stressed here. It is conventionally claimed that Voltaire's target in *Candide* is the philosophy of Leibnitz as reflected in *An Essay on Man* by Voltaire's friend Alexander Pope. Leibnitz-Pope is supposedly represented in *Candide* by Dr. Pangloss ("gloss over everything") who cheerily explains after every catastrophe that "everything is for the best in the best of all possible worlds." Pangloss, a "great German philosopher" from "Westphalia" (both of these identities seem funny to Voltaire) is untouchable by experience. Voltaire may have seen something here about a tendency in German philosophy toward abstraction. Jargon and preposterous abstraction stand between Pangloss and experience. Everything that happens, from natural catastrophe to slaughter, disease, the Inquisition and its auto-da-fé, corruption, hypocrisy, slavery, tyranny, avarice, cruelty—the list is endless— leaves Pangloss utterly unshaken. Even when he is hanged, dissected, loses his nose to syphilis, and is a slave in the galleys, his "metaphysics" remains unshaken and he himself serene. Everything has been arranged for the best, all events are interconnected, and even matters that seem plainly evil are, if rightly considered, somehow conducive to the benefit of someone somewhere and thus part of an overall rational design. When Pangloss loses his nose to venereal disease, he connects this with Columbus's discovery of America and easily rationalizes his sorry condition.

In all of this Voltaire's target is not Leibnitz or Pope but junk thought, complacency, a refusal to confront evil and suffering for what they are, and passivity before things that might be remediable. The positions of Leibnitz and the more clearly Christian Alexander Pope were, it is true, perverted by such popularizers as Soame Jenyns and Christian Woolf, who glibly glossed over suffering, but this is clearly not where Pope stood, even when he famously concluded Epistle 1 of *An Essay on Man* with these lines:

> And, spite of pride, in erring reason's spite
> One truth is clear, WHATEVER IS, IS RIGHT.[10]

This, it must be understood, is an ultimate statement concluding a poem in which a great deal is wrong. It is a final, an ultimate statement about divine Providence made after an agonizing inventory of suffering and catastrophe. It is an affirmation made "in spite of," and nothing could be further from Panglossian complacency. Virtually the entire body of Pope's other poetry satirizes "whatever is," and Pope's attacks upon knaves and fools are as savage as anything Voltaire ever attempted. When Handel set "Whatever is, is right" to music, he correctly interpreted it. He rendered "whatever is" a long and aggressively dissonant wail and then proceeded to "is right," and that on a minor chord. Pope and Handel thus affirmed "Being," affirmed, finally, the Creation—but without complacency. Alexander Pope did not consider his crippling hunchback, "this long disease my life," to be a trivial or benign matter, nor did he approve of quick trials in which "wretches hang that jurymen may dine."[11]

It takes nothing away from the power of Voltaire's performance in *Candide*, or the effectiveness of his satire on Panglossian junk thought, to point out, with John Butt, that Voltaire "makes no attempt to meet the traditional Christian argument, reinterpreted by Leibnitz, that evil cannot be excluded from a world in which we are free to choose evil or good, and that such a world is better than one where there would be no free agents, and therefore no evil and no good."[12]

Such junk thought as represented by Pangloss may derive at considerable distance from the thought of genuine philosophical minds, but it misunderstands them and falsifies their teaching. What John Dewey actually thought about education is unrecognizable in his popularizers. The thought of Nietzsche exists in the popular mind only in caricature. Few people actually read Freud, but everyone "knows" what he said. Even our Declaration of Independence, appealed to almost daily, is seldom accurately understood. In *Candide*, the process of intellectual devolution—vulgarization, dumbing-down—evokes Voltaire's scorn in the figure of Dr. Pangloss, who certainly has not read Pope or Leibnitz but, at best, only some popular pamphlets that misrepresent them. Along his comic way here, Voltaire picks off a shooting gallery of ripe targets, and the comic energies of the book are on their own showing an affirmation of mind and of life.

Voltaire's comic method is to exploit the absurdities and outrages of actual experience and then repeatedly raise them to a pitch that renders ridiculous any presumption that experience exhibits an obvious and benign order. His artistic strength resides in the energy of his imagination in raising things to such a pitch of delightful chaos and absurdity. He anchors his comedy in the actual, but like a gifted musician he produces cadenzas of the ridiculous without quite losing his hold upon the possible. Indeed, when the adventures and vicissitudes described here seem to cross beyond the border of the probable, involving shipwrecks, abductions, pirates, changing identities, beggars, kings, cannibalism, torture, much of this is not a great distance from eighteenth-century life as described in the picaresque adventures of such figures as Moll Flanders, Robinson Crusoe, Roderick Random, Peregrine Pickle, or indeed in the actual travails of historical individuals.

Here, in terms of the book, is an actual historical absurdity taking place. Candide, at Portsmouth in 1757, sees Admiral John Byng being executed for allowing the French to seize Minorca: "While they were talking, the ship reached Portsmouth. The waterside was crowded with a host of people who were gazing intently as a stout man kneeling, with his eyes bandaged, on the deck of a man of war. Four soldiers stood opposite him and fired three rounds each into his skull with the utmost composure, at which the crowd dispersed evidently quite satisfied."[13] The realistic absurdity of a passage such as this is much heightened in others: "My eyes were not always sore and bloodshot, my nose did not always touch my chin, and I have not always been a servant. I am the daughter of Pope Urban X and the Princess of Palestrina."[14]

Elsewhere the comic energies invested in absurdity achieve a pitch that becomes a metaphorical reflection of the absurdities of experience. Here is Dr. Pangloss, of serene vision about all being for the best, in one of his frequent re-manifestations: "While taking a walk one day, Candide met a beggar covered with sores. His eyes were lifeless, the end of his nose had rotted away, his mouth was all askew and his teeth were black. His voice was sepulchral, and a violent cough tormented him, at every bout of which he spat out a tooth."[15] And we can touch ground again in an episode that is both realistic and grotesque, as when the Prussians ("Bulgars") have been battling the French ("Abars"):

> When all was over and the rival kings were celebrating their victory with *Te Deums* in their respective camps, Candide decided to somewhere else pursue his reasoning into cause and effect. He picked his way over piles of dead and dying, and reached a neighboring village on the Abar side of the border. It was now no more than a smoking ruin, for the Bulgars had burned it to the ground in accordance with the terms of international law. Old men, crippled with wounds, watched helplessly the death-throes of their butchered women-folk, who still clasped their children to their blood-stained breasts. Girls who had satisfied the appetites of several heroes lay disemboweled in the last of their agonies. . . . Whichever way he looked, the ground was strewn with the legs, arms and brains of the dead villagers.[16]

Everything comes under Voltaire's comic gaze—monasticism, Islam, the vagaries of Eros—as in this marvelous episode, in which Candide has been wandering around in a South American jungle, and which is worth quoting at a bit of length:

> Just as the sun was setting the two wanderers heard some faint cries that sounded like women's voices. They could not tell whether they were of grief or of joy, but they rose hurriedly with that sense of anxiety and alarm that everything arouses in an unknown country. They found that the cries came from two naked girls who were tripping along the edge of the meadow, while two monkeys followed them nibbling their buttocks. Candide's heart was touched by the sight. He had learnt how to shoot by the Bulgars and could have hit a nut on a bush without touching the leaves, so, taking up his double-barrelled Spanish rifle, he fired and killed the two monkeys. . . .
> "A pretty piece of work, Sir!" said Cacambo. "You have killed those two young ladies' lovers."[17]

As Yeats once wrote, some women eat a crazy salad with their meat. But enough. One cannot go on quoting the entire book.

Yet some matters remain for reflection. Is there a vision here of some sort regarding man and society? As remarked earlier, the energies of the book are themselves a positive thing, a cleansing laughter both at junk thought and at the absurdities of human behavior. It also must be said that the characters in the book, as in the picaresque novel, exhibit a surprising resilience and durability, no matter what happens to them. In that sense, the comic spirit is never defeated. There remains, however, a large residue of contempt and disgust here; Voltaire's scorn can be devastating, an anger that often ranges beyond the lived fate of his France. Yet he was not a revolutionary and no doubt would have satirized Robespierre and Saint-Just had he lived to see them.

After three years in England, where he was astonished by the enormous consumption of gin and the frequency of suicide, Voltaire returned to France full of praise for the much freer political and social system he had seen. When A. R. J. Turgot, "the French Adam Smith," was appointed comptroller general in 1774, Voltaire considered it a great day in the history of France. He thought Turgot would introduce a freer economy on the English model. The king himself, Louis XVI, is popularly thought of as a legendarily blind autocrat, but in fact he was a reforming monarch on the order of Frederick of Prussia, Catherine of Russia, Joseph of Austria, and Gustavus of Sweden, all of whom looked to Enlightenment thinkers for guidance. Although Louis XVI was beheaded by the revolutionaries in 1792, he had known that the old French system badly needed reform and looked, like Voltaire, to England as a model. When Louis had ascended the throne in 1753 Voltaire hailed it as a day of deliverance for France.

By the time Voltaire died in 1778, it was clear that the old system probably could not be reformed. Government-protected monopolies constricted the economy, social class was rigid, public office could be inherited, the Church, impossibly, owned one-fifth of the land, and government debt had spun out of control through competition with a stronger England. There was no functioning legislature and no constitution. The royal court was decadent and lived in a dream world at Versailles. Of course, Turgot failed, like other economic and political reformers, despite the backing of the reformist King Louis XVI. *L'infâme* was more powerful than all of them. It seems likely that Voltaire would have settled for something like the English system of representative government, with the liberalizing economic measures advocated by Turgot and Adam Smith. Despite the rhetorical vigor and lasting fame of *Écrasez l'infâme*, Voltaire was no revolutionary utopian.

Finally, and this has given rise to a great many interpretations, Candide becomes the owner of a small farm in Turkey, living there with a circle of friends, including the long-desired but by now withered Cunégonde, and of course Dr. Pangloss, who retains all his illusions. At the end Candide tells his friends that we "must go and work in the garden."[18] Much speculation surrounds this enigmatic advice. Is Voltaire saying that all speculative philosophy, and not merely the junk thought of Pangloss, is futile? Is the "garden" a metaphor for France, Voltaire telling his readers to work to improve it? Could the "garden" imply revolution, a radical recovery of the garden of Eden, or else gradual reform, making things "grow better"?

On his estate at Ferney, Voltaire lived just inside the French border, too subversive for the authorities in Paris and Versailles but too French to live in Switzerland. In fact, he was proud of his own garden, which he considered to be laid out in the varied English manner, after the taste of Lord Burlington. Voltaire had visited England in 1726 and admired much that he saw. In his *Philosophical Dictionary* (1756) he wondered why the world could not be more like England, which he considered the model of freedom and tolerance. His heroes included Isaac Newton, John Milton, and George Washington. He considered the British mixed government—monarchic, aristocratic, and parliamentary—the best guardian of freedom and moderation. His own "English" garden at Ferney was a metaphor, modest in size compared with the vast expanses of a man like Burlington, but somewhat in the English taste and standing in contrast to the severe classicism of Versailles. Symmetry in landscape gardening was a metaphor for tyranny and absolutism.

Indeed, Voltaire cultivated the village of Ferney itself, turning it into a small example of Enlightened progress. He abolished the feudal tax burdens on the peasantry and provided a refuge for political and religious dissenters. In his old age, countless visitors flocked to Ferney to admire him, including Edward Gibbon, Charles Fox, James Boswell, Oliver Goldsmith, and John Wilkes.

We do not know the style of the garden Candide chose to work on at his farm in Turkey, or even whether it is meant as a political symbol in *Candide*. In his own politics, however, Voltaire, the admirer of the British system, belongs to the moderate tendency within the Enlightenment associated with such men as Montesquieu, Hume, Johnson, and Burke rather than with the utopian tendency associated with Rousseau and the Jacobins.

There is no need, moreover, to assume that Candide will remain in Turkey, of all places, indefinitely. He may only be telling his friends to do as well as they can by working where they are now. W. H. Auden seems to support this more modest view in his fine poem "Voltaire at Ferney":

> Yes, the fight
> Against the false and the unfair
> Was always worth it. Civilize.[19]

The Enlightenment was many sided, skeptical, fanatical, wise, destructive and creative, and indispensable.

CHAPTER TEN

Hamlet in St. Petersburg, Faust in Great Neck: Dostoyevsky and Scott Fitzgerald

The Novel as Epic of Empiricism

When we think about the post-seventeenth-century novel as a literary form and ask what assumptions underlie it, I think we must answer that it is different in important ways from all previous literary modes. We certainly find no rosy-fingered dawns here, and gray-eyed Athenas put in no appearances. Gods of any kind are difficult to smuggle into a novel. No rule of twelve or twenty-four books is laid down, and, in fact, rules about form seem absent. Much less than previous literature does the novel depend upon or refer to tradition. It does not observe literary ritual. The world of the novel is a world of fact. Facts constitute its reality, facts as if freshly observed. Every novel starts afresh. Imitativeness is a flaw. No good novelist wants to sound like Ernest Hemingway or James Joyce or redo Marcel Proust. That is, the novel constantly breaks with its own past. Unlike the literature of the past, the novel does not depend on a well-known story, such as are found in myth, legend, or the Bible. It may sometimes allude to them, but the primary reality of the novel is what the five senses disclose about reality—what you see, hear, smell, taste, and touch. A novel fundamentally does not "tell" a story, it "shows" it. Even thoughts are given by a voice we can "hear." Scholars do argue that the prose narratives of the ancient world, or the Middle Ages, or the Renaissance were novels. These arguments have merit, and one can wonder about Boccaccio and Cervantes, but something new, at least in felt degree, seems to happen in the early eighteenth century, and that new thing is the primacy of fact as the reality of the world.[1]

It is exciting to experience this new form as it emerges from tradition and literary convention. There are no sea coasts of Bohemia here, no Arcadias. The world in its resistant factuality is freshly grasped. There is something pristine, innocent here, as in the following passage from *Robinson Crusoe* (1719): "The sixth day of our being at sea we came into the Yarmouth Roads; the wind having been to the contrary, and the weather calm, we had made but little way since the storm. Here we were obliged to come to anchor, and here we lay, the wind continuing contrary, viz., at southwest, for seven or eight days, during which time a great many ships from Newcastle came into the same Roads, as the common harbor where ships might wait for a wind from the river."[2] This is the new world of novelistic fact, and no matter how refined it later becomes it remains the world of the novel. When Daniel Defoe wrote these words his sensibility was in the process of imaginatively appropriating the physical world. Not at all unrelated to this, science and technology in their early phases were seizing the world of nature, and the British navy was about to colonize much of the globe. The earlier magicians and alchemists certainly desired such possession, but the prose of Defoe assumes calm appropriation.

I hope it will not seem academically pretentious if I assert that the novel is the literary form most indebted to the worldview we call empiricism. The emergence of the novel is contemporaneous with the promulgation of John Locke's theory of knowledge, which holds that experience is registered in a human mind that previously had been a blank page. In Locke, the individual starts afresh and moves into experience. The novel proceeds with the same assumptions. We do not believe the tale until the teller tells it, and just as no two individuals are the same, no two novels are the same. In Locke's psychology, there are no inherited "innate" ideas; in the novel there are no prescriptive inherited conventions, as there are in such traditional literary forms as the epic, sonnet, ode, and so on. Allen Tate observed that the job of the novel is to "put man wholly into his physical environment."[3] Conventions are a barrier to the reality of the novel.

Tate's word "wholly" is important. Like empirical philosophy, the form of the novel is secular. Gods, goddesses, angels do not appear in serious novels. Miracles do not happen, and characters neither talk with God nor rise from the dead. The novel, in its form, cannot assume the existence of any reality beyond that of the five senses. In this it belongs to the powerful culture that gave rise to empirical science, saw it triumph in the time-space continuum and seize much of the world.

Yet, as we see the novel develop since Defoe, we see that often and, as the form develops, increasingly it presses against the limits of the time-space continuum. It must do so cautiously, or it would destroy its own formal empirical assumptions. Do we really believe that the dead lovers in *Wuthering Heights*, Cathy and Heathcliff, are seen together on the moors, that they really are unquiet in the quiet earth? I do not suppose we do. Very likely we attribute that idea to the superstition of the local peasants or to the imagination of the once stolid narrator, Lockwood. Yet we do not dismiss the idea either, perhaps want to believe it, and Heathcliff himself seems to come from a world elsewhere and to have connections with myth. The conclusion of *Wuthering Heights* opens a crack in the empirical world of the time-space continuum.

A great many other novels do this, setting up currents of resistance against the empirical worldview that gave them their birth. They do so, however, carefully, by providing possible empirical explanations.

If the novel is empirical, it is also individualistic, again in the spirit of Locke. You do not meet a character called Everyman or Sloth in a novel. G. K. Chesterton observed that the novel is interested in the ways people differ, whereas much earlier literature is concerned with the ways in which they are alike. The novel thus reflected the culture of an increasingly powerful middle class and its stress on individual achievement and identity. Yet older recognitions persist. Its characters cannot have names like Andrew Freeport, the merchant in Joseph Addison's and Richard Steele's novelistic essays. Yet the novel often seems to know that there is something beyond the time-space continuum and also beyond individualism. A Charles Dickens character can be named David Copperfield, but riskily Scrooge or Mr. Gradgrind. Here we are touching universal types, as in the old communal literature. Novelists who mean to press the edges of novelistic possibility, such as Joyce, go even further. His Leopold Bloom is an Everyman, and his story is involved with myth and with Odysseus.

As long as the novel continues to exist as a literary form it will remain fundamentally true to the commonsense world of Locke, the five senses, empiricism, secularism, and individualism. Yet it also registers a sense at some of its finest moments that these, though true and important, may also be limited and that perhaps a cosmos of meaning lies beyond them.

If one were designing an education in its most radical or fundamental sense, one would want, along with the important and indeed required books already discussed, to read a modern novel or two. One difficulty here is that there are so many novels, including indisputably great ones, that the choice becomes to a considerable degree arbitrary. For example, sheer length makes many great novels awkward to handle in a university course. *Middlemarch* is long, *Remembrance of Things Past* and *The Man Without Qualities* much longer. *Ulysses* is difficult and specialized. And so it goes. *The Red and the Black?* Of course that would be fine. Thomas Mann's *Magic Mountain,* or *Doctor Faustus;* or *Pride and Prejudice,* or *Huckleberry Finn* or *Moby-Dick?* All of these and many others are certainly worthy for the purpose. In this chapter I will consider quite briefly two novels, both illustrative of everything I have said here about the novel, both of incontestable importance, and both in different ways reaching toward depths beyond the deliberately set limits of Locke.

Hamlet in St. Petersburg

Johann Wolfgang Goethe (1749–1832) was a major figure of the Enlightenment and probably the greatest poet as well as the most learned man of his era. Yet when he projected his hero in his masterpiece, it was as the legendary figure Faust and not some version of such contemporaries as James Madison or Thomas Jefferson.

Both in art and in philosophy there proceeded, beginning in the late eighteenth century, a powerful reaction against the Enlightenment that attacked it as unheroic; narrowing; unreceptive to aesthetic, moral, and philosophical aspiration; and therefore inadequate to the entire human circumstance. The charge was that there had been depths and heights of human experience that the Enlightenment flattened and circumscribed. This is not surprising because that is what the Enlightenment had set out to do, as when Locke urged men to imagine the world in narrowly empirical terms.

The critique, when rational, could not dismiss the validity of Locke's empiricism, but it did seek to recover some of the ground of traditional philosophy as well as other registrations of human experience in religion and art. To risk a generalization again, this critique asserted that an inter-mediate realm does exist, one not dismissable as mere fantasy, and that in this intermediate area much of value has always existed. That there were wilder spirits urging this critique there can be no doubt, but the fact seems to be that the speculative mind, Locke to the contrary notwith-standing, had always pressed forward, apparently fulfilling the nature of mind itself, visible in its earliest beginnings, into areas that are to different degrees problematic. Mind itself has tried to achieve various modes of knowledge about those intermediate areas and symbolized that knowl-edge in different ways. Through different kinds of evidence, through speculation, and through reasoning by analogy, mind, historically con-sidered, does try to penetrate these problematic areas of knowledge.

Still another part of the critique of the Enlightenment has been that its ideal of the self was mediocre and ignoble. Its central image was the "citizen"—not in the total ideal of the man who could re-create his civilization if need be, but merely the "good" man, the man of a certain limited sort of reason, a man with a limited sense of possibility. There was no majesty of Achilles, no silence of the cloister, no nobility of soul, nothing beyond commonsense compatibility. Its "citizen" came to seem a much diminished thing, a mere "man in committee," and certainly not a man who plunges into the depths of hell and rises to claim a new life.

If one wanted a perfect example of a great novelist in rebellion against the formal presuppositions of the novel, it would be Fyodor Dostoyevsky. Intellectually, he believed the European Enlightenment to be shallow and, because shallow, dangerous. Although the novel as a literary form is empirical and secular, Dostoyevsky pushes beyond this, presses against the envelope of the time-space continuum, and gestures toward another sense of man's nature and destiny. This is clear in all his major novels. One thinks of the extreme fates of such figures as Raskolnikov and the nihilist Svidrigaylov. Of course not many Russian intellectuals carried the implications of their ideas to, effectively, suicide; but Dostoyevsky was concerned to work out the implications of those ideas. In this he was to a considerable degree like Dante, who throughout the *Divine Comedy* stripped souls down to their essential intentions. And we also have the extremism of such as the Marmeladov family, anarchic in a Dickensian way but endowed with the Russian intensity of a land on the outer edges of civilization. These tendencies in Dostoyevsky's fiction go to constitute a special world which, like that of all great novelists, is instantly recognizable.

For various reasons, including importance, narrative skill, and the practical consideration of manageable length, *Crime and Punishment* often was chosen as the final work in Columbia University's Humanities I–II course, which began with Homer. In fall 1956 when I introduced this novel to my students I was surprised by their enthusiasm, how passionately they received it.

Perhaps I should not have been so surprised. After all, the plot has a very strong forward movement, propelling the reader through its some five hundred pages. The book is full of vivid, not to say startling, characters. Its emotions are extreme, and much in it bears upon the great twentieth-century issue of totalitarianism and mass murder. On those grounds *Crime and Punishment* would appeal to students anywhere. Yet at Columbia this novel had a special edge, it even came to seem a Columbia novel.

Raskolnikov of course is a student, or former student; and the Columbia environment had both. Like many students, in their dormitories or off campus in rented rooms, he lives in a tiny and slovenly hovel. He is the absolute center of his own thoughts, lies in bed much of the time, and wonders whether he is a great man. The urban neighborhood around Columbia does not approach in degradation Raskolnikov's slummy milieu in St. Petersburg, but it does, here and there, hold out the possibility of a sleazy-romantic *vie de bohème,* at least to a degree that could not be approached in Princeton or Palo Alto. Of course Columbia had its great sunlit men of high culture like Jacques Barzun, Mark Van Doren, and Lionel Trilling, but it also had its nighttown possibilities, especially if students chose to supplement the campus with dives like the White Horse, the Cedar Tavern, and the San Remo down in Greenwich Village.

On top of all that, alert and literary Columbia freshmen were aware of Columbia's rich literary tradition, one recent strand of which was rather dark and had a Dostoyevskian coloration. In his memoir *Witness* published a few years earlier, Whittaker Chambers had included a scene describing how he had sat, as an undergraduate, one chilly day in the lovely Van Amringe Quadrangle in the middle of the campus and, gazing at the statue of Alexander Hamilton, that paragon of the Enlightenment, wondered whether he should commit suicide or join the Communist party. Could such a scene be imagined at Princeton or Amherst?

Columbia also possessed a new but by 1956 legendary tradition involving such figures as Allen Ginsberg, Jack Kerouac, and their friend William Burroughs (of the Burroughs business machine company and later author of the drug novel *Naked Lunch*), as well as lesser legendary figures who revolved in orbit around them. These personalities had once hung out in the West End Bar nearby on Broadway, in 1956 still a dive of some charm and considerable sleaziness.

The Ginsberg-Kerouac-Burroughs legend was that of the author-criminal in the antitradition of Villon, Baudelaire, Rimbaud, Genet. Ginsberg, an A student, had edited the college literary magazine; won prizes; repeatedly been disgraced, expelled, returned; was always in trouble; had been in an asylum, jailed, and even connected with a famous murder; and by 1956 was becoming famous as a "Beat" poet.

It certainly helped the dark glamour of these writers and their circle that the murder in question had actually happened. In 1944, an especially good-looking Columbia student named Lucien Carr—blonde, green eyes, sunken cheeks, artistic—had become the obsessive desire of a homosexual drifter named David Kammerer. One night after a long evening of drinking, the two found themselves in Riverside Park arguing and threatening. Kammerer wanted sex there and then. He threatened to kill Carr's girl. In a tussle, Carr stabbed him through the heart and killed him, then dragged his body to the edge of the Hudson River, weighted it, and threw it in. Carr ran first to his friend Burroughs, then to Kerouac, with whom he spent the night at bars in Harlem. Kerouac threw the fatal knife down a subway grate. He was often sleeping, against the rules, in Ginsberg's dorm room at the time. Carr plead self-defense, got two years; Burroughs and Kerouac were booked; Ginsberg was under some suspicion as knowledgeable.

Increasingly involved, though passively, with petty crooks who moved into his apartment and stayed, Ginsberg in 1949 was a backseat passenger in a getaway car and was arrested with the thieves. At that point Mark Van Doren told him sternly that he had to choose between criminals and society. If he believed that the criminals were in some way holy figures, then he should stick with that choice even if it meant going to jail. Van Doren also told Ginsberg that it might be a good thing for him to "hear the clank of iron." Lionel Trilling consulted Herbert Wechsler, an eminent law professor, who advised an insanity plea. Ginsberg took the advice and was confined to a clinic.

William Burroughs made more news in 1951 by killing his wife. They appear to have had a skit where he shot a water glass off her head with a pistol: William Tell. This came to an end when he put a bullet through her forehead. He got off by pleading a "firearm accident" and later said that this episode made him a writer and the famous author of the drug-soaked *Naked Lunch*.

Much of this tradition was known to my Columbia freshmen when we met to discuss Dostoyevsky and *Crime and Punishment*. Indeed, I often ran into some of my steadiest students when I was having lunch at the West End Bar or dropping in on the White Horse or the San Remo.

Toward the end of *Crime and Punishment*, when Raskolnikov is on the way to the police to turn himself in for his double axe murder, the following remarkable scene takes place at the junction of Sadovaya Street and Obukhovsky Prospect in a slummy district of St. Petersburg.

> He had suddenly remembered Sonya's words: "Go to the cross-roads; bow down before the people, and kiss the ground, because you are guilty before them, and say to all the world, 'I am a murderer!' " A shudder shook his whole body at the remembrance. He was crushed by the weight of all the unescapable misery and anxiety of all this time, and especially of these last hours, that he almost flung himself on the possibility of this new, complete, integral sensation. It had come upon him like a clap of thunder; a single spark was kindled in his spirit and suddenly, like a fire, enveloped his whole being. Everything in him softened on the instant and the tears gushed out. He fell to the ground where he stood. [No one can fail to be reminded here of Paul on the road to Damascus.]
>
> He knelt in the middle of the square, bowed to the ground, and kissed its filth with pleasure and joy. He raised himself and then bowed down a second time.
>
> "Look, here's a chap who's had a drop too much," remarked a youth who stood near him.
>
> Laughter answered him.
>
> "It's because he's going to Bethlehem, lads, and he's saying good-bye to his family and his country. He's bowing down to the whole world and kissing the famous city of St. Petersburg and the soil it stands on," added a workman who was slightly drunk.[4]

"Going to Jerusalem" indeed. This masterpiece has it in mind to go off like a bomb in the culture of rationalism and Enlightenment, has the intention of shifting the balance in the Western mind away from Athens and the "new ideas" and toward Jerusalem and Christianity. In this novel, the great Western cities of London, Paris, Berlin, and St. Petersburg are versions of Athens, while Russia and Christianity are Jerusalem and the deepest truth of things. At the end of his long interior journey Raskolnikov understands that in committing his brutal axe murders he also "killed myself." Through self-crucifixion and suffering he gains some access to his unconscious mind, finds there the eternal Jesus of suffering, death, and resurrection, and though imprisoned in Siberia for seven years, has begun his own resurrection from the grave. He had rid himself of his "bookish dreams," as the psychological detective Porfiry calls them, that is, the thought of the Enlightenment, and finds the fundamental truth of things. The former prostitute Sonya, who loves the self-crucified Raskolnikov, is his Mary Magdalene. Jesus entered Jerusalem riding on a donkey, and Raskolnikov kissed the ground at the cross made by Sadovaya Street and Obukhovsky Prospect as he is mocked by drunks in the crowd. It is through suffering that Raskolnikov has gained access to his unconscious mind and found the truth there, according to Dostoyevsky. The result is summed up by Dostoyevsky's biographer and critic Joseph Frank. In Dostoyevsky the unconscious mind "is never Freudian but always moral as in Shakespeare."[5] (By "Freudian" Frank means "amoral" and "anarchic.")

This is quite an argumentative bomb for Dostoyevsky to throw at the rationalism of the Enlightenment in 1866, and the remarkable thing is that a novelist who began with so sharply conceived a thesis—that the Western Enlightenment was shallow and dangerous—should have written not a polemical essay or a philosophical tale like *Candide* but a great novel full of the concrete detail that makes up actual life. He was able to do this because his appetite for the specificities of life was endless and because he used them to create a powerfully distinctive fictional world. Wherever you touch it, that world is like that of no other writer. You enter it instantly. All of the great writers of fiction have this power; Dostoyevsky had it to an extreme degree.

And he used it here to create a galaxy of characters who sometimes border on the fantastic, as they do in Dickens, but who are always held within the range of the possible. They seem larger than life, full of vast and different energies, but always contained within his imagined world. William Faulkner's Yoknapatawpha County has its startling characters. Dostoyevsky's St. Petersburg has Raskolnikov, Sonya, Marmeladov, Svidrigaylov, Porfiry, Razumikhin, Dunya, and many others vibrant with intense Russian life.

The city of St. Petersburg itself is an important presence both in its urban details and in its meaning. For Dostoyevsky, this city is an abomination, a corrupt Athens, and its actual history is important. It was built early in the eighteenth century by Czar Peter the Great, an enlightened modernizing monarch on the order of Frederick the Great, Louis XVI, and Catherine the Great. He located his new city near the Gulf of Finland and on the banks of the Neva River, which flows into the Baltic Sea. St. Petersburg rose out of a former marshland, and is crisscrossed by canals and rivers. During the summer, when the action of *Crime and Punishment* takes place, it was subject to oppressive damp heat, smells, and frequent epidemics, in this resembling the Venice of Mann's *Death in Venice*. Its slummy back streets were often putrid. Geographically it was the nearest important Russian city to Europe, and this is built into the meaning of the novel. Peter, the czar who built it, intended it to be the Russian gateway to Europe and European culture. In *Crime and Punishment* the city is a moral, social, and intellectual swamp, a sort of cosmic mistake. Its name of course honors the enlightened czar, but also recalls Peter who had the keys to another city. That possibility too is part of the novel as it presses against the edges of the empirical, commonsense world of the Enlightenment.

Raskolnikov, age twenty-three, a former promising law student at the university in St. Petersburg, but now gloomy and idle, living in a tiny hovel and part of a numerous and rootless student proletariat, brutally murders two marginal women with an axe, a repulsive old pawnbroker and her dim and passive sister Lizavéta. In the course of the novel, he offers a number of different motives for the crime but really holds to none of them. These rationalizations are mostly connected with important themes in the moral thought of the Enlightenment. In this novel Dostoyevsky reverses the usual situation in a detective story, in which the mystery to be solved is the identity of the criminal. Here the crime is committed early in the story, we know who the killer is, and the mystery involves a search for his motive. He himself never fully brings that motive to the surface, but the novel as a whole does so.

In Raskolnikov, Dostoyevsky gave us his own version of Prince Hamlet. In Shakespeare the question hovers of why the prince, after knowing the identity of the murderer, does not act against Claudius. In *Crime and Punishment* the question is why Raskolnikov acted the way he did in the first place. In pursuing this question Dostoyevsky plunges deeply into an exploration of human nature and engages psychological, philosophical, political, and religious issues. He also anticipates what would be the cataclysmic themes of the twentieth century—nihilism, mass murder, savage ideology, and totalitarianism.

In one direction, he competed with Shakespeare as an artist but also drew upon and competed with contemporary masters as well. Dickens is here, also Zola, Balzac, and Stendhal. His St. Petersburg is the Unreal City of Baudelaire and, later, T. S. Eliot. The Neva River flows through it as the Thames flows through Dickens's London, the Seine through Paris.

His challenge to Shakespeare, however, was, as Hemingway would say, for the championship. It has often been said that Dostoyevsky is an especially theatrical novelist; that is, he constructs his scenes using dialogue and soliloquy to present character. The big novel, however, was to the nineteenth century what the stage was to Elizabethan England, the preeminent vehicle for public expression in language. And so we have Raskolnikov, Dostoyevsky's salute to Shakespeare and attempt to rival him.

Prince Hamlet had been a student at the university in Wittenberg and was adept among the ideas of his day, including philosophy, literature, classical and modern history, and divinity. At about the same age, Raskolnikov has been studying law, has already published a notable if ominous article about crime, has a mind awash in the latest ideas, but is sunk in melancholy and spends most of his time like a "spider" thinking in his sordid room. Ideas matter to him, as they do to the prince, in that they are directly related to action. Prince Hamlet is plunged into the bottomless evil of Elsinore, where strangeness and evil are in the air. Raskolnikov is plunged into the strange and fetid world of slummy St. Petersburg while strange and radical ideas whirl through his mind. All around him, normality includes murder, suicide, extreme drunkenness, disease, prostitution, cruelty, indifference, official corruption, and pervasive filth. Raskolnikov is a prince in his way too. A promising graduate student, for his family he is the "future." His mother adores him, and his sister is willing to sacrifice herself to something like prostitution to sustain both her mother and Raskolnikov.

Shakespeare does not tell us exactly what Hamlet looks like, but Raskolnikov could play the prince. He "was pale, abstracted, and gloomy. . . . He looked like a man who has been wounded or suffered intense physical pain; his brows were knitted, his lips compressed, his eyes sunken. . . . Even his pale and gloomy countenance lit up for a moment at the entrance of his mother and sister, but this served only to give him an expression of more intensely concentrated torment instead of the diffused anguish that had been there before. The light soon faded, but the torment remained."[6] Like Hamlet, Raskolnikov dominates every scene in which he appears. It is as if he possesses a quality of intense being superior to everyone around him: "It was dark in the corridor; they were standing near a lamp. For almost a minute they looked at one another in silence. Razumikhin remembered that minute all the rest of his life. With every moment Raskolnikov's intent and fiery glance pierced more powerfully into his mind and soul. Suddenly Razumikhin shuddered. Something strange had passed between them."[7] Both Hamlet and Raskolnikov often seem insane, and indeed sometimes may be so. In both the question is raised about the boundaries between sanity and madness. Both have worried and undoubtedly sane close friends, Horatio and Raszumikhin, both of whose names connote "reason" (*ratio, raszum*).

No one can doubt that so comprehensive and learned a mind as Dostoyevsky's was aware of all these parallels between Raskolnikov and Hamlet and very likely aware of many more; and no one can doubt that

Dostoyevsky thought of his novel as aspiring to the greatness of Shakespeare's play. There exists a further resemblance between Shakespeare and Dostoyevsky, however. It is profound and not exactly demonstrable except by a grasp of an entire play such as *Hamlet* or an entire novel such as *Crime and Punishment*. I am certain, though I cannot prove it, that Dostoyevsky was aware of this kinship with Shakespeare. I cited earlier the remark by Joseph Frank that in Dostoyevsky the unconscious is "never Freudian but always moral as in Shakespeare." This does not mean anything so shallow as that Shakespeare and Dostoyevsky believed that human nature is essentially good. Everything they wrote denies that. It means that the unconscious knows things that the reason cannot formulate, and that in its depths the mind knows the profound difference between good and evil—and that the universe is the kind of place that gave rise to such a mind. How the individual acts on such knowledge is another thing, but in its unconscious depths the mind is moral. Joseph Frank does not go so far as to say so, but an intelligence such as Dostoyevsky's must have understood a similar recognition in Shakespeare.

Prince Hamlet, having seen Elsinore, knows that there are more things in heaven and earth than are dealt with in Horatio's restricted Stoic philosophy. Horatio's Stoicism is analogous to the Enlightenment in *Crime and Punishment*. If Hamlet finally acts, as some argue, because of a late and unconscious imperative of justice, leaving "books" behind, then he is analogous to Raskolnikov who, confused by theory and unacknowledged guilt, does in the end achieve at least a tenuous connection with his moral unconscious, acknowledges his guilt, kisses the ground at those "cross" roads, and gladly accepts justice for his crimes.

Early in the novel Raskolnikov murders the two women. He had planned to kill only the old pawnbroker, but when the time came he also killed her sister Lizavéta. Told with great economy and directness, this short scene is the most unambiguous thing in the novel. The sharpened axe does its work. In *Hamlet*, everything is ambiguous until the clink of steel at the end and the ensuing deaths.

The multiplicity of motives Raskolnikov ascribes to himself do not satisfactorily account for the murders, and assigning these motives an order of plausibility is difficult. The source of these motives, however, is important. They are based on notions in the air in intellectual St. Petersburg, and they derive, often crudely, from the Western Enlightenment. Yet their very multiplicity makes them seem superficial and points to something deeper and unacknowledged.

For example, Raskolnikov wonders whether, despite unpromising appearances, he might be a great man on the model of Napoleon, who indeed cast a long shadow over the European imagination. Hegel had seen Napoleon marching with his army through Berlin on his way to Russia after the battle of Jena. Hegel thought Napoleon embodied the world spirit, was the bearer of the French Enlightenment into the Eastern darknesses. Napoleon III had written a popular book about Julius Caesar, seeing him as a great man of the Napoleonic sort. Goethe's *Faust* was of course near at hand in all this. The point that impresses Raskolnikov is that such world spirits are destructive in order to be creative, and they are essentially amoral forces. His published article in the law journal had explored these themes, arguing that without the amoral destructiveness human progress could not occur. Thus Raskolnikov, according to this theory, commits the two murders to find out if he is such an amoral destroyer-creator, a bearer of human progress. His bungling of the crime and his subsequent torments indicate that surely he is not, but the experiment had to be made.

He has numerous rationalizations, however. Sometimes he says that he killed for money, to facilitate his career, which was surely more valuable than that of the old pawnbroker. On that rational calculus the murders were justified. But no, he does not resume his career, and he does not really believe money was his motive. He never looked in her purse to count the money, and he buried the loot without using any of it.

The idea of the amoral great man is connected with many of the ideas flowing out of the Enlightenment and into the intellectual atmosphere of St. Petersburg. The various forms of social Darwinism and utilitarianism may seem far from the heroic amoralism that Raskolnikov ascribes to Napoleon, but there are obvious links. William Godwin had famously argued in his *Political Justice* that he would leave his mother or sister in a burning building in order to rescue François Fénelon because this writer was of more use to mankind. That calculation might be justified according to the utilitarian premise of the greatest good for the greatest number, but there is a perversity and evil in its particular application.

The astute psychological detective Porfiry notices early in the novel that a key proposition in Raskolnikov's published article is that he "uphold(s) bloodshed as a matter of conscience." Indeed, Raskolnikov admits to Porfiry that he believes in the "New Jerusalem," the utopian society of the future, the ideal social order. Thus conscience could easily command "bloodshed" as a way of getting there. We see in the novel that his milieu is full of utopian ideas of various kinds, all of them destructive of ordinary morality. Raskolnikov himself might be called a proto-revolutionary. He believes in conscience-enjoined bloodshed. He is a utopian. He himself is not primarily political, but if he were, he would have been a violent extremist. These are what Porfiry (and presumably Dostoyevsky) calls "bookish dreams," and which are practical nightmares. From this perspective, Dostoyevsky can be read as a powerful antagonist to Karl Marx and his scientific utopianism, which was a specific product of the European Enlightenment.

There is also a further twist to this theme. At the bottom of Dostoyevsky's universe there resides nihilism, cold meaninglessness. In this he recalls Dante. Nihilism was a felt potential in much nineteenth-century thought—in Darwin, Huxley, Nietzsche—and Dostoyevsky's fictional world contains an impressive array of great Russian nihilists, monsters such as Stavrogin and Kirilov, and in *Crime and Punishment,* the memorable Svidrigaylov, who fights boredom through sensuality: he pursues preadolescent girls and finally commits suicide. The inference is that nihilism may be one aspect of utopianism, both expressing an acute hostility toward the actual and the possible, both being a negation of the givenness, the "isness," of the world.

Porfiry had spoken of the "bookish" dreams of Raskolnikov. But Raskolnikov had dreams that were not bookish at all, but redemptive.

For example, shortly before the axe murders, he had had a dream reflecting his childhood experience involving a group of rowdy and insensate peasants beating and killing a small mare in a street, beating it around the eyes and gratuitously smashing it to the ground. In the dream he adds something that had not happened. He dreams of cradling the bloody head of the mare in his arms and trying to comfort it.

This dream, a product of his moral unconscious, connects with much that follows about Raskolnikov. It may connect with his killing of the old pawnbroker, but more immediately with the murder of her passive sister Lizavéta. He had also at one point been engaged to marry the invalid daughter of a landlady. "I really don't know what drew me to her then. . . . She was always ill. If she had been lame or a hunchback, I believe I would have liked her even better."[8]

Ultimately this connects with Sonya, the saintly prostitute forced into the gutter by her irresponsible drunken father Marmeladov, who loves Raskolnikov, in her way, for his fellow suffering. The mare and the others are "poor gentle things . . . whose eyes are soft and gentle." One thinks of those haunting lines in T. S. Eliot about "The notion of some infinitely gentle / Infinitely suffering thing." This clearly is Dostoyevsky's vision of Christ, uniting humanity, and also the mare, in a vision of universal suffering.[9]

Yet the vision also includes Raskolnikov himself, as when he cries out to Sonya during his climactic confession: "Did I murder the old woman? I murdered myself, not her! I crushed myself, once and for all, forever."[10] Here Raskolnikov ceases to live in the present moment of misery and experiences the emotions of childhood, as in his dream of the tortured and slaughtered mare. The long-ago emotions of his childhood come at least partially to the surface.

On this point it is important to notice that the dream about the mare occurs before the murder, and that after the dream Raskolnikov experiences some moments of relief, as if returning to his true self. But when he soon learns that the old pawnbroker supposedly will be alone in her room, the conscious plan to murder her blocks out those early thoughts and feelings of relief. It is also important that when he goes through with the killings, Raskolnikov does so as if in a daze, as if an automaton. Not for an instant does he think of his great man, Darwinian, utilitarian, or utopian socialist rationalizations. Just why he goes through with the murder in this way is the subject of exploration throughout the rest of the novel. Among his deepest motives may be one he never articulates to himself, even at the end. Nevertheless, it seems implicit in his behavior that he understands unconsciously that he has turned his "loved" sister Dunya into a quasi-whore. She is the sole source of income and supports the promising but now idle Raskolnikov as well as his widowed mother Pulkheria. As an upper servant at a rural estate, Dunya is pursued sexually by the nihilist-sensualist Svidrigaylov, then passed off by Svidrigaylov's outraged wife, whom he later apparently murders, to a "respectable" but loathsome suitor named Lhuzin. It is inconceivable that Dunya would wish to marry Lhuzin, but she is prepared to do so for the income, some of which will go to support Raskolnikov. Raskolnikov does what he can to destroy the engagement, but when he succeeds, the perverted Svidrigaylov turns up in St. Petersburg to pursue Dunya.

The guilty role of Raskolnikov in living off the wages of Dunya's de facto prostitution has its parallel with the drunken Marmeladov and his family who live off the prostitution of his daughter Sonya. Marmeladov is a marvelous creation, a dark Russian version of Dickens's Mr. Micawber, his drunken rhetoric absurdly seedy-elegant. The parallel between Marmeladov, literally drunk, and Raskolnikov, drunk on ideas, is obvious, as is the parallel between Sonya and Dunya.

In all his discussion of his motives for the murders, for "killing himself," as he puts it, Raskolnikov never mentions his guilt over his dependence on Dunya's income. Apparently this remains unconscious knowledge to him. Yet his self-loathing turns into aggression directed outward, turns into the killings. It has reached the point where, as he walks through the streets of St. Petersburg, Raskolnikov is constantly aware of the 30,000 prostitutes historians inform us were working in that city. On this view, Raskolnikov could have committed suicide; instead he commits murder, a figurative suicide.

Since he is thus driven by unconscious drives, it is psychologically right that Raskolnikov confesses first to Sonya, then to the police, and accepts his sentence to seven years in a Siberian prison. Sonya is the only moral reality in his unconscious whirlwind, the center that holds. Through her he finds his way back to the sense of injustice present in his unconscious—as in his dream of the injustice done to the mare. And, accepting the universality of suffering as a human bond, he finds in his self-crucifixion a connection with his moral unconscious and a turn toward regeneration.

It seems clear that Dostoyevsky wins his argument with Marx. To achieve the New Jerusalem through reason and revolution, you have to kill too many old pawnbrokers and too many Lizavétas. The revolutionary must, in Thomas Gray's famous line, wade through slaughter to a throne. In purely rational and utilitarian terms, it may not matter how many Lizavétas and pawnbrokers you murder. The moral unconscious knows that it is wrong. When Raskolnikov rediscovers his moral unconscious he rediscovers himself. He was on the edge of becoming a zealous commissar until he found salvation in the acceptance of his own humanity through suffering. Dostoyevsky's God is like the God in Job, mysterious, and known through suffering.

In discussing this novel with students I find that I must allow that Dostoyevsky has made a telling argument against the Enlightenment. He has done so to the extent that we associate the project of the Enlightenment with utopian politics and with the deliberate restriction of "philosophy" to empiricism and rationalism. Along that restricting road we arrive at the condition of much analytical philosophy today, which does not regard Plato, Montaigne, or, for that matter, Nietzsche, Kierkegaard, or Heidegger as philosophers. Indeed, such characteristic Enlightenment philosophers as Hobbes, Locke, Bentham, and Mill, as well as, for example, Russell, have little serious to say about religion, tragedy, nobility of character, or a whole range of issues that have long occupied the human mind. The same is true of such figures as Darwin, Marx, and Freud, also products of the Enlightenment, who offered themselves as "scientists" but were also potent cultural prophets. In his attack upon the

Enlightenment, Dostoyevsky certainly did have hold of that important truth. He also saw that the Enlightenment could foster a certain dangerous kind of hubris, that, as Montaigne and Pascal said, made men seek to be angels but end up as beasts. *But also.* By this time in the college course I referred to at the beginning of this chapter the students have come to recognize that those words "but also" are a signature of wisdom; and having conceded that much to the great novelist, we have to add that if the project of the Enlightenment is more modestly defined, we must say that it conferred great practical benefits of a comprehensive sort, and that the criticism of the Enlightenment, as by Swift and Dostoyevsky, is part of the Enlightenment project itself, part of the Athens-Jerusalem dialectic. We have to recognize that none of us would care to live in a society that had not been shaped in important ways by the Enlightenment, which is to say that none of us would care to live in much of the world today. In fact, the Enlightenment was indispensable.

Faust in Great Neck

For a twentieth-century novel with which to conclude there are many possibilities in a variety of languages, but, in view of the shape of the twentieth century, an American novel seems appropriate. Again the possibilities are many, and perhaps *The Great Gatsby* seems a surprising choice. It is not epic in form like, for example, *Moby-Dick;* yet it is epic in its reach and seriousness and in its engagement with the themes of the Western consciousness explored here. F. Scott Fitzgerald's ambition was not minor. He spoke of aspiring to the heroic tradition of "Goethe-Byron-Shaw." He variously took among his models Keats, Stendhal, and Thackeray. If *The Great Gatsby* seems at first slight beside such a masterpiece as *Crime and Punishment,* then greatness can be displayed in the smaller as well as in the larger work. Fitzgerald himself did not blink at comparing *Gatsby* with *The Brothers Karamazov.*

Hemingway once compared Fitzgerald's talent to the dust on a butterfly's wing. Once the dust is gone the butterfly can no longer fly. Hem-

ingway was saying that Fitzgerald's talent was beautiful, delicate, somewhat mysterious, and highly perishable. Yet at its best, as in *The Great
Gatsby*, it was also remarkably strong and enduring. To choose another
simile, it was like a thin steel framework that looks light and fragile but at
the same time has great tensile strength and is surprisingly permanent.
Lionel Trilling thought that Fitzgerald's voice in his fiction had "gentleness without softness."[11] T. S. Eliot wrote that *Gatsby* "seems to me the
first step that American fiction has taken since Henry James."[12]

Published in 1925, *The Great Gatsby* is fast approaching the one-
hundred-year mark Samuel Johnson set for the determination of "classic" status. This was not an arbitrary figure. Johnson thought that if a
work retained its importance over that span of generations it had very
likely escaped from mere topicality and other transitory appeals and had
continued to appeal to intelligent permanent interest.

Gatsby remains in print and maintains large sales. It is widely assigned
to students. The amount of commentary on it has been and is enormous.
Although small in scale, it is highly concentrated because of techniques
Fitzgerald had learned from Joseph Conrad and T. S. Eliot. It lends itself
very well to classroom discussion. Its themes are major ones, and the
book easily locates itself thematically among the other works discussed
here. Though we come to it last, we do so, needless to say, not as a
culmination but as a work worthy of belonging in the conversation.

I took note of the enormous amount that has been written about *The
Great Gatsby*, so much indeed that it might seem impossible to say anything new about the book. Yet there is more to say about what is at its
center and radiates from there to suffuse and organize the whole. If *The
Great Gatsby* is not a religious novel, it nevertheless defines its themes in
religious terms; and in the end it may be religious after all. Indeed at its
center is what might almost be called a formal religion, one with a long
history, and that religion is magic.

Nick Carraway calls Gatsby a "son of God," explaining that he
sprang from a "Platonic conception of himself." As Yeats said, in dreams
begin responsibilities, and though James Gatz was the son of his father,
Jay Gatsby was self-created. If he was a "son of God," then the creative

imagination is God. If we think of Genesis, this may not be an altogether wild thought. God in Genesis is not merely reproductive but creative of novelty. We may well think here of Wordsworth's great poem "Resolution and Independence" and its famous line "By our own spirits are we deified."

Many readers have noticed that when we first meet Jay Gatsby gazing at the green light at the end of the Buchanan dock, the moment has a strange quality of religious awe, Gatsby trembling with emotion, his awe and expectation like that of a religious devotee. Nick was about to greet his neighbor, "But I didn't call to him, for he gave a sudden intimation that he was content to be alone—he stretched out his arms toward the dark water in a curious way, and as far as I was from him, I could have sworn he was trembling."[13]

One notices that Nick's language here seems slightly inadequate to the phenomenon he is witnessing. Gatsby is more than "content" to be alone; he implicitly insists upon it. The way in which Gatsby stretched out his arms was not "curious." It borders on ecstasy. Nick here stands outside Gatsby's imaginative world. He will not remain outside it, but will enter into it, participate in it, gain in knowledge of it, but retain his distance. His participation will also transform his language from commonplace to eloquence.

The green light at the end of Daisy's dock is important, and it connects with a great deal in this novel. Green suggests "go" and looks forward to the role automobiles play here, the green optimistic light leading to disaster. There are no red danger lights in Gatsby's world. Everything is go, all things are possible. Gatsby expects to press down the accelerator, reverse time, return to 1917 and remembered romance. The drunk in chapter 3, who has hit a stone wall and knocked a wheel off his car, thinks he can put it in reverse and "go." The color green also connects with the eternal green of the unfallen Eden of which the Dutch sailors dream at the end. And the color green, far from incidentally, is the color of the American dollar, which is the agent of transformation throughout the novel.

When Nick first sees his "neighbor," a weighted word here, Gatsby is reaching out his arms to that intensely optimistic (but also dangerous and even sinister) green light. We now know that we are in the presence of something unusual, a world of optimism and transformation that is a powerful presence throughout the novel. And we come to recognize that the idea of magical transformation describes much that is characteristic of modernity. It has its claims on reality.

In *The Great Gatsby*, the idea of magical transformation constitutes a parallel and rival religion competing with Christianity, and magic is implicit in the imagery with which Fitzgerald surrounds Gatsby when Nick first glimpses him. Indeed, magic has an ancient theological history, traceable at least as far back as the account of Simon in the book of Acts. Consider the paragraph immediately before the one just quoted from about Gatsby trembling with emotion: "The wind had blown off, leaving a loud bright night, with wings beating in the trees and a permanent organ sound as the full bellows of the earth blew the frogs full of life. The silhouette of a moving cat wavered across the moonlight, and turning my head to watch it, I saw that I was not alone."[14]

This passage has connections not only with the world of romance but with the world of folklore. Gatsby is here associated with witchcraft in its mystery and cruelty, wings, blown frogs, cats, the moon, and, more certainly, with magic. We notice that the moon and the cat are in the same sentence with that neighbor. (Nick will be his neighbor in a more than geographical sense as the narrative unfolds.) Gatsby is a "son of God," indeed, and attempting a magical victory over time and mortality. He is himself the divinity of a world whose distinguishing motif is magical transformation.

Consider the famous paragraph near the beginning in which we meet Daisy Buchanan (née Fay—or "fairy elf") sitting on a couch in the Buchanans' East Egg mansion with her friend Jordan Baker: "They were both in white and their dresses were rippling and fluttering as if they had just been blown back in after a short flight around the house. I must have stood for a moment listening to the snap of the curtains and the groan of a picture on the wall. Then there was a boom as Tom Buchanan shut the rear window and the caught wind died out about the room, and the two women ballooned slowly to the floor."[15] The language here renders this a magical castle, and even the landscape is in motion, alive with spirits. Here is how Nick Carraway approaches the Buchanan place, stepping through the looking-glass into that strange world: "And so it happened that on a warm windy evening I drove over to East Egg to see two old friends whom I scarcely knew at all."[16] Indeed, he does not know them. Daisy "Fay" may belong to Gatsby's world of imagination and magical transformation, though Daisy (and Tom) Buchanan do not qualify.

When Nick first approaches the Buchanan house in East Egg, something suddenly begins to happen and you sense it in the prose. "Their house was even more elaborate than I had expected, a cheerful red and white colonial mansion, overlooking the bay. The lawn started at the beach and ran toward the front door for a quarter of a mile, jumping over sun dials and brick walls and burning gardens—finally when it reached the house drifting up the side in bright vines as though from the momentum of its run."[17] There is strange commerce here between actuality and metaphorical reach. The prose is full of strange possibility, and while it does not lose its hold on literal description it nevertheless renders the scene alive, in motion as if inhabited by spirits. We sense that house and grounds may themselves be on the verge of transformation into something else.

Magical transformation, indeed, is the subject of *The Great Gatsby*, such transformation viewed as the essence of modernity. We need to support that claim here with only a few examples from the multitude that fill the narrative. There are those three Negroes Nick sees while crossing the Art Deco Queensboro Bridge toward the startling skyscrapers of Manhattan. He is a passenger with Gatsby in his fabulous Rolls. As they cross the bridge, Nick muses, "Anything can happen. . . . Anything at all." Then he records: "As we crossed Blackwell's Island a limousine passed us, driven by a white chauffeur, in which sat three modish Negroes, two bucks and a girl. I laughed as the yolks of their eyes rolled toward us in haughty rivalry."[18]

In their own way, these are black Gatsbys, their social positions transformed by money. In Manhattan, the "grey old man" from whom Myrtle Wilson buys a pup "bore an obscure resemblance to John D. Rockefeller," a farcical variation on the theme of transformation. Nick's own family, the Carraways, participates in this comprehensive magical process: "The Carraways are something of a clan and we have a tradition that we're descended from the Dukes of Buccleuch, but the actual founder of my line was my grandfather's brother, who came here in fifty-one, sent a substitute to the Civil War, and started the wholesale hardware business that my father carries on today."[19] This sentence is beautifully split into two parts by "but the actual," from the fictitious Gatsbean ancestry over to the gritty facts. Nick himself knows what "actuality" is. He has not, to use Conrad's phrase about Mr. Kurtz, "kicked free of the earth"; and Gatsby has many connections with Kurtz. It is Nick's hold on the actual that partially excludes him from Gatsby's magical world. The culminating example of transformation in the book is of course Jay Gatsby, formerly Jimmy Gatz. Even his name beautifully embodies it. "Gatsby" is a prettied-up "gat," or pistol, with an English suffix, a name splendidly appropriate to a crook, a gangster, and a would-be Oxford man. Such a name change, not incidentally, must be for the most part peculiarly American, as Weinstein becomes Winston, Schwartz becomes Black, and former Africans become George Washington Smith and Grover Cleveland Jones.

In a brilliant passage at the beginning of chapter 3, Fitzgerald employs the repeated possessive pronoun "his" to create a world centered on Gatsby and follows it with a beautiful metaphor of magical transformation: "There was music from my neighbor's house through the summer nights. In his blue gardens men and girls came and went like moths among the whisperings and the champagne and the stars. At high tide in the afternoon I watched his guests diving from the tower of his raft, or taking the sun on the hot sand of his beach while his two motor boats slit the waters of the Sound, drawing aquaplanes over cataracts of foam. On weekends his Rolls Royce became an omnibus."[20]

That is Gatsby's empire; Fitzgerald learned such use of "his" from Conrad on Kurtz's Congo "empire." Then comes the sacrament of magical transformation: "Every Friday five crates of oranges and lemons arrived from a fruiterer in New York—every Monday these same oranges and lemons left his back door in a pyramid of pulpless halves. There was a machine in the kitchen which could extract the juice of two hundred oranges in half an hour if a little button was pressed two hundred times by a butler's thumb."[21]

As the divinity of his magical world, Gatsby has manifestly divine trappings. He rides in a chariot, a fabulous cream-colored Rolls, bright with nickel, swollen here and there in its monstrous length with triumphant hat boxes and tool boxes and terraced with a labyrinth of windshields that "mirrored a dozen suns." It gives out "a burst of melody on its three-noted horn." It has "fenders spread like wings," and it radiates its light through the dusty neighborhood of Astoria as they drive toward the magical bridge. For the time being, the divine Gatsby is invulnerable. When a motorcycle cop stops him, Gatsby shows him his card from the commissioner: "Know you the next time, Mr. Gatsby. Excuse *me*."[22] And like any magician he wears garments rich and strange. "He took out a pile of shirts and began throwing them, one by one before us, shirts of sheer linen and thick silk and fine flannel, which lost their folds as they fell and covered the table in a many-colored disarray. . . . Suddenly, with a strained sound, Daisy bent her head into the shirts and began to cry stormily. . . . 'It makes me sad because I've never seen such—such beautiful shirts before.' "[23] Daisy understands the meaning of the shirts: that they are all for *her*, that they are Gatsby's absurd and beautiful tribute; she worships at this shrine of magic and recovers for a moment her lost self, "Fay," from the all too earthy and material Tom Buchanan.

Fitzgerald was far from the first to see that the idea of magical transformation and the idea of modernity are profoundly connected. Goethe's *Faust* is a trumpet blast and a manifesto of the modern spirit, and at the beginning of part 2 it is much to the point that Mephistopheles shows up at the emperor's court and relieves the bankruptcy there by introducing paper money—backed by fictitious treasure, supposedly "buried in the Emperor's ground." This sleight of hand overcomes skepticism about the soundness of the kingdom and produces instant prosperity. "Tens, Thirties, Fifties, Hundreds," reports the lord treasurer to the emperor. "Your city, else half molded in stagnation,/Now teems in prosperous jubilation."[24]

Goethe saw that paper money, a fiction in itself and intrinsically worth nothing, tended to make society, heretofore hierarchical and relatively unchanging, itself fictional and highly mobile. In a brilliant climax to the introduction of paper money, the court fool transforms himself into a noble lord and purchases a "grange with game preserves." Mephistopheles comments sardonically, "Now who will deny our Fool is wise and witty?" Goethe sees that money—un-real estate—has a strange transforming power. One's own appearance, if accepted by others, becomes the social reality. One can invent oneself, as the fool does.[25]

In *The Great Gatsby*, too, it is money that creates possibility and a considerable freedom, such as the three Negroes in their limo with a white chauffeur enjoyed. Money is the liberator of spirits pure and impure, and Gatsby is the Faust of this world of magical transformation. He has his Mephistopheles, a minor devil, in the form of Meyer Wolfsheim and other underworld minor devils on the phone from Philadelphia.

At the outset of the story, Nick begins his initiation into the magical world of money and magic. "I bought a dozen volumes on banking and credit and investment securities today and they stood on my shelf in red and gold like new money from the mint, promising to unfold the secrets that only Midas and Morgan and Maecenas knew."[26] Most sentences in Gatsby are rich in meaning, but that one is especially so. J. P. Morgan was an actual person. Nick could have read about him in the rotogravures, though perhaps with a touch of magic to him if we think of Morgan le Fay; but Midas was a mythical figure (and also a magician who performed transformations); and Maecenas was historical but also legendary, the man whose wealth at Augustus's court made it glitter with artistic greatness. The alliteration assimilates the historical Morgan into this legendary and magical company. The supposed boundaries of the stable old "real" world begin to blur and the historical and time-bound begins to mix with the legendary and magical.

It is not ordinarily noticed that our familiar one-dollar bill is in its way a magical document. Appropriately it is colored green and constitutes a ticket of admission to this entire magical world. Flowers like Daisy and Myrtle may grow in that magical soil. On our dollar bill there is reproduced the great seal of the republic. On the front there is the familiar eagle, but the reverse side is strange and not a little sinister. It shows a pyramid with a human eye at its apex, this symbol being framed by two Latin inscriptions from Virgil. One, *novus ordo seculorum,* means "new order of time." The other, *annuit coeptis,* means, roughly, "begun under divine auspices." Thus time will begin again in uniquely favored America. The greenness of Eden will be restored. This, symbolically on the one-dollar bill, is the dream of Eden entertained by the seventeenth-century Dutch sailors on the last page of *The Great Gatsby.* Appropriately enough, and democratically, this dream is announced on the one-dollar bill and endorsed by the father of his country, George Washington, whose portrait is on the face of the bill. On the higher denominations, things get more complicated, but on the one-dollar bill, in "the beginning," anything is possible—or almost anything.

The fact that magic is the essence of modernity is the perception that shapes *The Great Gatsby.* From his perspective as a sociologist and theologian, Peter Berger put it this way:

> *The City is a place of magic.* . . . I don't mean occultism, though there is enough of that around as well. I mean magic in a more ample sense, namely the quality of the surreal, the intuition that reality is manipulable, unpredictable, subject to the strangest metamorphoses at any moment. If you will, I mean what Rudolf Otto called the *mysterium fascinans.* The British author Jonathan Raban, in his curious book *Soft City,* argues that modern urban life is characterized by magic, and not (as it is customarily thought to be) by rationality. I think that there is much to be said for this view; Raban also maintains that New York

has this magic in a particularly potent form. The magic of the city can be summed up in a sentence that sums up a recurring experience: *Anything can happen here—and it could happen right now.*[27]

Not surprisingly, Nick first sees Gatsby at night, trembling with desire under a moon; and Gatsby's strongest moments in the novel take place after dark. During the daylight hours, he seems ineffectual, in disarray. He is not, after all, J. P. Morgan, who could stem a bank panic by signing a few documents about gold and who controlled the White Star Line, which in turn owned the *Titanic.* Jay Gatsby is a spirit. He is painfully ineffectual during the scene in Nick's cottage, where he meets Daisy for the first time after five years of his self-invention, or at the Plaza Hotel, where Tom Buchanan brutally faces him down and recovers Daisy. Gatsby is strong under the moon of romance; in the daylight, he is a crook.

If Gatsby is a god of magical transformation, he is not the only character in the book who has designs of that sort upon reality. Even the earthy-muscular Tom Buchanan seeks "a little wistfully, for the dramatic turbulence of some irrecoverable football game."[28] Daisy carries her own dreams, and they are poignantly evoked by the sounds of a waltz. Meyer Wolfsheim magically transforms the World Series through money, changing the White Sox of 1919 to the Black Sox of history. Jordan Baker cheats at golf.

The desire for Eden is also pervasive. Gatsby has an "Adam Study" and surrounds himself with forty acres of garden. The odors of jonquils, hawthorn, plum blossoms, and—yes—kiss-me-at-the-gates pervades his mansion. His bedrooms are swathed in rose and lavender silk, and his closets are filled with apple-green, lavender, and orange shirts. He pursues "Daisy" and Tom has a mistress called "Myrtle." The seventeenth-century Dutch sailors are not the only ones who long for a past moment of intensity and innocence. At the end, Gatsby gazes at a ruined garden: "He must have looked up at an unfamiliar sky through frightening leaves and shivered as he found what a grotesque thing a rose is and how raw the sunlight was upon the scarcely created grass."[29]

As against that desire to recover the moment of lost innocence and remembered intensity, a powerful countercurrent runs through the book and asserts itself against the unlimited possibility of transformation as held out by the magic of modernity. This countercurrent asserts the claims of actuality. The book handles Jay Gatsby with great tenderness, but it also judges him, even while holding open the possibility that his magic, after all, may—actually!—prevail. The book does not foreclose on Gatsby.

All of Gatsby's central propositions prove fallacious: that time is not real, that Daisy never loved Tom, that crime and idealism can really coexist, that he is an Oxford man. Gatsby's whole project to roll back the clock to 1917 and the period before Daisy's marriage to Tom is really an attempt to deny the reality of man's objective existence in time and to assault man's mortality. Throughout the book Fitzgerald makes time a powerful undercurrent. Nick Carraway's voice is full of aphorisms, suggesting experience distilled by time, and the book opens with a banal aphorism delivered by his father: "Whenever you feel like criticizing anyone, just remember that all the people in this world haven't had the advantages that you've had."[30] Nick thinks enough of this lame truism to put it at the beginning of his narrative.

And the power of actuality pulls strongly against Gatsby's magic. The entire story is told in the past tense, often with an elegiac tone. The narrative itself moves through the change of seasons, beginning in spring 1922 and moving through that strange summer and into fall, with signs of winter present. Nick can recall the names of Gatsby's guests, a superb comic catalogue inspired by a similar one in Thackeray's *Vanity Fair* but with the theme of magical transformation woven in. They had come to Gatsby's parties in "that summer" of 1922; he had written them down (perfect touch) in the blank spaces of a *timetable*. "It is an old timetable now, disintegrating at its folds, and headed: 'This schedule in effect July 5, 1922.' But I can still read the grey names."[31]

In the climactic scene, which approaches a sort of wild genius, in which Gatsby at long last meets Daisy in Nick's cottage, time in various forms pervades the language describing the scene, until Gatsby tries to conceal his nervousness by feigning ease and leaning back against the mantelpiece: "His head leaned back so far that it rested against the face of a defunct mantelpiece clock, and from this position his distraught eyes stared down at Daisy, who was sitting, frightened but graceful, on the edge of a stiff chair. . . . Luckily the clock took this moment to tilt dangerously at the pressure of his head, whereupon he turned and caught it with trembling fingers, and set it back in place. Then he sat down rigidly. . . . 'I'm sorry about the clock,' he said. . . . 'It's an old clock,' I told them idiotically."[32]

This is an astonishing piece of writing, surpassed if possible by that scene in which, as the guests leave one of Gatsby's parties, a drunken driver runs his car into a stone wall and knocks one of the wheels off. The drunks are so besotted that they fail to appreciate the nature of the damage they have caused to their car. One of the drunks gets out and after a ludicrous exchange with the crowd admits that he was not the driver. The drunken driver is still in the car.

> At least a dozen men, some of them little better off than he was, explained to him that wheel and car were not joined by any physical bond.
> "Back her out," he suggested after a moment. "Put her in reverse."
> "But the wheel's off."
> "No harm in trying," he said.[33]

The next paragraph delivers a fine elegiac vision of Gatsby, still in control, drunk in his own way, and unaware that he has a wheel off too. "The caterwauling horns had reached a crescendo and I turned and cut across the lawn toward home. I glanced back once. A wafer of a moon was shining over Gatsby's house, making the night fine as before, and surviving the laughter and the sound of his still glowing garden. A sudden emptiness seemed to flow from the windows and the great doors, endowing with complete isolation the figure of the host, who stood on the porch with his hand up in a formal gesture of farewell."[34] The host, the wafer, the moon, and a benediction are there as Gatsby says farewell, sacraments in the parallel and parodic religion of magic. The drunken driver, of course, is a comic version of the tragic Gatsby. He ignores the detached wheel, and Gatsby, himself drunk on imagination and possibility, ignores the reality of time. But is there, as the drunk says, "No harm in trying"?

Certainly Gatsby's magical aspiration spreads corpses along the North Shore of Long Island. At the end, he himself lies dead and bleeding in his swimming pool, surrounded, like some dying god of spring and fertility, by the fallen leaves of autumn. (On this I think Fitzgerald had read *The Waste Land* with attention.) Nick, in an epiphany, says that Gatsby is "worth the whole damn bunch put together."[35] We also hear Nick's point translated into language. We seldom hear Jay Gatsby speak. But when he does utter words, they are often astonishing: "Her voice is full of money."[36] Jay Gatz could never have dreamed that up. "Can't repeat the past? Why of course you can."[37] What calm assurance. Is it possible he is right? Was Daisy's love for Tom only "personal"?[38] Gatsby is breathtaking. He not only pushes the edge of the envelope, he shreds the edge of the envelope and moves in language into some other realm. This in fact is characteristic of Fitzgerald's own style. Again and again, not only in his best stories but even in his magazine stories, he does strange things with his prose. Magical? On the evidence of his manuscripts at the Firestone Library in Princeton he also worked very hard for them. He revised and revised until the strange phrase came to him. Hemingway thought his talent was like the dust on a butterfly's wing. It was much more enduring stuff than that.

Compared with Gatsby, Nick Carraway is banal until not quite the end, and perhaps most banal at the very beginning when he quotes with apparent reverence his father's boring chestnut of advice. Yet at the end, good old Nick, like Hamlet's friend Horatio, somehow is moved to completely unexpected eloquence. Against all odds, Nick Carraway's reflections on what he has seen are astonishing, his prose moving toward song, an operatic prose aria, about the Dutch sailors and their own moment of wonder as they gaze upon that fresh green breast of the New World. This voice is a startling thing for Nick to find, ordinary Nick, son of a banal father who opens the novel with a cliché. This new and lyrical

Nick must have found his voice only through his total experience of Jay Gatsby. The example of Hamlet's friend Horatio is apposite. He too is moved to eloquence by his experience of the prince: "And flights of angels sing thee to thy rest."

Writing in 1924, Fitzgerald both learned much from Eliot's *Waste Land* and meant to challenge it thematically. He learned techniques of concentration and juxtaposition, the creation of landscapes that seem phantasmagoric, the interweaving of popular tunes, the use of myth: Gatsby is born in the spring of the novel and dies in the fall in his swimming pool, yet is reborn at the end as his moon of magical transformation rises again over his Long Island. Fitzgerald called his valley of ashes a "waste land," had the absent God preside over it in the form of the empty eyeglasses of Doctor Eckleberg, and included a "journey to the underworld" to see Meyer Wolfsheim.

Yet Fitzgerald challenged Eliot with an answer to *The Waste Land*. That moon, rising over Long Island at the end, is the Gatsbean moon of magical transformation, that "wafer" as it had been called, of the religion of magic. Fitzgerald tells us that the transforming imagination is immortal.

And so, in that waste land, it indeed proved to be. Fitzgerald's waste land, the dusty dwelling place of George and Myrtle Wilson, in 1924 was a landfill in which coal ashes and other waste material were being used to make available for building a marshy area known as Flushing Meadows. One has noticed that in 1922 Fitzgerald has Nick exclaim to Gatsby that his lighted mansion "looks like the World's Fair." That, in conjunction with "Flushing Meadows," suggests the firmness of the book's purchase on the essence of modernity. Imagination and money transform reality.

The moon of magical transformation indeed rose over Flushing Meadows. The old marshland became in 1939 and 1940 the New York World's Fair, arguably the greatest of all world's fairs, at least the equal of the London Crystal Palace. The richly symbolic Trylon and Perisphere, designed by Wallace Harrison and André Fouilhoux, has been considered an epiphany of the modern movement in architecture. After that,

Flushing Meadows would become Shea Stadium, then the National Tennis Center, with stadia named after Louis Armstrong and Arthur Ashe. Those three blacks with their white chauffeur, driving in their limousine over the Art Deco Queensboro Bridge, might justifiably gaze in haughty and moneyed rivalry at Jay Gatsby in his Rolls chariot.

Fitzgerald's answer to Eliot's desert of the heart was thus romantic imagination, that "intense life" which Nick sensed in Daisy and Gatsby when they were reunited, if only for a brief period.[39] Gatsby's magical wafer moon, that symbol of the romantic imagination, would always rise over those "inessential houses," as it does on the last page. The imagination changes the self as it changes the world, and Fitzgerald had the Goethean insight that money is a prime agent of transformation, money being a concretization of freedom. Whether the transformation be for good or ill, beautiful or grotesque, depends on the quality of the imagination.

Thus the title *The Great Gatsby* can be read as ironic, sounding like a carnival barker introducing a second-rate magic show. But that title may really not be ironic, and Gatsby may be great after all.

Afterword: Today and Tomorrow

I first saw the Columbia University campus as I climbed up out of the New York City subway at 116th Street and Broadway, up from men and bits of paper, whirled by the cold wind. And there was the university, McKim, Mead, and White's buildings and geometrical lawns and paths austerely beautiful in their varied neoclassicisms. This was not Arnold's Oxford, "steeped in sentiment . . . spreading her gardens to the moonlight" nor Fitzgerald's neo-Gothic Princeton, that "meadowlark among the smoke stacks." This was not alma mater but dura matter, insisting on its place, a fortress within the swirling metropolis. On the frieze of Butler Library the university declared itself with names carved in stone: Homer, Voltaire, Aristotle, Plato, Shakespeare, Newton, Rousseau, Sophocles, Dante, Cervantes, Goethe . . . The names were thus proudly and apparently permanently proclaimed.

As I soon came to understand, they were not a closed list of genius. Very far from it. Many other names from the past could have been added, and in fact their works were within the library. The assumption was that the human intellect will continue its work, and names now unknown would be equivalent in excellence to those on the frieze. These names were chosen because they represented intellect operating at its maximum power, establishing a standard of excellence to which the university aspired in every area of its activity. Although the great city swirled outside its gates, here on the campus were time and quiet space to approach the work of intellect at its highest reach, which is, as Arnold wrote, to strive "in all branches of knowledge, theology, philosophy, history, art, science, to see the object as in itself it really is." We all know that this goal is difficult to attain, perhaps impossible. The human lens is often clouded. But the goal of intellect is always there: cognition, the self-cleansing act of trying to see the object of knowledge as clearly as possible.

Perhaps it would suffice to say that the major works discussed in this book speak for themselves, do so magnificently, and make the case for their own importance. They have done so since they were written, immediately recognized as masterly; and none was written for a university specialist. They stretch the abilities of even the best reader, and they are strong and resilient enough to survive even the worst efforts of an inferior teacher. Battered by the most egregious interpretive invasions, they tend in my experience to snap back into shape with a reassertion, often an increment, of power. Each of these authors has found a form and a language fully adequate to the experience expressed in the work. And taken in the aggregate, these books provide an account of Western thought and feeling at its most intense and along the course of its historical development.

Of central importance here has been the power and tension of Athens and Jerusalem, cognition and spiritual aspiration, refracted through the changing circumstances of history and the perceptions of the individual writer. There is not a writer dealt with here who did not express, though sometimes by implication only, this sense of a dialectic, knowing even while writing the presence of other possibilities. Achilles dies for honor but can mock it. Abraham argues and bargains rationally with God and even laughs at him. The tension was there early and memorably.

Given such tensions, it is not surprising that major works often disagree with one another. We have Augustine's *Confessions* but we also have Voltaire's *Candide*. There is Dante, but also Montaigne, each of them projecting a powerful account of human actuality. The Western mind is permanently in tension; it is dialectical, as Leo Strauss and many others have said. It embodies an argument at the core of its being. Strauss maintains, indeed, that freedom exists because of the tension between the rival claims. That is, a society organized according to unmitigated rational authority would look something like Plato's *Republic,* probably with the addition of recent developments in genetics, while a society organized for spiritual aspiration would be a sort of monastery. Although it is clear that an individual forced in an either-or situation to make a choice must choose between the rival authorities, Strauss thought, persuasively I think, that culture and society must remain open to the two possibilities, maintain the tension.

The very power of the important books works to make their readers fair-minded. It demands that the books be heard. The reader experiences the desire to come up to their power of mind. You listen to them, putting aside your own opinions, desires, and causes. There occurs the thought that there is no need to assign Plato or Montaigne, Dante or Dostoyevsky to some political category, at least before waiting a very long time. This amounts to the cultivation of fairness, or disinterestedness, and it attacks the fortress of every provincialism.

These concluding comments may well strike the reader as self-evidently true. So indeed they seemed to the consensus of those who read the report made by Harvard University in its famous publication *General Education in a Free Society* (1948), with a general introduction by James Bryant Conant, the university's president. A distinguished committee had deliberated for three years and unanimously endorsed detailed proposals for Harvard's undergraduate curriculum. Its central assertion was this: "It is proposed that the course in the area of the humanities required of all students will be one which will be called the Great Texts of Literature." President Conant, a chemist of world stature, in endorsing this proposal and implementing it, did not mean that students be engaged only with literature, that is, philosophy and history as well as imaginative works. He was well aware of the other responsibilities of such a university as Harvard to other areas of study, including the various cultures of the world's people past and present. Yet he and those who advised him also knew that the "great texts," as they were called here, are at the core of Western civilization.

It is not at the present moment obvious that anything germane to this position has changed since the Harvard report set forth its arguments. By 1948, World War II had been fought and won, and we had full knowledge of the horrors of the death camps and other dark passages. For the most part, these did not cause a loss of civilizational nerve. What we had not experienced in 1948 was the Vietnam period and its tumultuous emotions, which involved rebellion against institutions and authority. Beyond the borders of the United States, in addition, there were the international uprisings of 1968, which often have been compared in intensity and effect to the European rebellions of 1848. The effects of these events are still felt in terms of university authority and intellectual integrity.

To continue President Conant's line of thought in a slightly different terminology, I would say that the education in the liberal arts for which he called assists mightily in making the student or anyone else a "citizen," as I have used that term in my opening chapter—that is, a person who can recreate Western civilization if need be. Of course, far short of that possible achievement, a citizen understands the vital components of that civilization as well as its history and is thus located in time as well as place. Such a citizen is not a transitory "fly of a summer," to use Burke's phrase. "He who is ignorant of what happens before his birth," wrote Cicero, "is always a child."[1]

Since 1948 a very large development has taken place which reinforces the position of the Harvard report. Today, important elements of Western civilization are becoming characteristic of world civilization, at least among the advanced nations. Representative democracy, together with its many presuppositions, appears to be the only remaining legitimate form of government, at least among civilized and civilizing people. To that form of government, Western political philosophy and Western ethical principles, evolved over centuries, are fundamental. Tribal rule and other collectivities do not flourish among these presuppositions about ascertainable general truths, about individual worth and individual responsibility. In addition, Western science and mathematics are universal and essential to modern development. There is no distinctive Chinese mathematics or African physics. To the now considerable extent that economics is a science, Western analyses are prevailing in the world today. It is true that the apocalyptic Nazi eruption remains a shock, but it was crushingly defeated as part of a struggle against totalitarianism worthy of being described by Thucydides.

What we are seeing is at least a partial globalization of Western culture, however refracted by local conditions. This process will entail, at least among the educated, an understanding of Western experience at its profoundest levels, not only its scientific procedures and discoveries but also its moral and psychological explorations that are coordinate with them and probably inseparable from them. The distinguished social philosopher Robert Nisbet often wrote profoundly about this, and I will quote him very briefly here: "The ideas that come forth from Socrates and then from Plato and Aristotle were to form the essence of the Western philosophical tradition. To try to imagine what we know as Western philosophy apart from Socrates and his followers would be impossible. The same applies to the drama that took form under Aeschylus, Sophocles and Eurypides in the same period. Its essential problems were those of spirit and conscience precipitated by two powerful and, for a time, almost equally evocative social and moral orders, the one a reflection of sacred tradition, the other of individual release."[2]

It would be onerous here to dwell at length on the recent past in liberal education. There cannot be anyone who is unaware that since around 1970 we have gone through a peculiar phase in the life of the university and in liberal education. In one of its aspects this has involved a turning away from the kind of fundamental works discussed here. We have had various "postmodern" literary theories, which cast doubt on the very nature and value of literature. We have had fantastic egalitarian denials that one work can be superior to another. These challenges have met with extensive rebuke, which over the years has been so successful intellectually that the position of literature has no doubt emerged stronger than before.

It is telling that ideological impositions on literature tend to depend on what has frankly been called "thin reading" by its advocates. They mean skimming, or a deliberate inattention to the literary text. What this allows for is a perpetual hunt for the villain in whatever is under discussion. In principle, because one always knows that the villain will be exposed, and who the villain is, there is really no reason to read more than one book since the plot is always the same. Critics of this sort often speak of "interrogating" the work of literature, and one can imagine rubber truncheons and bare light bulbs. Their own tone is often snarling and accusatory. Needless to say, the villain always turns out to be variously white, male, Western, racist, imperialist, sexist or homophobic—or, with luck, all of them together. The result of this is not literary experience but an endless repetition of slogans and clichés. Careful reading of important works resists and undercuts these muralistic cartoons.

It is a matter of consensus that in the United States, at least, this academic mutation, and mutilation, had its roots in the era of the Vietnam war. Yet other factors than that war must have been operating because, as has widely been noticed, in that pivotal year 1968 there were near-apocalyptic student-faculty explosions in most of the advanced nations, that is, in nations where Vietnam did not figure on the national agenda, and where the stated rationales had little to do with that war. What these eruptions appear to have had in common was an antinomian dislike of rules, a rebellion against genuine learning and authority, and an egalitarian abandonment of distinctions between the important and the unimportant, even between the prose on a cereal carton and the poetry of Shakespeare. In their overall thrust, which amounted to a kind of reverse sentimentalism and unjustified rage, these moods appeared to be hostile to Western civilization itself.

Finally, in this vein, we have also had the ideology of "multiculturalism." Thus we have had a sort of manifesto by the very estimable Nathan Glazer entitled *We Are All Multiculturalists Now*. It is certainly true that various cultures, even primitive cultures, have produced stunning works of art. But when Glazer is ill he does not go to a witch doctor, he does not tune into a tom-tom instead of Mozart on his CD equipment, he does not vacation in Uganda or Borneo, and he does not go to multiculturalist conferences in an oxcart.

No one can doubt the attraction and interest of works of art springing from cultures past and present and at all degrees of development. Artistic achievement does not necessarily correlate with achievement in science, life expectancy, political organization, philosophy. It is possible that the *Iliad* and the Pentateuch are the greatest works discussed in this book. They have at their centers Achilles and Moses, Bronze Age figures as transmitted by later oral cultures. Yet apart from art, other cultural and civilizational achievements are variously distributed.

A suspension of judgment regarding various cultures is a useful operational procedure for an anthropologist who is studying them. Such an observer tries to see these cultures on their own terms and find out how they function. There would be no reason for an anthropologist not to approach the culture of Pol Pot's Cambodia this way, or the culture of the Aztecs. But it is obvious nonsense to say that they are all equal, or equally desirable. In fact, multiculturalism is a purely Western invention and has varied ideological roots. None of the cultures we are supposed to be "multi" about is at all itself multicultural—certainly not an African tribe, certainly not China or Japan, certainly not Hindus or Muslims. In fact, multiculturalism is an ideological academic fantasy maintained in obvious bad faith. It really amounts to a form of anti-Westernism. That is, all cultures are to be respected and valued except the civilization of the West, to which, not surprisingly, the actual inhabitants of those other cultures are trying to migrate in large numbers.

It is my perception that all of this is coming to an end, though with agonizing slowness. It has been subject to a devastating intellectual critique. And the best students, given the choice, are voting with their course selections in favor of fundamental courses instead of the faddish ones. Universities are discovering that they need to require non-Western, multicultural, and other du jour courses, which usually consist of complaints against the West, in order to fill the seats. Although the students do not possess anything like a rationale for doing so, they are choosing to an increasing extent the cognitive rather than the ideological courses because they find that, more and more today, these are taught in a fair and disinterested way. Good thought, like courage, usually wins in the end.

And so I will conclude with a word on behalf of that almost forgotten word, that almost always misused word, *disinterestedness*. This signifies a condition of mind in which one puts aside personal passion and personal claims or "interests" and endeavors to see and hear as accurately as possible. The judge in a court of law is supposed to put aside his prejudices and opinions, his economic status or gripes, his religion, race, or politics and try to assess the case before him.

In all areas of knowing and understanding, such disinterestedness is absolutely fundamental. The person who would be disinterested in the service of knowing must strive to cleanse the cognitive gaze of prior attitudes and assumptions, the buzz of fashion and considerations of current opinion, and try to see through an unclouded mental lens. It is beyond tribe and nation, beyond personal attachment, and might conceivably be inimical to survival in a Darwinian sense. The lion and the alligator can never be disinterested. It was no bad theoretician of knowledge who said, "Unless you change and become as children you shall not enter the kingdom of heaven." The cognitive gaze must try to be the innocent gaze. I will say here that I consider cognition, knowing, one of the very highest pleasures, and that I think of the university as the place devoted at its core to cognition.

One of the most sympathetic portraits of a university man to appear in European literature is Chaucer's vignette of the "clerc" (scholar) of Oxford. This penurious young man was probably an advanced student who supported himself by tutoring. He is, as Chaucer says, thin as a rake and even looks hollow. Yet at the head of his bed he has twenty volumes of Aristotle bound in black and red leather, his most precious possessions. We are left to imagine that he starves himself to buy these expensive books. Then come Chaucer's love-struck lines:

Of studie took he most cure and most hede.
Nought o word spak he more than was neede . . .
Souninge in moral vertu was his speche.
And gladly wolde he lerne and gladly teche.[3]

That young scholar from the reign of Richard II is well worth our contemplation. "And gladly wolde he lerne and gladly teche." The repetition of the word "gladly" suggests that he does not "lerne" or "teche" for external, ulterior reasons. "Gladly lerne" and "gladly teche" are parallel phrases, related by symmetry. Thus learning and teaching seem to be part of a continuous process, parts of a self-validating whole. Each implies the other. His behavior constitutes a circle spinning gladly, but must be energized by his splendid books. I do not think it going too far in interpretation to say that the circle defined by "gladly . . . gladly" may be seen as the traditional circle of perfection, infinitely expandable. Thin as he is, and poor, Chaucer's scholar is totally devoted to cognition, and in his chosen activity inhabits a version of eternity.

Notes

Chapter 1: Athens and Jerusalem

1. Lionel Trilling, "The Meaning of a Literary Idea," *The Liberal Imagination* (New York: Viking, 1950), p. 283.

2. Paul A. Cantor, *Hamlet* (Cambridge: Cambridge University Press, 1989), p. 64.

3. Edward Grant, "When Did Modern Science Begin?" *American Scholar* (winter 1997), p. 105.

4. Grant, p. 105.

5. Grant, p. 107.

6. Grant, p. 107.

7. Leo Strauss, "Jerusalem and Athens: Some Preliminary Reflections," in *Studies in Platonic Political Philosophy*, ed. Thomas I. Pangle (Chicago: University of Chicago Press, 1983), pp. 147–71. A useful analysis of this essay appears in Susan Orr, *Jerusalem and Athens: Reason and Revelation in the Works of Leo Strauss* (London: Rowman and Littlefield, 1995). Gregory Bruce Smith, in "Who Was Leo Strauss?" (*American Scholar* [winter 1997], pp. 95–103), gives a good overview of Strauss's work, including his emphasis on maintaining the tension between Athens and Jerusalem.

8. Friedrich Nietzsche, *Thus Spake Zarathustra*, *The Portable Nietzsche*, ed. and trans. Walter Kaufman (New York: Penguin, 1954), pp. 170–71.

9. Thomas Babington Macaulay, quoted in J. H. Plumb, *Men and Places* (London: Cresset Press, 1963), p. 258.

10. Robert Frost used this striking phrase in a public performance. He was speaking of a visit to Jerusalem during which the press asked him what literature accomplished. He gave this answer. He said the press reported him as saying, "to a higher level," which he regarded as absurd (LP recording, not available).

11. C. S. Lewis, *The Allegory of Love* (Oxford: Clarendon Press, 1936), p. 1.

Chapter 2: Athens: The Heroic Phase

1. *Nomos:* the musical symbol of the cosmic harmony. See Eric Voegelin, *Plato and Aristotle,* vol. 3 of *Order and History* (Columbia: University of Missouri Press, 2000), p. 322.

2. Homer, *Iliad,* trans. Robert Fagels, intro. and notes by Bernard Knox (New York: Penguin, 1990), book 22, ll. 31–33, 38. All passages cited from the *Iliad* are from this translation.

3. A very fine discussion of *areté* can be found in Werner Jaeger, *Paideia: The Ideals of Greek Culture,* vol. 1 (Oxford: Basil Blackwell, 1939), chap. 1.

4. Jaeger, p. 8.

5. Jaeger, pp. 5–8.

6. Jaeger, p. 33.

7. *Iliad,* book 6, ll. 288–93.

8. *Iliad,* book 6, ll. 556–67.

9. *Iliad,* book 21, ll. 119–24.

10. Michel de Montaigne, "Of Experience," *The Essays: A Selection,* trans. and ed. M. A. Screech (London: Penguin, 1991), p. 425.

11. Blaise Pascal, *The Provincial Letters, Pensées, Scientific Treatises* in *The Great Books,* publisher William Benton (Chicago: Encyclopedia Britannica, 1952), *Pensée* 358, p. 235.

12. Bernard Knox, introduction to Fagels's translation of the *Iliad,* p. 45.

13. Homer, *The Odyssey,* trans. Robert Fagels, intro. Bernard Knox (New York: Penguin, 1996), book 4, ll. 135–50.

14. *Iliad,* book 9, ll. 386–91.

15. Christopher Logue, *Kings: An Account of Books I and II of Homer's Iliad* (New York: Farrar, Straus, Giroux, 1991), p. 8. Used here with the permission of the publisher.

Chapter 3: Moses as Epic Hero

1. Cyrus H. Gordon and Gary A. Rendsburg, *The Bible and the Ancient Near East* (New York: Norton, 1997), pp. 95–96.

2. Gordon and Rendsburg, p. 109.

3. Gordon and Rendsburg, pp. 20–23.

4. Robert Jastrow, *God and the Astronomers* (New York: Norton, 1978), p. 12.

5. Job 40:31–34. New International Version used throughout.

6. Paul Tillich, *The Courage To Be* (New Haven: Yale University Press, 1952), p. 187.

7. John Milton, "On the Morning of Christ's Nativity," ll. 190–94.

8. Jack Miles, *A Biography of God* (New York: Alfred A. Knopf, 1995), pp. 96–97, 136–37. This fine work of scholarship has been valuable to me throughout. The God of Genesis 1, however, there before the beginning, cannot really have a biography. His encounters with humans in the Bible, as Miles brilliantly shows, have been represented in different ways.

9. Cited by Frederick Coppleston in *Medieval Philosophy* (New York: Doubleday, 1993), p. 341.

10. Miles, pp. 26–27.

11. Søren Kierkegaard, *Fear and Trembling*, ed. and trans. Howard V. Hong and Edna H. Hong (Princeton: Princeton University Press, 1993), pp. 15–23 and 54–81.

12. Miles, p. 58–59.

13. Gordon and Rendsburg, pp. 141–43.

14. Gordon and Rendsburg, pp. 151–52.

15. Eric Voegelin, *Israel and Revelation*, volume I of *Order and History* (New Orleans: University of Louisiana Press, 1950), pp. 393–95.

16. Voegelin, pp. 102–10 gives a brief but detailed account.

17. Voegelin, pp. 392–93. I am especially indebted to Robert Alter, *Genesis: Translation and Commentary* (New York: Norton, 1996). The commentary on Genesis and Exodus in *The New Interpreter's Bible*, vol. I (Nashville: Abingdon Press, 1994), has been consistently valuable. *The Oxford Companion to the Bible*, ed. Bruce M. Metzger and Michael C. Coogan (Oxford: Oxford University Press, 1993), has been an authoritative guide.

18. Miles, pp. 102–5.

19. Voegelin, pp. 406–8; also Gordon and Rendsburg, pp. 104–7.

20. Voegelin, p. 406.

21. Miles, pp. 136–38.

22. C. S. Lewis in *Reflections on the Psalms* (New York: Harcourt, Brace, 1958), pp. 155–60, comments on this psalm.

23. To compare large things with small, indeed with gossip, W. H. Auden recalled that in his first meeting with his editor Charles Williams, "For the first time in my life [I] felt in the presence of sanctity." T. S. Eliot has testified that Williams had an extraordinary radiance about him. Auden elaborated: "I had met a good many people before who made me ashamed of my own shortcomings, but in the presence of this man—we never discussed anything but literary business—I did not feel ashamed. I felt transformed into a person who was incapable of doing or thinking anything base or unloving. (I later discovered that he had a similar effect on many other people.)" Humphrey Carpenter, *W. H. Auden: A Biography* (New York: Houghton, Mifflin, 1981, p. 224). The halo in Renaissance art no doubt reflects an intense version of such sanctity.

Chapter 4: Socrates and Jesus

1. Nichols College, Dudley, Massachusetts, 1997.
2. Professor Marjorie Nicolson, a follower of Lovejoy, in lecture at Columbia University, ca. 1958.
3. Quoted by T. S. Eliot in one of his epigraphs to *Four Quartets*, citing Diels: *Die Fragmente der Vorsokratiker (Herakleitos)*.
4. Diogenes Laertius, *Lives of the Philosophers II*, cited in Jonathan Barnes, *Early Greek Philosophers* (New York: Penguin, 1987), p. 100.
5. Plato, *Parmenides* 127A–128D, cited in Barnes, 150–53.
6. Plato, *The Symposium*, trans. Walter Hamilton (New York: Penguin Books, 1951), p. 108. The reference is to line 272 in book 4 of the Fagels translation.
7. *Symposium*, pp. 108–9.
8. *Symposium*, pp. 92–95.
9. Aristotle, *The Ethics of Aristotle: The Nicomachean Ethics*, trans. J. A. K. Thomson (London: Penguin, 1955), p. 312.
10. Henry Vaughan, "The World," ll. 1–7.
11. Plato, *Apology*, in *Plato: The Last Days of Socrates*, trans. Hugh Tredennick and Harrold Tarrant (London: Penguin, 1993), pp. 53–54.
12. Rudolf Otto, *The Idea of the Holy*, trans. John W. Harvey (Oxford: Oxford University Press, 1924).
13. John Murray Cuddihy, *No Offense: Civil Religion and Protestant Taste* (New York: Seabury, 1978), pp. 198–99.
14. C. S. Lewis, *Reflections on the Psalms* (London: Geoffrey Bles, 1958), p. 26.

Chapter 5: Paul

1. Here I wish to express my indebtedness to two books by the great Saint Paul scholar Arthur Darby Nock, viz., *St. Paul* (New York: Harper, 1938), and *Early Gentile Christianity and Its Hellenistic Background* (New York: Harper, 1964). Both books exemplify formidable scholarship and steady judgment. I have also found especially valuable Werner Jaeger's series of Harvard lectures published as *Early Christianity and Greek Paideia* (Cambridge: Harvard University Press, 1964).
2. Jaeger, p. 4.
3. Nock, *Early Gentile Christianity*, p. 31: "Lucian speaks of Christ as introducing a new *telete* (that is, a new rite or initiation), into the world" (*Peregrin* II).
4. Jaeger, p. 39.
5. Jaeger, p. 11.
6. Nock, *Early Gentile Christianity*, p. 108.
7. Nock, *St. Paul*, pp. 143–44.
8. Jaeger, p. 62.

9. John Milton, *Paradise Lost,* book 1, l. 16; book 8, ll. 173–74. Johann Wolfgang Goethe, *Faust,* part 2, l. 11582.

Chapter 6: Augustine Chooses Jerusalem

1. In his excellent *St. Augustine* (New York: Viking, 1999), Garry Wills argues for *The Testimony* as the better title. I retain the familiar *Confessions* on the ground that for most readers the focus is not on sexual excess. The best way to regard the *Confessions* as a genre is probably as a "long prayer."

2. *Confessions* X, vii, 15. All quotations from the *Confessions* here come from *The Confessions of St. Augustine,* trans. John K. Ryan (New York: Doubleday, 1960).

3. The sentence that concludes the previous book is: "I made myself a barren waste." It is not widely recognized that these passages are a main source of the title and principal themes of *The Waste Land* by T. S. Eliot.

4. Peter Brown, *Augustine of Hippo* (Berkeley: University of California Press, 1969), pp. 35–39.

5. *Confessions,* 70.

6. Brown, p. 83.

7. *Confessions,* p. 136.

8. *Confessions,* pp. 221–22.

9. Brown, p. 131.

10. *Confessions,* pp. 144–45.

11. *Confessions,* p. 195.

12. *Confessions,* p. 195.

13. *Confessions,* p. 202.

14. *Confessions,* p. 202.

15. *Confessions,* p. 202.

16. T. S. Eliot, "Little Gidding," section V, *Four Quartets.*

17. Dante, *Inferno,* Canto V, l. 138.

Chapter 7: Dante, Rome (Athens), Jerusalem, and *Amor*

1. John Keats, "On First Looking into Chapman's Homer," ll. 9–10.

2. George Santayana, *Three Philosophical Poets* (Cambridge: Harvard University Press, 1910); T. S. Eliot, "Dante," in *Selected Essays* (London: Faber, 1932); and Mark Van Doren, "The *Divine Comedy,*" in *The Noble Voice* (New York: Holt, 1946). In mentioning these three essays I am very far from ignoring the indispensable contributions made by a great many scholars, such as, most recently, Charles Singleton, Robert Hollander, and John Freccero, among many others. Centuries

of commentary on the *Divine Comedy* is available on the Internet from the Dartmouth Dante Project.

3. Eliot, "Dante," p. 268.

4. Eliot, "Dante," p. 252.

5. All quotations from the *Divine Comedy* used here are from the translation by John D. Sinclair (Oxford: Oxford University Press, 1961). This sentence is from the *Inferno,* Canto I, p. 23. Lines are not numbered in this prose translation.

6. Robert Frost, "Birches," ll. 43–58.

7. *Inferno,* Canto I, p. 23.

8. *Inferno,* Canto I, p. 22.

9. *Inferno,* Canto IV, p. 63.

10. *Inferno,* Canto IV, p. 63.

11. As with all the major writers considered here, the commentary on Virgil is vast. I have found especially valuable Richard Jenkyns, *Classical Epic: Homer and Virgil* (London: Duckworth, 1992). Jenkyns presents in general a consensus view of Virgil and avoids idiosyncracies. His observation here is on page 53.

12. Mark Van Doren, "The Aeneid," in *Noble Voice,* p. 97 and elsewhere in this essay. Van Doren describes Virgil's style well, but he is too concerned to assert the superiority of Homer, which Virgil surely would admit.

13. Virgil, *The Aeneid,* trans. Robert Fitzgerald (New York: Random House, 1983), book 12, ll. 349–52, p. 402.

14. Jenkyns, p. 69.

15. T. S. Eliot, "Virgil and the Christian World" in *On Poetry and Poets* (New York: Farrar, Straus, and Cudahy, 1957), p. 138.

16. C. S. Lewis, *The Allegory of Love* (Oxford: Oxford University Press, 1951), p. 4.

17. Santayana, p. 91.

18. Dante, *La Vita Nuova,* ed. Pasto Milano (New York: Penguin, 1947), p. 618.

19. Lyndall Gordon, *T. S. Eliot: An Imperfect Life* (New York: Norton, 1998), p. 13.

20. Santayana, p. 118.

21. *Inferno,* Canto X, p. 135.

22. *Inferno,* Canto IV, p. 63.

23. *Inferno,* Canto IV, p. 65.

24. Santayana, p. 129.

25. *Inferno,* Canto V, p. 75.

26. *Inferno,* Canto V, p. 75.

27. *Inferno,* Canto V, p. 77.

28. *Inferno,* Canto V, p. 77.

29. *Inferno,* Canto V, p. 77.

30. *Inferno,* Canto V, p. 79.

31. *The Confessions of St. Augustine,* ed. and trans. John K. Ryan (New York: Doubleday, 1960), p. 202.

32. *Inferno,* Canto XV, p. 193.

33. *Inferno,* Canto XV, p. 193.

34. Robert M. Durling and Ronald Martinez, *The Inferno,* vol. 1 of *The Divine Comedy of Dante Alighieri* (Oxford: The Oxford University Press, 1996), 557–60.

35. *Inferno,* Canto XV, p. 197.

36. *Inferno,* Canto XV, p. 199.

37. *Inferno,* Canto XV, p. 199.

38. *Inferno,* Canto XXVI, p. 327.

39. Cited by John D. Sinclair, *Inferno,* p. 331.

40. *Inferno,* Canto XVI, p. 327.

41. Cicero, *De Finibus* V, xvii, 48.

42. *Inferno,* Canto XVI, p. 327.

43. *Inferno,* Canto XVI, p. 325.

44. *Inferno,* Canto XVI, p. 327.

45. *Paradiso,* Canto XXX, p. 483.

46. *Paradiso,* Canto XXX, p. 483.

47. *Paradiso,* Canto XXX, p. 483.

48. *Paradiso,* Canto XXX, p. 485.

49. Van Doren, "*Divine Comedy,*" p. 230.

50. Eliot, "Dante," p. 268.

51. Eliot, "Virgil and the Christian World," p. 146.

Chapter 8: Hamlet's Great Song

1. *The Life of Henry V,* act 1, scene 1, ll. 1–2.

2. *Hamlet,* act 1, scene 1, ll. 1–2. The rest of the dialogue discussed here follows immediately upon this opening, concluding with line 13.

3. Act 1, scene 5, ll. 84–86.

4. Paul A. Cantor, *Hamlet* (Cambridge: Cambridge University Press, 1989), p. 26. Professor Cantor, while giving due weight to other sources of contradiction in the prince, sees the great difficulty of obedience to this command as particularly important.

5. Act 1, scene 4, l. 39.

6. Act 1, scene 5, ll. 165–66.

7. Act 1, scene 2, ll. 129–59.

8. Act 1, scene 2, ll. 129–30.

9. Act 3, scene 1, ll. 66–68.

10. Act 1, scene 5, ll. 187–88.

11. John Donne, *The First Anniversary: An Anatomy of the World*, ll. 213–15.

12. Act 2, scene 2, ll. 307–13.

13. Act 3, scene 4, ll. 32–33.

14. Act 3, scene 4, l. 213.

15. Act 5, scene 1, l. 77.

16. Act 5, scene 1, ll. 190–92; 198–200.

17. Act 3, scene 1, ll. 154–62.

18. Cantor, p. 54.

19. John Hale, *The Civilization of Europe in the Renaissance* (New York: Atheneum, 1994), p. 189.

20. Storms rage in *Othello, Macbeth*, and climactically, in *Lear*. Elsinore appropriately is wrapped in murky weather.

21. Act 1, scene 5, ll. 84–85.

22. Act 1, scene 5, ll. 85–86.

23. Act 5, scene 2, ll. 226, 10–11.

24. Cantor, p. 64.

25. Act 5, scene 2, ll. 347–52.

26. Act 5, scene 2, ll. 362–63.

27. Act 5, scene 2, ll. 362–64.

28. Act 5, scene 2, ll. 398–403.

29. Mark Van Doren, *Shakespeare* (New York: Holt, 1939), p. 196.

30. Act 5, scene 2, l. 361.

31. T. S. Eliot, "Dante," in *Selected Essays* (London: Faber, 1932), pp. 264–65: "And take the *Comedy* as a whole, you can compare it to nothing but the *entire* dramatic work of Shakespeare. The comparison of the *Vita Nuova* with the *Sonnets* is another, and interesting, occupation."

32. This view of *The Tempest* is at least implicit in T. S. Eliot's use of the play in *The Waste Land*. Robert Hunter develops it persuasively in *Shakespeare and the Comedy of Forgiveness* (New York: Columbia University Press, 1965).

33. Act 1, scene 2, ll. 376–81.

34. Act 1, scene 2, ll. 396–402.

35. *The Waste Land*, ll. 124–25.

36. *The Waste Land*, l. 191.

37. *The Waste Land*, ll. 316–19.

38. Act 4, scene 1, ll. 23–24.

39. Act 4, scene 1, ll. 104–105.

40. *Doctor Faustus*, in *The Works of Christopher Marlowe*, ed. C. F. Tucker Brooke (Oxford: Clarendon Press, 1910), act V, l. 1477.

41. Act 5, scene 1, l. 57.

42. Act 5, scene 1, ll. 182–85.

43. Act 5, scene 1, l. 186.
44. *The Tempest, epilogue*, ll. 1, 16–20.

Chapter 9: The Indispensable Enlightenment

1. James Boswell, *The Life of Samuel Johnson*, ed. Louis Kronenberger (New York: Viking, 1947), p. 114.
2. John Locke, *An Essay Concerning Human Understanding*, ed. John W. Yolton (London: Dent, 1961), vol. 1, p. 6.
3. Molière, *The Misanthrope and Other Plays*, trans. and intro. by John Wood (London: Penguin, 1959), p. 38.
4. *The Misanthrope and Other Plays*, p. 42.
5. *The Misanthrope and Other Plays*, p. 75.
6. *The Misanthrope and Other Plays*, p. 75.
7. William Blake (untitled): "Mock on, Mock on, Voltaire, Rousseau! / Mock on, Mock on; tis all in vain. / You throw the sand against the wind, / And the wind blows it back again."
8. Boswell, p. 137.
9. Voltaire, *Candide, Or Optimism*, trans. John Butt (London: Penguin, 1947), p. 104.
10. Alexander Pope, *An Essay on Man*, epistle 1, ll. 293–94.
11. Alexander Pope, *Epistle to Arbuthnot*, l. 132; *The Rape of the Lock*, Canto 3, l. 23.
12. Voltaire, p. 8.
13. Voltaire, p. 110.
14. Voltaire, p. 49.
15. Voltaire, pp. 27–28.
16. Voltaire, pp. 25–26.
17. Voltaire, p. 69.
18. Voltaire, p. 144.
19. W. H. Auden, "Voltaire at Ferney," ll. 10–12.

Chapter 10: Hamlet in St. Petersburg, Faust in Great Neck

1. Ian Watt, *The Rise of the Novel* (Berkeley: University of California Press, 1957). In general I follow Watt on this subject, though well aware that claims have been made that earlier prose fiction can be called novels. Nevertheless, I think Watt is correct in his focus on the sharpening of the sense of the phenomenal world in the post-seventeenth-century novel.
2. Daniel Defoe, *Robinson Crusoe*, (Mineola, N.Y.: Dover, 1998), p. 6.

3. Allen Tate, "Techniques of Fiction," in *Critiques and Essays on Modern Fiction,* ed. John Aldridge (New York, 1952), p. 41.

4. Feodor Dostoyevsky, *Crime and Punishment,* ed. George Gibian (New York: Norton, 1989), pp. 444–45.

5. Joseph Frank, "The World of Raskolnikov," *Encounter* (June 1966), pp. 30–35; reprinted in Norton edition op cit., pp. 567–78. Frank's discussion of the moral unconscious may be found on p. 574.

6. Dostoyevsky, p. 188.

7. Dostoyevsky, p. 265.

8. Dostoyevsky, p. 195.

9. T. S. Eliot, "Preludes III," in *The Complete Poems and Plays* (New York: Harcourt, Brace, Jovanovich, 1980), p. 13.

10. Dostoyevsky, p. 354.

11. Lionel Trilling, "F. Scott Fitzgerald," in *The Liberal Imagination* (New York: Viking, 1950), p. 244.

12. F. Scott Fitzgerald, *The Crack-Up,* ed. Edmund Wilson (New York: New Directions, 1945), p. 310.

13. F. Scott Fitzgerald, *The Great Gatsby* (New York: Scribner's, 1953), p. 21. Notably, at the end of *This Side of Paradise,* Amory Blaine "stretched out his arms to the crystalline, radiant sky."

14. *Gatsby,* p. 21.

15. *Gatsby,* p. 8.

16. *Gatsby,* p. 6.

17. *Gatsby,* p. 6.

18. *Gatsby,* p. 69.

19. *Gatsby,* pp. 2–3.

20. *Gatsby,* p. 39.

21. *Gatsby,* p. 39.

22. *Gatsby,* p. 68.

23. *Gatsby,* pp. 93–94.

24. Johann Wolfgang Von Goethe, *Faust,* trans. Cyrus Hamlin (New York: Norton, 1976), p. 153, ll. 6075–76.

25. *Faust,* p. 153, ll. 6160–71.

26. *Gatsby,* p. 4.

27. Peter Berger, *Facing up to Modernity* (New York: Basic Books, 1997), p. 218.

28. *Gatsby,* p. 6.

29. *Gatsby,* p. 162.

30. *Gatsby,* p. 1.

31. *Gatsby,* p. 61.

32. *Gatsby,* p. 87.

33. *Gatsby,* p. 56.

34. *Gatsby*, p. 56.
35. *Gatsby*, p. 154.
36. *Gatsby*, p. 120.
37. *Gatsby*, p. 111.
38. *Gatsby*, p. 152.
39. *Gatsby*, p. 97.

Afterword

1. Mark Van Doren, *Liberal Education* (New York: Holt, 1943), p. 118.
2. Robert Nisbet, *The Sociological Tradition* (New York: Basic Books, 1966), p. 315.
3. Geoffrey Chaucer, "General Prologue," *The Canterbury Tales*, ll. 303–4, 307–8.

Index

Page numbers with *n* refer to note numbers on that page.